D0108837

IN THE FIRE OF THE HEART

IN THE FIRE OF THE HEART

BY

RALPH WALDO TRINE, 1866-

Author of
In Tune with the Infinite, What All the World's a-Seeking, Character-Building Thought Power, etc.

NEW YORK
McCLURE, PHILLIPS & CO.
MCMVI

PREFACE

This little volume deals with certain facts and forces in connection with both our individual lives and our common social life. It deals with the latter first. It will have principally three types of readers. The first, that large class of open and fair-minded people who love justice and honour, who believe in the great principle of equal opportunities for all and special privileges for none, who believe that one great class of people are not to be used simply as a grist for another class, who believe that there is nothing just, or wise, or safe, much less common-sense, in permitting a social and political state where there are little groups of men and families grown so enormously rich and powerful that their very riches and privileges and excesses become a menace to their own welfare, as well as to that of the people at large and to the very State itself.

The second, that class, perhaps comparatively small, possibly already much larger than we realize, whose members have been so long schooled in privilege on their own part, or from their ancestors, or from their associations, that they come actually to believe that they in some way are better than the rest of the people, that somehow it was, or is intended, that they be sort of custodians of the welfare of other and less favoured people, and that they become dispensers of bounty to them in the degree that it will not affect their own accumulations, or ease and proprietary standing. By them the book will be strongly criticised, but their criticisms will be honest, the same as their prejudices are honest.

The third will be the class — though the readers of the book from this class will be very small — who by fair means and foul, chiefly foul, and dishonest, and devilish, manipulate to get the great natural properties that should be owned by and administered for the welfare of all the people into their own hands for their own personal and excessive enrichment, who debauch and poison as they go, who are criminals in practice and many at heart, though eminently "respectable" and smooth and suave and plausible in their methods, and who strike out vigorously and viciously at everything that would present truthfully and impartially the forces that are at work in our social state, and that would seem to disturb or menace or curtail their privileges and their methods; who own a portion of the public press for the direct and deliberate promotion of their ends, or who in one form or another influence or control sufficiently some other portions — though not all by any means — as to have it belittle and belie any and all attempts to present true conditions and feasible remedies to the people. The book will be criticised by them, condemned even as being something given to exaggerating sonditions or dangerous to the social order — there are numbers of expressions and forms that form sort of stock phrases that are always ready and at pen's point for this purpose. The major portions of the criticisms and statements from those of this class will be falsehoods — deliberate and vicious — and the interesting part of it is that they know they are such, even while they are uttering them.

It perchance may not be unwise or amiss to say that those of the class first mentioned, as well as that portion of the public press that is not owned or controlled, or whose policies are not shaped by, or their cues taken from, the forces of greed and privilege and public debauchery, but that stand true to the higher manhood and for the higher public welfare, while they will agree with and sanction the general purpose of the little book, will not agree with the author in all particulars. Nor is such to be expected.

Again, it may not be amiss to say by way of foreword, that on the part of those or rather many, in the Academic world, the little book will not be accepted, on the ground of its being not "scientific," or "scholarly" (or orthodox ?) but "popular." The author wishes to acknowledge at once this criticism, and to state most frankly that he has not aimed to make it academic, or technical, or orthodox, but that he has deliberately aimed to make it a simple, concrete little volume along the lines with which it deals, "popular," in the sense of its being for that splendid great "common people" that has made this, as well as every nation of importance and power in the world's history, and upon whose welfare all depends; and who, moreover, are now getting such awakenings, as well as facts and forces into their possession, as will yet save and redeem the nation, and with it their own great common interests.

Ralph Waldo Trine

Sunnybrae Farm
Croton Landing, N. Y.
November 1, 1906

College professors moan because no one reads their bloodless and wordy books on economics, but economics when dealt with straight from the shoulder by men who know the facts is to-day more popular than the most popular fiction, more interesting than the most interesting travels, better selling than any other form of literature. This is significant. The American people are gathering facts for future action. They want to be absolutely sure before they act, and then, get from under. — FROM A CURRENT EXCHANGE.

CONTENTS

IN THE FIRE OF THE HEART

I

WITH THE PEOPLE: A REVELATION

A DREAM, or a vision, or fancy, I know not; but it seemed to be amid surroundings unknown before and yet it seemed very like this world. But there was a difference — to travel one had in thought but to see one's self in a desired locality, or in the presence of the desired person, and he was there.

It seemed to be where one could look for a long distance, yet it was not a hill, and men and women were coming and going. It seemed to be neither day nor night, for one could discern no sun nor moon, neither were there stars, and yet it was light.

And I heard heavy trampings as of men clad in coarse nailed boots. I looked and presently I beheld the form of a man, but bent, and he looked closely to the ground before him as he walked. Though he seemed tired, weary, and as if he would be glad to lie down and sleep for a thousand years, yet he seemed to be hurrying along as if he might be late to something. In his hand he carried a pail.

And as I looked I saw others, and still others. Some were coming, some were going. All seemed encased in the same coarse garments, many were weary, and all seemed bent toward the ground and all were hurrying along.

And as I wondered pityingly — for pity seemed to pervade all things then — there appeared before me one who seemed to come to satisfy my questionings. He was not one of those I was looking upon, although it seemed as if at one time he might have been. His face was as if at sometime he had known great suffering, but there was now a look of strength and compassion, there was such beauty in his face that I wondered at it all. Moreover he seemed to know all things and my thoughts as quickly as I knew them myself. I was about to make inquiry of him when he approached nearer and said: "These are of a company numbering many millions upon the earth who do its heaviest and most important work. Were they not to go to their work daily the industries of the world would stop, and great suffering and privation would result." Why do they seem so eager I thought, and why are they bent so to the ground?

"Their work is heavy. Their hours are long. They have but little time with their families, for they must work diligently and faithfully while work lasts, for later on work stops and for some, for weeks, and for some, for months, there is no work, and their pay were they to work every day in the year is not enough to keep them in comfort."

But why I thought, and I contemplated the vast millions made from industry even in my country every year, is their pay so small?

He smiled; it seemed to be a pitying smile, but he did not answer my thought, and I knew not at the time why he smiled and said nothing.

While I was meditating upon all this I heard a great commotion as if outside of great gates, and I heard voices and the cries of excited men by the score. My companion said, "These are men out of work. A few are to be taken to-day, though it will be scarcely one from a score, and the others will tramp on as they have for many weary days to other works."

Scarcely had the noise subsided and the eager multitude of men gone on its way when I heard excited and angry shouts. I looked and beheld a man not yet in the prime of life. His face was haggard and white and as he ran he was followed by a crowd of shouting and excited men and boys. I heard a dull sound and then I saw a stone fall to the ground and one corner of it was wet and very red. I saw the man stagger and fall forward, and from the back of his head blood flowed. A woman rushed from the crowd. "It's John, I feared the look in his eyes this morning." She kissed the white face and with her lower skirt wiped the bruised and bleeding head. And the child she carried in her arms looked on in wonder.

Then I heard the clang of a gong and horses hoofs striking the hard pavement, and as the rapidly gathering crowd separated I noticed that the man's form was very thin. My companion said: "Long out of work and with hungry mouths to haunt him, he has stolen bread. It's common.'

And I saw — I knew not whence they came or whither they went — a large company that seemed to be neither men nor women for they were not grown, nor were they erect. They did not seem to be children, for they had neither children's faces nor movements. "These were children," said my companion, "put to work before their time. Some are old and broken now, and though still young, are scarcely able to keep up in the race, and from them a brood still worse will come." But there are not so many, I ventured. "In your country alone there are at this moment nearly two million." God, Heaven and Hell, I cried, if —

"Wait," he said, and before he had spoken his thought I heard a commotion as of doors breaking open, and under lurid lights and amid strains of coarse quick music I saw bedraggled and flushed faced and harsh voiced women that were pushing and pulling one another, and when one fell others seemed even with vile words to kick and beat her. With a sense of horror, I thought, What is this?

"This is a low dance hall. They are fighting for a brute of a man." I heard the same music and the same noise and revel from other places. I looked and saw place after place of the same type. So many, I said, and how came they here? "In this section are over a thousand to-night and there will be to-morrow; the ranks are always full. They start in different ways and from many different places." I looked at a group with whom were still traces of refinement. The faces were some marred, but the hair of some had great beauty in its colour. "These," he said, "were employed in large and well-known stores and establishments at wages so small that when food was gotten, all was gone. They struggled for a while, many bravely, but they grew weary when they could make no headway, for the grace, the attraction, the fire and the dreams of youth were with them. Men were ready to give them money. For a while they found the way less hard and dreary. They never dreamed of these places; but all find their way here in time." All? I said. "Sometimes a rough black wagon carries a rudely stained box out through a long street and through a gateway edged with drooping trees, and some are spared these resorts." Then I became conscious again of the sights and ounds about me.

So horrible it all seemed, that I said, cursed be greed and those that — "Lightly," he said, "a wealthy owner of one of the large establishments in which some of these were at one time employed, has built a most beautiful chapel in one of our large churches and has just had it dedicated to Christ. In all charity he is most liberal." I sat musing but I could *not* comprehend. Then anger seemed to vie with reason, when I was brought again to myself by the sound of horse's hoofs hurrying by. They drew a strange looking wagon. It was followed by two rattling carriages that were drawn by poorer looking horses. In the first was a gentle looking woman and with her were three children. In the second were women who looked something like those that were in the places about us, but they seemed to be of a more gentle type. "I said," volunteered my companion, "that sometimes a rudely stained box is carried out through a long street, and some are spared these resorts. She was so gentle and beautiful and was filled with such compassion and kindness. So young, only in the early twenties. The care of the family fell largely upon her, but she was never strong and by and by she fell weary. Then kind gentlemen helped her, though they received more than they gave. She went away for a time, but her help never failed to reach the little home. By and by she returned, but all hands were raised against her, and her fine sensitive spirit could not stand before it. Again she went away and soon the White Plague came to be her companion, but it did not stay with her long. She seemed not to care, nor had she any fear. From her savings a letter carried each fortnight the same old help to the little home, until two days ago, from a public institution, where even with a sad and sweet smile she left it, her body with a little envelope enough to bury it, was sent back to her mother's home." And as I thought of her bravery, her goodness, and her youth, then "All hands were raised against her" rang in my ears and anger seemed to seize me. "It is the way of the world," he said, "but few are wise enough or themselves stainless enough to unders and.' But we all have our failings and none are perfect, I volunteered. I wept and found relief, then involuntarily I cried, Jesus and Mary Magdalene. "Jesus was wise and full of compassion, and more, *his own life was without error.*"

And as I pondered and repeated to myself his words, my companion seemed to be forgetful of my presence and stood looking out into the space before us, while a strange expression covered his face. I looked at him but said nothing. Presently and without any other movement, even of the head, he placed his hand upon my forehead and said, "yonder!" My surroundings seemed changed and it was not as on the earth. I looked and beheld a company in very white garments and in their midst was one who seemed as if she had come a long distance, for she walked as if weary, and as she turned her face I saw that it was sad, and yet not sad, for joy was in it.

And two were leading her by the hand and they went along a path that was very bright and that became brighter as they went. And there walked beside them one whose form was not that of a woman and He was clothed with a greater light. I wondered upon it all and when I perceived again I saw that some were seated and others were reclining as on a bank. Then He whose form was not that of a woman bent over and kissed the forehead of the one; and I saw Him no more.

Looking again I could no longer distinguish from the others the one that had been led. And I thought — she must be rested now. And immediately they seemed to be joined by hosts of others, and among them were little children and young men and maidens, but I saw no aged there. I must have slept, for when I recalled my surroundings my companion was taking his hand from my forehead and as he did so I heard him say, "They are returning." I looked and saw the strange looking wagon and the two rattling carriages as they retraced their course along the road. "And her mother never knew it," said my companion. "And may she not until she is welcomed and cared for by the one who was welcomed and cared for to-day, and then to know will not hurt her." I am grateful for this revelation, I said. Would that all could have witnessed it. "All," he replied, "who, imperfect themselves are prone to judge or condemn another. Henceforth you shall be a better man." Amen and amen, I shouted, and so loudly it seemed as the whole city must hear. Then I thought, but I did not feel ashamed.

I heard a low rumble, the grinding as of iron upon iron, a sudden jerking sound. A crowd quickly gathered. A woman rushed through it and bore something from the track. There was blood upon the track. The form was limp and blood trickled down upon her dress. Pale and trembling, she bore it through a door, the entrance to a long dark passageway. My companion said: "To-morrow they will cart it away to the Potter's Field. He was such a bright lad, and of great promise." But the father? I said, "He is away to his work." But the father's work? "You do not understand," he said, and again he smiled. But surely, I persisted, there should be no Potter's Field in a country such as this. "In your own great city," he said, "one in every ten is buried in the Potter's Field. This year many thousands will be hauled there. It is the last indignity the poor fight against but the living must have bread and they cannot help it." The crowd still looked at the blood upon the track, but the car had moved on.

What a place, I thought, for a child to play, for the

street was not wide, and it seemed to be very dirty and it was very hot, and many teams were going and coming, and through them cars that seemed never to end their clanging, were threading their way. The noise and now and then the smells were something frightful. "Look about you" he said. I looked and in the one block there were over a hundred children at play. Why do they play here? Why do they not go to the parks, and to the prairies about the city, and out into the country? And again he smiled and said nothing. The air was close and it seemed as if we were in some strange place underground where there was no light nor air, only noise and commotion and smells indescribable.

And I saw a little cortege similar to the one we had seen before but it was longer as it threaded its way along. "Another victim of the plague." The plague? "The White Plague. This time it is a mother. She worked until a few days ago. Last year the father went with it and two children. Three are left. In the same tenement over a dozen have gone with it in a third as many years. This is its home. These houses, these rooms were built for it. From here it spreads itself throughout the city. Three times as many take it here as in other parts." I said, Why have they not houses with more light, more air, more open space? And again he smiled, and said nothing. It seemed as if my brain were on fire and I longed for full breaths of pure air. "We must change," said my companion, and turning he led the way.

There was the mingling of sounds as if pieces of fine

metal were striking one another in the air; and out from under the shade of wide-spreading trees and along a smoothly paved road a low hanging carriage rolled, almost without noise. In it were four men. All looked so comfortable, so big, and so well-to-do. Hope seemed to seize me and I said, if only these men knew of the conditions we have been witnessing, *they* would go to their relief. My companion listened, but he did not seem to share in my enthusiasm, and at the time I knew not why. "One," he said, "is owner of the mills from which you saw the coarsely booted and clothed men with pails in their hands coming and going, the men whose wages enable them to live only in the most meagre comfort if they work every day in the year which they never do. Very large sums are saved by closing the mills for a portion of each year and even when they are running, some work always on part time only."

"His companion on the seat with him is owner of works where many hundreds of children and many women are employed. Though others manage the works for him, they have machinery which children can tend that saves a million a year over what adult labour would cost. It is very hard and exacting work for the little ones and many come out of the works crippled or stunted and deformed for life, but it is a great saving for the owner!

"The other is very rich and prominent, the owner of many apartment houses as he calls them, in the portion of the city we have just been visiting. Tenements and lung-blocks those who live in or near them call them.

The Honourable Joseph, his friends and charitable institutions know him as. Slimy Joe his tenants and those who have close dealings with him, call him!

"The fourth is a man who has never worked at all. He inherited properties worth many millions. Managers attend to these and collect his incomes. Among them are many extensive railroad properties. His father was known as the great corruptionist. His managers follow in his father's practices. He is a lavish spender and loves sport. Though large and strong looking, he is never well."

But all the rich are not like these, I volunteered. "By no means," he replied. "These are only the parasitic, the low down rich, those whose God, whose religion, whose life is greed, and who know no more. But their name is legion, though they are never happy, never at peace."

The people, the people, I cried, musing on the great inequality that seemed to haunt me. "The people are a fool. They do not think. They have little imagination, scarcely enough to know their power. But some day"—and a strange light passed over his face and he seemed filled with great emotion, but did not finish his thought. Presently he continued, "A large hospital that many of the rich help support was destroyed some days ago, and a large charity ball is being given to help rebuild it. They are on their way to it now. A little later as you look in upon it you will see women, wives and daughters of these, and others, clad in garments costing almost fabulous prices, and decked with jewels and gems sufficient in value to feed and clothe the portions of the city we have just been in for years. I will point out to you a young man who has recently come into possession of over thirty millions, who has never done a useful day's work in his life and who perhaps never will. I will point out to you a lad of but twelve years who upon his father's demise will fall heir to properties worth over a hundred million, all made from values created by the people of the city where his properties lie. Among those whom you will see to-night you will notice many most vulgar in their excessive display, and others gross and vulgar in their appearance, for excessive wealth makes gluttons and abnormals of many. And when you see the haughty, self-important air on the part of many, remember it is merely one of the weaknesses of human nature to which the excessively rich are easy victims, and that it will be more or less balanced by the presence of many admirable and sensible people, who will be there to-night. There are few of the very rich and none of the excessively rich that do not pay heavy penalties for their abnormal hold on life, the same as the excessively poor. In this they are alike. Rejoice that you are of neither and use the knowledge you have gained for the good of both. With the common people their redemption lies."

I thought on the times when to my questions he smiled and said nothing, and then I seemed to understand clearly.

"With the people," repeated my companion, as he touched his hand upon my head. I seemed for a while to be absorbed, yet not in thought. Presently I perceived that I was alone, when a strange fascination took possession of me, and it holds me still. "With the people." "With the people."

II

THE CONDITIONS THAT HOLD AMONG US

WE should be a very great and a uniformly prosperous people. As a nation we have had advantages and opportunities that have never been equalled perhaps, by any people thus far in the world's history. We have been free from the cast systems and certain progress strangling customs of the old world countries; we have enjoyed from the beginning practically full civil and religious liberty; we started free from that dreary, grinding, hopeless, drink-impelling poverty, that is the bane and the curse of so many of the old world countries; we have had almost universal free educational opportunities for our boys and our girls, for our young men and our young women, and even for the older when they have so chosen. Our natural products from soil, and stream, and mine have been almost *fabulous* in their returns.

We should be a uniformly free and happy and prosperous people. But we are not uniformly free, neither happy nor prosperous. These statements may seem to some the product of a mind ill at ease, or given to misstatement or to exaggeration. Shall we see?

For all practical purposes, we do individually as well as collectively, enjoy civil freedom. But he who is not economically free, is in a slavery of the most haunting and endeavour-crushing type.

And over ten millions of our people are in a state of chronic poverty at this very hour — almost one out of every seven, or, to make full allowance, one out of every eight of all our people are in the condition where they have not sufficient food, and clothing, and shelter to keep them in a state of physical and mental efficiency. And the sad part of it is that large additional numbers, — numbers most appalling for such a country as this, are each year, and through no fault of their own, dropping into this same condition.

And a still sadder feature of it is, that each year increasingly large numbers of this vast army of people, our fellow-beings, are, unwillingly on their part and in the face of almost superhuman efforts to keep out of it till the last moment, dropping into the pauper class, — those who are compelled to seek or to receive aid from a public, or from private charity, in order to exist at all — already in numbers about four million, while increasing numbers of this class, the pauper, sink each year, and so naturally, into the vicious, the criminal, the inebriate class. In other words we have gradually allowed to be built around us a social and economic system which yearly drives vast numbers of hitherto fairly well-to-do, strong, honest, earnest, willing and admirable men with their families into the condition of poverty, and under its weary, endeavour-strangling influences many of these in time, hoping against hope, struggling to the last moment in their semi-incapacitated and pathetic manner to keep out of it, are forced to seek or to accept public or private charity, and thus sink into the pauper class.

It is a well authenticated fact that strong men, now weakened by poverty, will avoid it to the last before they will take this step. Many after parting with everything they have first, break down and cry like babes when the final moment comes, and they can avoid it no longer. Numbers at this time take their own lives rather than pass through the ordeal, and still larger numbers desert their families for whom they have struggled so valiantly, — it is almost invariably the woman who makes her way to the charity agencies. The public and private charities cost the country during the past year as nearly as can be *conservatively* arrived at, over $200,000,000.

Moreover, a strange law seems to work with an accuracy that seems almost marvellous. It is this. Notwithstanding the brave and almost superhuman struggles that are gone through with, on the part of these, before they can take themselves to the public or private charity for aid, when the step is once taken, they gradually sink into the condition where all initiative and all sense of self-reliance seems to be stifled or lost, and it is only a rare case now and then that they ever cease to be dependent, but remain content with the alms that are doled out to them, — practically never do they rise out of that condition again. Talk with practically any charity agent or worker, one with a sufficiently extended experience and you will find that there is scarcely more than one type of testimony concerning this. And as this condition gradually becomes chronic and endeavour and initiative and self-respect are lost, a certain proportion then sink into the condition of the criminal, the deseased, the chronically drunk, the inebriate, from which reclamation is still more difficult.

There are reasons for these conditions coming about, and one reason chief among them all, that we shall consider most fully in its proper place. First, however, let us look still more minutely into the conditions of the type we have been considering that we may have before us facts sufficient in number and in power to impel us to an examination of the *causes* which have brought about these conditions.

As has been stated, there are at the present time over ten million of our fellow-beings living in a state of poverty, that is, without sufficient of food and clothing and shelter to keep them in a first-class condition even as animals are kept, — to keep them in a state of efficiency to compete in the struggle for work; and when at work, the rush and the strain in many centres has become so great, and the competition for even a mere livelihood so keen, that no one can afford to be even for the shortest period, in anything but a state of full and complete efficiency.

The above estimate is based, among others, upon the careful estimates made by Mr. Robert Hunter, in that late and very admirable book, "Poverty,"* and has been formulated from a very wide range of statistics and facts and observations. Moreover, as this estimate has been made only on the basis of the distress which manifests

*Macmillan & Company, New York and London.

itself, such as pauper burials, yearly evictions, the numbers applying for public charity, the vast armies out of employment for some portion of the year, it must be most clearly evident that there is a very large additional number who are in great need, many in dire distress, who suffer keenly but bear it bravely, and suffer and struggle on, without its ever becoming evident to the world.

After stating that in 1903, 20 per cent of the people of Boston were in distress; in 1897, 19 per cent of the people of New York State; in 1899, 18 per cent of the people of the New York State; in 1903, 14 per cent of the families of Manhattan were evicted; and every year 10 per cent (about) of those who die in Manhattan have pauper burials,— facts taken *directly* from city and state statistics, and the pathos and tragedy and suffering they stand for so plainly evident, Mr. Hunter goes on to say: "These figures, furthermore, represent only the distress which manifests itself. There is no question but that only part of those in poverty, in any community, apply for charity. I think anyone living in a Settlement will support me in saying that many families who are obviously poor — that is, underfed, underclothed, or badly housed — never ask for aid or suffer the social disgrace of eviction. Of course, no one could estimate the proportion of those who are evicted or of those who ask assistance to the total number in poverty; for whatever opinion one may have formed is based, not on actual knowledge, gained by inquiry, but on impressions, gained through friendly intercourse. My own opinion is that probably not over half of those in poverty ever apply for charity, and certainly not more than that proportion are evicted from their homes. However, I should not wish an opinion of this sort to be used in estimating from the figures of distress, etc., the number of those in poverty. And yet from the facts of distress, as given, and from opinions formed, both as a charity agent and as a Settlement worker, I should not be at all surprised if the number of those in poverty in New York, as well as in other large cities and industrial centres, rarely fell below 25 per cent of all the people."

Speaking of unemployment,* and when one's wage is about a "living wage," that is, sufficient to keep him and his family in fair condition, providing he loses no time whatever, we can easily see what unemployment even for a very short period must necessarily mean. Mr. Hunter says: "The figures of unemployment, although very imperfect, show that the evil is wide-spread, even in times of prosperity. . . . In the last census (that of 1900) the number found to be unemployed at sometime during the year was 6,468,964, or 22.3 per cent of all the workers over ten years of age,engaged in gainful occupations. Thirty-nine per cent of the male workers unemployed, or 2,069,546 persons, were idle from four to six months

*At this present time—a period of unusual commercial and industrial activity—less than the average number are out of employment. But with our present methods, this dreaded and hard condition, that has in the aggregate affected millions among us, is liable to repeat itself at any time. Any fair dealing, therefore, with the economic conditions of the nation cannot omit a consideration, or at least a mention, of these conditions.

of the year. These figures are for the country as a whole, for all industries including agriculture. In manufacturing alone the unemployment rose to 27.2 per cent of all the workers. In the industrial states of the East and North the percentage of unemployment is larger than for the country as a whole. The Massachusetts census for 1895 showed that 8,339 workmen were unemployed continuously during that year, and that 252,456 persons were irregularly employed. This means that over 27 per cent of all persons covered by the inquiry were idle some portion of the year. That this is not exceptional is shown by the Massachusetts census for 1885. At that time over 29 per cent of the workmen were irregularly employed. In other words, the annual wages of more than one workman in every four suffered considerable decrease by reason of a period of enforced idleness, extending in some cases over several months. In the industrial towns, such as Haverhill, New Bedford, and Fall River, the irregularity of employment was even greater. In these towns from 39 to 62 per cent of the workmen were idle during some part of the year."

That very large numbers of workers, heads of families, receive for their work an insufficient amount to keep themselves and their families in comfort as well as in a state of efficiency, is a well-ascertained fact. Very large numbers are not receiving what is known as a "living wage." That there are those who do receive enough to keep themselves and their families in comfort, but who fail to do so, either on account of intemperance, or bad management, or misfortune of some kind, or through lack of an ordinary good management, or by reason of some other cause or causes, is undoubtedly true, and to deny it would be entirely useless. That, on the other hand, there are vast numbers who are receiving a wage insufficient even by the utmost economy, good management and self-denial, to keep themselves in a state of comfort and efficiency is most abundantly true. Were this number very small instead of being of such enormous proportions, it would be a menace to the highest welfare of the country as well as a disgrace so great as to demand that its causes be ascertained and eradicated.

It would be a very hard matter, as can readily be seen, to establish a necessary or "living wage" that would be such for all portions of the country, because living expenses in some sections are necessarily considerably higher than in others. We can approach, however, to an average necessary wage by ascertaining what good authorities, as well as careful investigators, have practically decreed as a necessary wage in various employments as well as sections of the country. John Mitchell has said, in his book on "Organized Labor": "For the great mass of unskilled workingmen, . . . residing in towns and cities with a population of from five thousand to one hundred thousand, a fair wage, a wage consistent with American standards of living, should not be less than $600 a year. Less than this would, in my judgment, be insufficient to give to the workingman those necessaries and comforts and those small luxuries which are now considered essential."

It has been shown by the Massachusetts Bureau of Statistics of Labor (1901) that $754 a year is required for a family of five persons to live on. An able official of one of the largest New York City charities states that as a result of his observations two dollars a day, or about $624 a year, is necessary for a family of five in New York City. Without going farther into the matter this would establish an average necessary wage of about $659 a year. And while this may be greater than *necessary*, as it undoubtedly is for some localities, it is not too high an amount for many others.

In the light of this it will be interesting as well as valuable to see what in various localities, as well as lines of work, the actual wages received are. The census of 1900 shows that the average yearly earnings of each of 5,308,406 persons engaged in manufacturing was $437.96. The previous census, that of 1890, showed that it was $444.83 per worker. This slight difference, the census bureau says: "was only an apparent one, due partly to the exclusion of high-salaried foremen and managers from the returns of the census of 1900, partly due also to the more complete returns of the lower-paid labour in the south.

The following table (the census of 1900) subdivides the census compilation for a number of cities as follows:

	Average No. wage-earners.	Average yearly wages.
The 10 largest cities	1,412,831	$489
154 next largest	1,599,033	445
Outside these cities	2,294,279	400
	5,306,143	

For this number of wage-earners, a little over five million, the average wage therefore, was in round numbers, $445.

Dr. Peter Roberts says that the average yearly wage in the anthracite coal district is less than $500, and that about 60 per cent of the workers receive less than $450. The Federal census for 1900 states that 11 per cent of the male workers, over 16 years of age employed in the New England cotton mills, received a rate of pay amounting to less than $6 a week,— about $300 a year. This, it must be noted, was their rate of pay, that is, what they would have earned had they worked every day in the year, hence not the actual wage received.

In the Middle States nearly a third of all the workers are receiving a rate of wages less than $300 per year, and in the Southern States, considerably over half — 59 per cent — are receiving less than this amount. When the time that they cannot work is taken out, we can readily see what this amount means. In many cases it means at least one fourth less in actual wages received. In the shoe-making industry less than $300 a year is received by 51 per cent of unskilled workers, in the Central States by 80.3 per cent, and in the Middle States by 87 per cent of this same class of workers.

Testimony was presented before the Industrial Commission showing that the 150,000 track hands working on the railroads of the United States received wages ranging from 47½ cents a day for the South to $1.25 a day in the North. The highest wage they would receive then would be about $150 a year for the South, and a little less than $375 for the North. Testimony was given by the same witness that these wages were also paid to the carmen and shopmen in the North and South, numbering about 200,000 men. Before the same Industrial Commission, testimony was given that the wages of the street-car employees ranged from $320 to $460 a year.

From this we are able to get some idea of what the needs of some millions in the country are compared to what they are able actually to receive to meet these needs. And then when sickness comes, or death, or accident, or misfortune of any type as well as being temporarily thrown out of employment, which is many times a misfortune of the gravest moment, we can readily see what distress and uncertainty must result. Certainly we need brought about in the nation a condition that gives an economic and industrial state which guarantees at least a fairly decent living wage and a regularity of employment to the great hosts who today are denied them. This, indeed, is fundamental. I can scarcely resist here the impulse to quote another paragraph or two from Mr. Hunter's admirable work:

"Among the many inexplicable things in life, there is probably nothing more out of reason than our disregard for preventive measures and our apparent willingness to provide almshouses, prisons, asylums, hospitals, homes, etc., for the victims of our neglect. Poverty is a culture bed for criminals, paupers, vagrants, and for such diseases as inebriety, insanity, and imbecility; and yet we endlessly go on in our unconcern, or in our blindness, heedless of its sources, believing all the time that we are merciful in administering to its unfortunate results. Those in poverty are fighting a losing struggle, because of unnecessary burdens which we might lift from their shoulders; but not until they go to pieces and become drunken, vagrant, criminal, diseased, and suppliant, do we consider mercy necessary. But in that day reclamation is almost impossible, the degeneracy of the adults infects the children, and the foulest of our social miseries is thus perpetuated from generation to generation. From the millions struggling with poverty come the millions who have lost all self-respect and ambition, who hardly, if ever, work, who are aimless and drifting, who like drink, who have no thought for their children, and who live contentedly on rubbish and alms. But a short time before many of them were of that great, splendid mass of producers upon which the material welfare of the nation rests. They were in poverty, but they were self-respecting; they were hard-pressed, but they were ambitious, determined, and hard working. They were also underfed, underclothed, and miserably housed,— the fear and dread of want possessed them, they worked sore, but gained nothing, they were isolated, heart-worn and weary."

It is true, as can be readily established, that during the past few years there has been on the whole an increase of wages,— though by no means in all cases,—

but at the same time through various other combinations of economic causes there has been an increase in the prices of the various commodities as well as actual necessities of life, many of which have been enormous and out of all keeping with whatever advance there has been in wages. Under the title, "Wages and the Cost of Living," the following paragraph appeared in the *Arena* for November, 1903. "The special pleaders for corporations and trusts have made a great deal of capital out of the fact that between 1897 and 1901 the wages in New York City have in sixteen trades risen from an average of $2.78 to $2.91 a day, and this fact has been broadly heralded through Great Britain as an argument in favour of protection and monopoly. But these special pleaders for plutocracy fail to mention another fact, and one which entirely changes the nature of the case. They fail to state that during this period the cost of living in the Empire City increased 10 per cent above the increase in wages, while since 1901 the cost of living has steadily risen. Dun's Agency places the increase at over 33 per cent." And according to the Dun Mercantile Agency report on March 1, 1906, the cost of living for the entire country was then the highest it has been during the thirty years it has kept a record. This coupled with the uncertainty of employment in so many lines of work, that is, the necessary non-employment during a certain number of weeks in the year, works in many cases, as we can readily see, almost untold hardships.

We are still considering this vast army of over ten millions in our country who are living in poverty in the face of our great apparent prosperity, much of which is indeed *apparent* when the facts are carefully looked into. There has been of late years a great prosperity, but confined so generally to such a small group, or to such small groups of people, that its force is to a great measure lost when considered in connection with the great mass of the people.

The number of propertyless persons, that is, tenants, in a state or country, is many times a good criterion of the real standard, or rather the diffusion of its prosperity. The census returns for 1900 show that 8,365,739 families, or 54 per cent do not own the homes in which they live, that is, they are continually paying rent. Those owning and occupying mortgaged homes were 2,196,-375; while those living in homes that were wholly and actually their own were 4,761,211, or but 31 per cent of the total number of families in the country. Of course, the number of families owning their own homes is much smaller in the cities than in the smaller towns. In several of our larger cities, probably 99 per cent of the *wage-earners* do not own the homes in which they live, but are each year paying out, sometimes as much as 40 per cent of their earnings, in rent. I have seen it estimated that the amount paid in rent and in interest on mortgaged homes is at least two billion dollars per year,— less the amount paid in taxes,— and this vast amount is annually transferred into the pockets of 10 per cent of the population, the rent paid for property used as *homes* only.

The last Federal census shows the following percentage of homes rented in the various cities, enumerated:

Boston	81.1
Chicago	74.9
Cincinnati	79.1
Fall River	82.0
Holyoke	80.6
New York (Manhattan)	94.1
Philadelphia	77.9

In 160 cities, of at least 25,000 inhabitants each, the average number of tenants is seventy-four in every hundred.

Professor J. G. Collins, a statistician who had charge of some of the inquiries of the census of 1890, estimated that only about 10 per cent of the population of the country were landlords, and that these owned and controlled somewhere near 90 per cent of the nation's total land values.

The idea I think quite generally prevails that the great agricultural population of the nation is in a generally prosperous condition, and that there are but few who do not own the farms upon which they live and which they till. Certainly it is natural to suppose that such is the case. The total number of farms in the United States is 5,737,372, supporting a population of about 28,000,000 people. Mr. George K. Holmes, a very cautious and careful investigator, has shown that on the basis of the census of 1890, over 34 per cent of our farmers are tenants, and an additional 18.6 per cent have their farms mortgaged. Accordingly over one-half of the farmers of the country have only a partial ownership in their farms or are propertyless.

When we consider the great numbers of families

whose wages or incomes are scarcely sufficient to keep them above continual want, or in other words, above the poverty line, and then only when they are working every work-day of the year, we can see what havoc is wrought when any extra calls are made or burdens thrown upon them, when sickness or accident comes, or death takes place, either on the part of the breadwinner or in his family. When one is receiving just a living wage, or as in so many cases, less than a living wage, it means untold hardship when any of these come. This undoubtedly is one of the great agencies that keeps a large number of this great army in poverty.

The frightful killings and maimings that are continually going on in connection with our railroads and various other large industries,— and we are the most backward country in the world in our gross neglect in compelling greater safety and care,— is also responsible for untold hardship and suffering. To show how dangerous and uncertain the work of a railway employee is, the following facts will indicate. The Interstate Commerce Commission for the year 1902 reported among employees 53,493 injured or killed, among passengers 7,028, other persons, 12,729, with a total of 73,250. These figures are indeed, scarcely believable. And in the previous year, out of every 399 employees, one was killed, and one out of every 26 was injured. The trainmen,— engineers, firemen, conductors, brakemen, etc., are the greatest sufferers. Among these one was killed for every 137 employed, and one was injured for every eleven employed. It is indeed difficult to believe that in this day and age such slaughter, and much of it so unnecessary, is permitted to go on year after year: and strange as it may seem the railroad owners or managers resist, and resist most powerfully, practically every attempt that is made to compel them to adopt various, and many times well known, safety devices.

The Accident Bulletin issued by the Commission for the *three months* ending March 31, 1906, shows the total number of casualities to passengers and employees to be 18,296 (1,126 killed and 17,170 injured). In closing the Bulletin says:

"The most disastrous accident reported in the present bulletin — a collision, causing thirty-four deaths and injuring twenty-four — was due to the striking failure of the train-despatching system. A telegraph operator at a small and lonely station, who had been on duty all day and more than half the night, fell asleep, and on awaking misinformed the train despatcher as to what had occurred while he was asleep. It is pertinent to observe that the block system repeatedly advocated by the Commission, is the true means that ought to be adopted for such distressing disasters as that reported in Accident Bulletin No. 19, just made public."

"These injuries to railway workmen are more serious than at first appears, for very few of the men who are injured are over thirty-five, and most of them are in the twenties. This period — between twenty and thirty-five — is the most important period of a workman's life. It is the time when he is of utmost value to his family, since the children are still too young to take up the support of the family.

"The responsibility of the railroads for poverty, resulting from injuries or casualties, is of three kinds at least. First: In many cases they overwork their employees. Dr. Samuel McCune Lindsay says: 'Emergencies frequently occur due to accidents or condition of weather when men may be required to work continuously from twenty to thirty hours, and, in exceptional cases, men have been continuously at work in train service for thirty-six hours.' Second: Many railroad systems have resisted and violated the law compelling them to put on automatic couplers, and they are now fighting the introduction of the block system, both of which improvements are designed to prevent accidents and injuries. Third: In case of accidents, 'company' physicians and lawyers hasten immediately to the place of the accident, and, if possible, persuade the workmen to sign contracts by which they agree, for some small immediate compensation, to release the company from any further liability. I have known many, many cases where workmen have, for a few dollars, signed away their rights to sue when their injuries have been as serious as the loss of a leg or arm. In the seventeen years ending June 30, 1902, 103,320 persons were killed, and 587,028 injured by the railway industry."*

Of the anthracite regions, Dr. Peter Roberts, who has made a very careful study of the industrial and social conditions there, says: "Nearly half the employees have no provision for either the incapacitated through accident or for the maintenance of widows and orphans

* "Poverty"—Robert Hunter, p. 38.

when death befalls those who provide for them in this hazardous calling. Many operators display generosity worthy of emulation; others manifest criminal indifference to the sufferings of employees and their families because of accident. . . . To leave these men to the mercy of overbearing operators in case of injury and death is unworthy of the civilization of the century in which we live."

From these facts and figures we can see what a large number of semi-incapacitated, and in case of the death of the breadwinner what a large number of practically dependent people are thrown each year upon the public for support, or who have to accept the condition of the pauper. We have much to learn from the German system in this respect. As a result of statistics gathered in connection with its splendidly growing insurance systems,—for old age, accident, sickness, infirmity,—it has made an effort to find out who is responsible for the suffering, and to demand accordingly compensation for the injured. In other words it has fixed not upon the individual, who is many times entirely helpless in regard to the matter, but upon industry and upon society the responsibility for much of its poverty and attendant suffering. It found that 80 per cent of all accidents in industrial lines were due to the "professional risks" of industry itself, and as a consequence the industries of that nation must bear the cost of these accidents,* and not the workingmen themselves. How different from our almost barbarous conditions in this respect.

*"Workman's Insurance Abroad" by Dr. Zacher, 1898, Berlin.

Certainly the criminal negligence of the railroads as well as other great lines of industry in this terrible and to a large extent preventable slaughter,– at the cost of slightly reduced dividends only, is indeed appalling, and is equalled only by the stupid negligence of the public in allowing it to continue. A change will come, however.

Sickness means far more to the wage-earner than to any other class, and for two, if not indeed for more, reasons. In the first place the loss of the wage if it be the wage-earner, or the increased expenses if it be one of his family, means immediate hardship where there is no reserve power, as in such large numbers of cases where one is receiving just a living wage there cannot be; and in the second place, the care and attention that can be secured are not at all equal to those that can be had by the more well-to-do. Especially is this true when so many hundreds of thousands are compelled to live in the types of tenements landlords are permitted to extract their rent from. But this is again the result of our general economic condition, for people would not live in these,— some would, but very, very few,— if their incomes or wages permitted them to live in quarters any better.

These conditions to a great extent are responsible for that slowly devouring, subtle, but most deadly modern plague among us,— tuberculosis, sometimes called the "Great White Plague." It will in this twelvemonth claim in New York City alone not less than fifteen thousand of its people, in the United States not less than one hundred and fifty thousand, in the world over a million. And yet it to a very great extent is an entirely preventable disease. Social and economic conditions far below what they might be are to a very great extent responsible for its never diminishing prevalence. Of it Mr. Hunter,* who has had perhaps as great opportunities for observing its growth and its methods as anyone not directly connected with the medical profession, says: "It is a needless plague, a preventable plague. It is one of the results of our inhumane tenements; it follows in the train of our inhumane sweatshops; it fastens itself upon children and young people because we forget that they need playgrounds and because we are selfish and niggardly in providing breathing spaces; it comes where the hours of labour are long and the wages small; it afflicts the children who are sent to labour when they should yet be in school; the plague goes to meet them. It is a brother to the anguish of poverty, and wherever food is scant and bodies half clothed and rooms dark, this hard and relentless brother of poverty finds a victim. . . .

"The extent of the White Plague is one of the best tests of a high or low state of society; in many ways it is the truest and most accurate of social tests. The number of its victims will indicate the districts in which sweat-shops flourish, and the streets in which the double-decker tenement, the scourge of New York, is most often found. Where the death rate from the plague is greatest there ignorance prevails; drunkenness is

* "Poverty," page 164.

rife; poverty, hunger, and cold are the common misfortune. . . .

"Tuberculosis is more common in the cities than in the country. The death rate from this disease in the cities of over twenty-five thousand inhabitants is about twice that of the rural districts of the state. The tenement districts suffer much more from the disease than do the well-to-do districts. In Paris the death rate is three times as great in the poorest quarters as it is is in the well-to-do quarters. In Hamburg the proportion is almost the same. In the First Ward, near the Battery in New York City, fourteen times as many people die from tuberculosis, in proportion to population, as in a certain ward adjoining Central Park. Obviously it is a plague which exists much more among the poor than among the rich. . . .

"The disease is one which affects especially residents of the tenements and the workers in certain trades, as, for instance, printers, tailors, bookkeepers, dressmakers, bakers, cigar-makers, potters, stone-cutters, file-grinders, dyers, wool-carders, etc.

"To know why these classes of people are affected, let us for a moment consider how the disease is spread. A person having consumption can, it is said, expectorate in a day seven billions of germs or bacilli. These germs or bacilli are the only cause of the disease. The sputa or expectorations from the diseased lungs dry and afterward become a pulverized dust which is blown about through tenements, theatres, street cars, railway trains, offices, and factories. In fact, the infection is disseminated wherever tuberculosis sputum becomes dry and pulverized. The germ is killed by sunlight and lives but a short time in the open air, but it will live for months in darkness or in places artificially lighted. . . .

"This dry, pulverized dust is the most important of the means of spreading tuberculosis throughout all parts of the city, so that, I do not doubt, a consumptive of the sweat-shop, spraying the garments he sews by sneezing or coughing, may convey to some delicate lad or girl in a far-distant part of the country or in a wealthy part of the city the disease which the sweat-shop has given him. A virulent cause of consumption is the spray discharged from the nose, lungs, or mouth of the consumptive invalid. As before mentioned, those near the person suffering from tuberculosis are very likely to contract the disease. Children playing about on the floor, kissing or embracing the diseased mother or father, taking the milk from a tuberculosis mother, so often contract the disease that the mass of people have an almost unshakable belief that it is inherited. Eminent physicians, however, say that the disease is not inherited. . . . It is cheaper in every way to cure a consumptive in a sanatorium than it is to let him die in a hospital or in a public institution of some kind, but to let him die in a hospital or institution of whatever kind is cheaper than to let him die in his tenement. What we are doing now is just the wrong thing. . . . It is unquestionably the duty of society to care for the victims of this disease. It is a social disease. Society is responsible for its continuance. . . .

"It will be stamped out when the humane work of the Tenement House Department and the Health Department of this city, and of every other city, is victorious over opponents; when there is established in the mind of everyone that vital principle of an advanced civilization, namely, that the profits of individuals are second in importance to the life, welfare, and prosperity of the great masses of people. It will disappear from that community which demands the destruction of an insanitary tenement regardless of inconvenience to individuals and which also demands that there shall be no dark and windowless rooms within its boundaries under any condition whatsoever, as a result of any plea, or as a favour to private interests great or small."

Certain tenements as well as workshops become infected with the disease. We have heard of the "Lung Block" and also of the "Ink Pot" in New York, both with their frightfully large numbers of deaths from tuberculosis. Mr. Ernest Poole, in describing the conditions in this latter tenement, says: "It has front and rear tenements five floors high, with a foul, narrow court between. Here live one hundred and forty people. Twenty-three are babies. Here I found one man sick with the plague in the front house, two more in the rear — and one of these had a young wife and four children. Here the plague lives in darkness and filth — filth in halls, over walls and floors, in sinks and closets. Here in nine years alone twenty-six cases have been reported. How many besides these were kept secret? And behind these nine years — how many cases more?

"Rooms here have held death ready and waiting for years. Up on the third floor, looking down into the court, is a room with two little closets behind it. In one of these a blind Scotchman slept and took the plague in '94. His wife and his fifteen-year-old son both drank, and the home grew squalid as the tenement itself. He died in the hospital. Only a few months later the plague fastened again. Slowly his little daughter grew used to the fever, the coughing, the long, sleepless nights. The foul court was her only outlook. At last she, too, died. The mother and son then moved away. But in this room the germs lived on. They might all have been killed in a day by sunlight; they can live two years in darkness. Here in darkness they lived, on grimy walls, in dusky nooks, on dirty floors. Then one year later, in October, a Jew rented this same room. He was taken, and died in the summer. This room was rented again in the autumn by a German and his wife. She had the plague already, and died. Then an Irish family came in. The father was a hard, steady worker, and loved his children. The home this time was winning the fight. But six months later he took the plague. He died in 1901. This is only the record of one room in seven years."

Professor Koch, who a little over twenty-two years ago discovered the cause of tuberculosis, says in an interview on the subject: "In all other infectious diseases we attack infection at its source; cases of small-pox, of leprosy, of diphtheria, of plague, are isolated, but cases of tuberculosis in their last stages, the most deadly stage of the most deadly disease of all, are still allowed throughout Europe to spread further infection broadcast in the midst of their already destitute families. This fact does not yet seem to be learned. When it is, and when we have these homes for the hopeless cases adjoining every city, then tuberculosis will pass from the midst of us." Again, he says: "It is not cruelty to isolate these cases; it is the truest and highest kindness."

I have dwelt at length upon this great "White Plague" — consumption — because its prevalence and its non-abatement are so directly caused by social and industrial conditions that the individual himself is powerless to escape, and which only a united public action can end. There are public spirited and earnest people in some of our states, however, who are already aroused to the importance of this great, and, to a large extent, unnecessary evil, and who are already beginning to put into operation agencies that promise much for its amelioration. Much, however, must be done; and a great part must be along the lines of better social and industrial conditions under which so many millions of our people live.

Did space permit we could also consider at length the diseases resulting to workmen from various types of employment, for some are in time inevitably health-breaking, and some are invariably most deadly. But generally for those who are striken through these employments, no provisions of any type are made, and when no longer strong or capable the worker is thrown out upon himself. Unable in his weakened or diseased condition to find other employment, he many times becomes a public charge. "Parasitic" employments, with no further responsibilities for those whose health they undermine, are all too common in this day of enlightenment. The public must demand greater protection from and responsibility on the part of these. Mr. John Graham Brooks, in his admirable work, "The Social Unrest,"* has spoken most strongly of that frightful list of striken labourers that are now thrown back upon themselves or their families with recompense so uncertain and niggardly as to shock the most primitive sense of social justice. Speaking of what comes under the head of accident injuries in connection with the progress of German insurance, Mr. Brooks further says: "Previous to the accident insurance in Germany it was thought that there might be thirty or forty thousand injuries due to machinery that would be covered by the insurance. The first investigation showed three times this number; when the investigation became more complete, six times the number . . . Most civilized communities outside of America have already made the same acknowledgment by framing new laws that mark an era in a juster social legislation."

Switzerland came first in 1881, then Germany, Austria, Norway, England, France, Italy, and Denmark. They have all taken definite steps along the lines of the securing of justice in this matter of industrial accidents. The United States, the nation above all others that one would naturally think had greatest cause for taking such a step, has as yet done practically nothing.

* Macmillan and Company, New York and London

Undoubtedly lack of regular employment, sickness or weakness, combined with the receiving of a mere living wage, which leaves no opportunity to meet any emergency successfully, is responsible for the great proportion of the poverty and resultant pauperism that is in existence in our own as well as in so many other countries to-day. The uncertainty and darkness that the combination brings into the lives of millions of otherwise strong, honest, hard-working, and withal deserving, people, is almost indescribable. We make it hard for many a man to be honest and independent and self-respecting, and when with all his magnificent struggles he eventually goes under, we throw the role of the criminal or the pauper upon him and those dependent on him.

We have the rush and strain in so many lines of work, the boom and then depression, men rushed and driven and then no work. There is no time for culture and advancement while the rush and strain is on, and the uncertainty of existence — to meet one's honest obligations, and many times the search for work when unemployment comes, leaves no time for culture or advancement, or even for the normal enjoyment of life, which should be in any enlightened country at least the portion of every endeavour. I think one of the saddest and most unjust features of our present day life is the contemplation of the thousands of thousands who are working from early to late year after year merely to get bread and clothing and shelter for the next day's work — nothing more, lives void of all art, learning, rest, or hope.

Think what a loss it means to even an average standard of citizenship. Think what it means for the future. Think what a thing human life on this basis has become, compared to what it might and should be.

I have an infinite respect for that great body of labour striving in the face of such great odds to remain diligent, honest, self-sustaining, fighting continually to retain their places as self-supporting members of the community, and to give whatever opportunities they are capable of giving to their children — this vast army of heroes, heroes in the common life, the highest type there is. Many of them, however, on account of sometimes shabby clothes and a less prosperous appearance, are looked down upon by many more well-to-do and better kept, but who in a similar test would fall far below them in the measure of heroism. It is of this great army that Mr. Hunter speaks as follows: "In the same cities and, indeed, everywhere, there are great districts of people who are up before dawn, who wash, dress, and eat breakfast, kiss wives and children, and hurry away to work or to seek work. The world rests upon their shoulders; it moves by their muscle; everything would stop if, for any reason, they should decide not to go into the fields and factories and mines. But the world is so organized that they gain enough to live upon only when they work; should they cease, they are in destitution and hunger. The more fortunate of the labourers are but a few weeks from actual distress when the machines are stopped. Upon the unskilled masses want is constantly pressing. As soon as employment ceases, suffering stares them in the face. They are the actual producers of wealth, who have no home nor any bit of soil which they may call their own. They are the millions who possess no tools and can work only by permission of another. In the main, they live miserably, they know not why. They work sore, yet gain nothing. They know the meaning of hunger and the dread of want. They love their wives and children. They try to retain their self-respect. They have some ambition. They give to neighbours in need, yet they are themselves the actual children of poverty. . . . The necessities for maintaining physical efficiency are very different from those essential to mere living. A Hottentot, a Lazzarone, or a vagrant may live well enough on little or nothing, because he does not spend himself. The modern workman demands a far higher standard of living in order to keep pace with intense industrial life. Physical efficiency, not mere existence, is to him vital. His necessities are necessities! It is a terrible word, for "Necessity's sharp pinch" is like that of a steel vise. There is no give to it. Necessity is like flint or granite. It is irresistible. It cannot be shuffled with nor altered. If physical efficiency is an absolute and vital necessity to the workman, so to him are certain necessities for maintaining that physical efficiency. The fundamental thing in all this is that every workman who is expected by society to remain independent of public relief and capable of self-support must be guaranteed, in so far as that is possible, an opportunity for obtaining those necessaries essential to physical efficiency. Such a standard is the basis of almost everything; for, unless men can retain their physical efficiency, they must degenerate. To continue in poverty for any long period means in the end the loss of the power of doing work, and to be unable to work means in the end pauperism."

There is a very direct connection between uncertainty of employment and increased vagrancy and increased crime, especially theft and those things pertaining thereto. This is always noted in connection with any unusual industrial depression, and also in lesser degree in connection with the closing down of any particular work or works. We allow to be built up an economic and industrial system that makes it hard and next to impossible for a man to be honest, self-supporting, and therefore self-respecting, and then punish him for it.

Several years ago, the case of a workman and his connection with the Associated Charities in Boston came under my observation. He was a strong, splendid type of man, driver of a team in connection with one of the large lumber firms. One day in handling a load of heavy timbers, through some mischance, his shoulder was dislocated and he was laid up for some weeks. His family consisted of a wife and three children, one of them a babe. They lived in three neatly kept small rooms in a section of low-priced tenements. As soon as his little reserve power was exhausted, in order to keep above want, they had to apply for aid to the Charity Organization. When he was finally capable of resuming work, it was found that his place had been filled by another. I have known this man to get up and be out of his house long before light, and with practically nothing for breakfast, regularly day after day for several weeks, in his vain endeavour to find work. Wherever he could get track of any possibility of work, he was there early among those seeking the same. He was not a shiftless man, caring little whether he had work or not, but a strong, sober, earnest man, who felt the responsibility of the family dependent upon him. This weary, fruitless search for work, is a tale that is repeated over and over every day in any large centre.

Sometime ago it was my privilege to sit with a friend, a Municipal Judge in the Borough of Brooklyn, as he despatched his daily round of cases. There were numbers whose troubles could be traced directly to a lack of regular employment. Among them was an unusually strong, splendid looking man, of about middle age, a blacksmith by trade. His work had been chiefly in connection with the handling the large forge pieces that form part of the work of various machine-shops. Through some shifting of forces — he was not a man who drank — he was thrown out of work. The weary, fruitless search for work and the increasing want — notwithstanding his splendid physical build he was a sensitive man — enabled depression finally to take strong hold of him, and after struggling with this for some days he finally one evening got his bottle of poison and quietly lay down on the kitchen floor to end it all. He was found before the end came, was resuscitated, and the next day was taken before the Municipal Judge on the charge of attempted suicide. It was indeed pathetic to see this splendid looking man, dejection and quiet written in every movement and on every feature, careless now as to what disposition would be made of him, having no choice now as to whether it was confinement or freedom. Fortunately he was before a Justice of unusual type, one who used his office primarily for the good he could do to that weary and never ending round of fellow creatures that came before him daily. That same day agencies were put into operation to help the man find work — the only thing needed — and thus restore him as nearly as possible to his family and to his former independent position.

How frequently men drop on the streets of the cities of this, in many respects, great nation, from hunger, in addition to that greater number of men and women who suffer quietly and unknown to the world, in a country where there is plenty for all a thousand times over. They prefer hunger and starvation to theft or begging, and thousands upon thousands prefer it to becoming a pauper. Such are indeed heroes of the highest mould.

We must learn that the duty of our industries is not done with the payment of just a living wage. Compensation must be adequate to enable something to be laid by for the emergency that comes to every individual and to every family.

There is a necessary and there is an unnecessary poverty. The former is that that comes about through intemperance, shiftlessness, laziness, depravity. This I suppose will always be with us. There is no power that can shield men or women from the penalties or the inevitable results of the violation of natural and moral laws. There is on the other hand, and it is unhappily the very great portion of it all, an unnecessary poverty. The great bulk of the vast amount of poverty in the country to-day, as well as that in every other country is of this unnecessary type. It results through no fault of the individual, in fact through agencies that the individual as such cannot cope with and cannot escape. It is due to certain social and industrial evils and wrongs that a truly great or even self-respecting nation cannot continue to permit. We must find and put an end to the causes that deliberately make paupers out of the citizens of a great and free nation, and then turn around and take care of them out of the public funds.

An industrial system that takes out of a man all the vitality and energy and good there is in him and then throws him out and onto the public as a public charge, is not of a high order, and as it is not necessary it certainly cannot much longer be permitted. We must make provisions for old age. When vast numbers are receiving merely, and still other vast numbers not even, a living wage, and can scarcely keep even with the daily demands of life, how then, broken and helpless — many long before their time — can they expect to live, self-supporting, and in even the crudest form of comfort, in their later years. We must learn from Germany and other countries, and take up the matter of old age pensions. We must make provisions for old age and for the helpless outside of pauperism, this in addition to a fairer living wage. A noted writer has recently said that the whole matter resolves itself into the matter of fair wages and regular employment. Then too we must stop killing as well as injuring the breadwinners in such wholesale numbers, or if not, then industry *must be compelled* to make just and full and quick recompense to those that through this agency become dependents. Prof. Edward D. Jones, speaking of the fairer wage, says: "The necessity for higher wages is based upon the observation that, in the purchase and sale of labour upon the market, all the necessary and legitimate costs of producing labour are not provided for in the wages received. Such transactions are not complete economically, and do not meet the claims of social justice. Fair wages must include more than enough to support the labourer while working, and must cover compensation for seasons of idleness due to sickness, old age, youth, lack of work, or other causes beyond the control of the labourer."

We are still considering the actual conditions that exist in a country supposedly very great and uniformly prosperous. In the United States to-day there are over four million paupers. The average person would scarcely believe that in New York in the year 1897 over 29 per cent of the people and in 1899 over 24 per cent of the people found it necessary to apply for relief. And yet, these figures given by the State Board do not include the relief rendered by the trade unions, various small clubs, circles, and committees, nor the relief given by individuals. During the year 1903 in Boston, more than 20 per cent of the inhabitants were rendered aid by the public authorities alone, and in addition to these it is estimated that during that year 336,000 persons were aided in private institutions, such as hospitals, dispensaries, asylums, etc., and these are not, except by duplications, contained in the above figures. Estimating that these figures are correct as published, it will be found that the number of people in the State of New York in distress and requiring aid in 1897, and the number in Boston in 1903 equalled proportionately the number of those in poverty in London.

The Charity Organization Society in New York finds that from 43 to 52 per cent of all applications for aid need work rather than relief. The United Hebrew Charities in the same city say the distress and poverty among their people is due mainly to the inability to find opportunities to become self-supporting. This applies not only to New York, but equally well to Chicago and to various other cities. There is then a direct connection between irregularity or lack of employment and pauperism, the same as there is a very direct connection between irregularity or lack of work and vagrancy. If so large a proportion of those applying for aid need work rather than relief, nearly or practically one half, then it certainly is encumbent upon society to provided a solution of the problem. Want and a lack of regular employment precede both poverty and vagrancy more often than they follow it.

There is also a very direct connection between want

and an adequate means to supply it and drunkenness. It is the cheerless, dreary condition in men's lives, in the lives of both men and women, that is responsible for the great bulk of intemperance that we find. Underfed, underclothed, cold without sufficient heat, no hope, despondency, this is the chief road to intemperance and degeneracy. Were we to know all the facts we would find that drink precedes but rarely. Poverty precedes more often than it follows. The great evil of intemperance which is the bane in the lives of such vast numbers of working people in this country, as in England, and every country where it has reached similar proportions, is to a vast extent due to the dreary and hard and underfed and hopeless conditions in so many hundreds of thousands of lives. Cold without sufficient heat, a desire to get away from, to forget the dull, weary hopelessness. Wise, indeed, was the Bishop of the English Church when he said, "If I lived in the slums I should be a drunkard, too."

Dr. Henry van Dyke, preaching the baccalaureate sermon at one of our leading universities some time ago, gave utterance to this same great truth when he said: "There are monstrous evils and vices in society. Let intemperance be for us the type of all, because so many of the others are its children. Drunkenness ruins more homes and wrecks more lives than war. How shall we oppose it? I do not say that we shall not pass resolutions and make laws against it. But I do say that we can never really conquer the evil in this way. The stronghold of intemperance lies in the vacancy and despair of men's minds. The way to attack it is to make the sober life beautiful and happy and full of interest." But the lives of this vast army of men and women that we are considering, those continually in or continually face to face with want, are not beautiful, neither are they happy nor full of interest. They should be; they could be.

Mr. Arthur W. Milbury, Secretary of the Industrial Christian Alliance, has said: "I have had a long and intimate personal experience with the class of men referred to, and I give it unhesitatingly as my testimony that not many men are 'lazy' in the sense in which this word is commonly used. I have dealt with thousands of such men and have almost invariably found them willing and anxious to work. I know that a great many people engaged in charitable enterprises have much to say about lazy people, but I am inclined to think that it is not so much laziness that is at fault as the efforts so many of us make to put square pegs in round holes. All men are not born with the same energy and the same intelligence, and what might be called laziness in me might be called superhuman energy in other men. In this institution, we do not put at chopping wood or shoveling coal, if we can possibly help it, the man whose only occupation in life has been that of bookkeeper or clerk and who has never had any hard physical labour. We endeavour, as far as possible, to put men at the work they are best fitted for. Perhaps this is one reason why our experience leads us not to consider laziness as prevalent a vice as some other people."

The conditions that surround the lives of the children

of any country, especially the play-life, constitute a very great factor in determining the immediate future conditions of that country. In the early days of the American nation the fields, and all that this conveys, were the playgrounds of the children. As the city began and grew the Common was given them in place of the fields; this was succeeded many times by the small yard of the home. But as the cities have grown and land has become more valuable, and population denser and continually denser, the children have been gradually pushed out into the streets, until in Greater New York for example, the street and all that that means is the chief playground for not less than half a million children. This is also true, to a greater or less extent, of certain portions of every great city in the country,— the street with its noises and all of its dangers, its dust and its dirt, and many times its stifling atmosphere, as well as all of its moral dangers, is the playground of at least seven million of our children to-day. After saying that, "The younger criminals seem to come almost exclusively from the worst tenement-house districts," an eminent authority even many years ago gave before a New York Legislative Committee, testimony as follows: "By far the largest part, 80 per cent at least, of crimes against property and against the person are perpetrated by individuals who have either lost connection with home life, or never had any, or whose homes have ceased to be sufficiently separate, decent, and desirable to afford what was regarded as ordinary wholesome influences of home and family."

It is the life in the streets of the large city where the needs of the children seem to have been so generally forgotten, that develops as Mr. Jacob A. Riis has so authoritatively said, "dislike of regular work, physical incapability of sustained effort, misdirected love of adventure, gambling propensities, absence of energy, and untrained will, carelessness of the happiness of others."

Such are the baneful influences that surround the lives of these almost unbelievably large numbers of our quickly coming men and women, a number so large as soon to constitute the determining factor in the nation's life.

For one to realize that there are hungry people, and even among the children, who *especially* need proper and sufficient nourishment to insure fully developed and enduring bodies as well as brains, to realize that there are the hungry and the chronically hungry, resulting from poverty, in a country of such supposedly universal prosperity, is at first almost startling. It was estimated during a recent winter — at a period of more than ordinarily average prosperity that there were more than seventy thousand children in New York City who arrived at school hungry. I have seen attempts made to deny this, but so far there have been no successful ones. When asked his opinion as to the correctness of this statement the City Superintendent of Schools said: "With regard to Mr. Hunter's statement, I beg leave to say that a statement of this kind must necessarily be an estimate and only approximately correct. Mr. Hunter, however, has had unusual opportunities for forming a judgment in this matter and I should think that he would be more likely to underestimate than to overestimate the number." It is the opinion of the Superintendent himself, that there are hundreds of thousands of children in the city schools who cannot study because they are always hungry. Commenting upon this same matter at about that time, an editorial in one of our most influential New York daily papers said: "The fact that seventy thousand children go to school hungry is established. . . . They say the people of England are deteriorating because many of them live in a constant state of half-starvation. . . . If conditions are not changed, the next five years will find the number of half-starved children in New York doubled. These conditions will put 100,000 children in Chicago on half rations, and they will create a starving population in every city of this marvelously prosperous country. . . . It is not a part of the common lot of life. There is no excuse for anyone starving in the United States. Destitution is a removable calamity. It is a political and economic disease. A correct system of government and a correct enforcement of proper laws will remove it." In addition to this army of underfed children in our schools, there are undoubtedly very large numbers of the underfed among those who are not in the schools at all.

The number of children not in our schools is perhaps much larger than the average person has any conception of. A careful estimate in connection with New York City, shows that fourteen out of every hundred of all children of eleven and twelve years of age, over twenty-five out of every hundred of all children of thirteen years, and more than fifty out of every hundred children of fourteen years of age are not in attendance at the public schools. I have no facts of a similar nature that pertain to other cities, before me, but I dare say that in some cases at least, perhaps many, the numbers would be quite as large.

Our modern life is becoming so intense, and the struggle for existence is becoming, especially in some centres, so keen and so sharp, that no one growing into manhood and womanhood can afford to enter upon the stage of activity in anything but a thoroughly first-class and sound condition, both mentally and physically. Each should have an equipment of only the very best in a country supposed to be among the best. Nevertheless there are at this present hour over 1,700,000 boys and girls under fifteen years of age at work in our mills and our mines and various industrial establishments and works of all types. At this point space does not permit of any enumeration of the conditions under which vast numbers of these children of from five to fifteen years of age are working, nor any detailed enumeration of the broken condition of so many of them so long before their time, sometimes even before they have entered upon young manhood and womanhood.

The cotton mills of the South, many owned or controlled by wealthy Northern capitalists, have of recent years brought about a condition of child slavery that was scarcely surpassed by a similar condition in England during its darkest period of child labour so many, many years ago. The greed for gain when it once takes possession of a man is never satisfied, and the *only way many times* to protect the helpless from the brute for society itself to stretch forth its strong mandatory arm.

In addition to the almost unspeakable evils resulting to the child himself and later to the man and woman, is the competition that this army of over 1,700,000 child workers throws out against adult labour, and especially is this a matter of no small import when there are continually such large numbers of men and women out of employment as we have already noted. Greater profits is the one and practically absolute cause, for in this age of modern machinery the children can many times be hired for a third of the man's normal wage.

In view of the facts presented in that much discussed and very suggestive and valuable book, "The Present Distribution of Wealth in the United States," published sometime ago, by Mr. Charles B. Spahr, we can scarcely cease wondering that our Federal Bureaus have not even before this made an effort to find the present drift of matters in this respect in the country. Mr. Spahr's findings revealed the fact that even so far back as 1890, considerably over one-third of the families in the United States, or 41 per cent, are entirely propertyless: that seven-eighths of the families hold but one-eighth of the national wealth: and that on the other hand, one per cent of the families own more than the entire remaining 99 per cent.

Another suggestive way of presenting the matter is that the "wealthy" and "well-to-do" classes, that is, 1,500,000 families hold in wealth over $56,000,000,000, while the remaining "middle" and "poorer" classes, that is, 11,000,000 families, own but $9,000,000,000, and of course, in this latter number of families are not included the 41 per cent of the families that are entirely propertyless, which, as is apparent, would greatly swell the inequality.

Other estimates including those of Mr. George K. Holmes, an expert statistician employed on the census, revealed facts of a very similar nature.

These are indeed not only significant but most portentous facts, and if the above are the facts as far back as 1890, they have undoubtedly been accentuated with great force since then, for there has been no decade in our entire history in which so many great private fortunes have been built up or have been added so powerfully to as that between 1890 and 1900, and since. A well-known man in the financial world in reviewing some of our present day conditions has recently made a statement to the effect that it is only a matter of simple mathematics to ascertain the day, and that only a few years away, when ten men will be practically owners of the United States. He has indeed much basis, in view of present conditions and the present trend of matters, for this statement.

The fact of the matter is that in face of the great and

unprecedented growth of wealth in the United States, resulting in large measure from its youth and wonderful natural resources and opportunities, the increase has been so *unequal* that the vast millions have flowed into the pockets of the few, while the few millions have gone to the lot of the many. The rich have grown richer at a rate and to a degree that is almost astounding, and while it is not true that the poor have on the whole grown poorer, *it is true* that the increase going to their lot has been so exceedingly small in comparison — in some cases not even sufficient to be noted at all — that practically the same effect has come about. In other words the increase in general prosperity and of those at the upper end has been out of all proportion to that of the great labouring and middle class. The masses of the people are not getting their just relative increase. Were it not at the risk of dealing too much with statistics and figures, it would be most interesting to calculate and consider the total amount of wealth created each year or each decade, and the amount of it that actually goes to the great mass of the producers of that wealth.

A Fabian Tract says that there are about one million rich men in England who do nothing, hence live on the labour of others. The vast tracts of land that in great estates, sometimes even in large cities (over 600 acres in the heart of London is held by a single individual), that are held by rich or titled families, and thus kept away from the people to whom the land should rightly belong or for whose benefit it should be used, is undoubtedly one of the great causes of the great inequality of conditions in Great Britain. I have passed partly by one estate in North Britain, eighteen miles wide and a hundred miles long. There are numerous estates of vast numbers of square miles each, even comprising whole villages where no single dweller owns the house in which he lives, nor can he even drive a nail in it without permission.

In view of the above facts it is interesting to note the following, a conversation between the well-known author of that widely circulated little book, "Merrie England," and one of the subjects, a working-man subject, of the King. The title of the chapter in which it occurs is, "Who Makes the Wealth, and Who Gets It?"

"Now, John, what are the evils of which we complain? Lowness of wages, length of working hours, uncertainty of employment, insecurity of the future, low standards of public health and morality, prevalence of pauperism and crime, and the existence of false ideals of life.

"I will give you a few examples of the things I mean. It is estimated that in this country, with its population of thirty-six millions, there are generally about 700,000 men out of work. There are about 800,000 paupers. Of every thousand persons who die in Merrie England over nine hundred die without leaving any property at all. About eight millions of people exist always on the borders of destitution. About twenty millions are poor. More than half the national income belongs to about ten thousand people. About thirty-thousand people own fifty-five fifty-sixths of the land and capital of the kingdom, but of thirty-six millions of people only one and one-half millions get above $15 a week. The average income per head of the working classes is about $85 a year, or less than twenty-five cents a day. There are millions of our people working under conditions and living in homes that are simply disgraceful. The sum of crime, vice, drunkenness, gambling, prostitution, idleness, ignorance, want, disease, and death is appalling. . . . To what are the above evils due? They are due to the unequal distribution of wealth, and to the absence of justice and order from our society.

"Political orators and newspaper editors are very fond of talking to you about 'your country.' Now, Mr. Smith, it is a hard practical fact that you have not got any country. The British Islands do not belong to the British people; they belong to a few thousands — certainly not half a million — of rich men."

The poverty and wretched conditions in London and other large centres in Great Britain is indeed very great in its proportions, but we in the United States are rapidly approaching it in many centres, and in some, according to all available facts and statistics, we have reached it already. Sometime ago a well-known English philanthropist and sociologist, who was travelling in this country studying the conditions of the working classes, publicly declared while in Washington, as the result of his investigations that there are worse places in that city than the worst quarters of London.

Said Jacob A. Riis: "I am not easily discouraged.

But I confess I was surprised by the sights I have seen in the national capital. You people of Washington have alley after alley filled with hidden people whom you don't know. There are 298 such alleys.

"They tell me the death rate among the negro babies born in these alleys is 475 out of a thousand before they grow to be one year old. Nearly one-half! Nowhere I have ever been in the civilized world have I ever seen such a thing as that."*

The luxury on the one hand and the poverty on the other, and it has been the history of the world that where the former has grown great the latter has grown great also and as a consequence, that we find in the American nation to-day, and within a period so comparatively short, is simply enormous in its proportions.

While in this country we are not labouring under the caste system that exists in England,and has there become almost as fixed and pronounced as it has been for untold generations in India for example,we are already feeling a similar bearing and power on the part of the very rich, both as families and as individuals, and some such state is now as for some time past it has been, in process of rapid formation in this country.

Sometime ago I noticed the definition that an eminent writer gave to the word loafer, and as nearly as I can recall — a loafer — one who works not himself but lives on the work of others, either as a gentleman, or as a tramp or a beggar or a pauper — both classes are kept through the support of others.

*Washington Times, Dec. 16, 1903.

The upper and lower ends are borne by the great middle classes,— and the growth and increase of the upper tends continually to increase the number of the lower — These great extremes result primarily from the unequal distribution of the profits resulting from the handling of earth's products. This is the reason of the one per cent of the families owning already more than the remaining 99 per cent.

It is from this that the "smart" set comes, sometimes called the "brainless" set, sometimes the "thoughtless." The maker of the fortune, the father or the grandfather, many times made from the most common clay stuff, but with an ability in manipulating, in accumulating, sometimes with a working knowledge of scarcely one of the ten commandments, was the one who did the work; and the descendants become dwellers in idleness, and worse than idleness, for the old gentleman has helped them onto the backs of other people and from this position they refuse politely to descend, and will remain there until the people bring about a different set of conditions on the one hand, or until idleness and luxury, so many times descending into vice, has sapped the vitality and the common level is found again. It was John Stewart Mill who pointed out the following facts:

"When men talk of the ancient wealth of a country, of riches inherited from ancestors, and similar expressions, the idea suggested is, that the riches so transmitted were produced long ago, at the time when they are said to have been first acquired, and that no portion of the capital of a country was produced this year except so much as may have been this year added to the total amount. The fact is far otherwise.

"The greater part in value of the wealth now existing in England has been produced by human hands within the last twelve months. A very small proportion indeed of that large aggregate was in existence ten years ago; of the present productive capital of the country scarcely any part, except farmhouses and factories, and a few ships and machines, and even these would not in most cases have survived so long, if fresh labour had not been employed within that period in putting them into repair.

"The land subsists, and the land is almost the only thing that subsists. Everything which is produced perishes, and most things very quickly.

"Capital is kept in existence from age to age, not by preservation, but by perpetual reproduction."

A great deal of very bad sense and a lack of discriminating thought is shown at the present day in an indiscriminate vituperation of the rich, as if all were of the same class. It is by no means true. They cannot be indiscriminately classed together nor spoken of in the same category any more than various types of business enterprises, those that though large are straightforward and honourable, and those that seem to be the very epitome of hell in their methods.

Among the rich are some of the finest and noblest types, and most valuable in the social structure. Moreover, it seems to me that there should be not only no indiscriminate vituperation, *but none at all.* Whatever blame there is should rightly rest upon those sitting quietly by and allowing a system of social and economic injustice and inequality to be built up that enables a few to become so enormously and so drunkenly rich that even they themselves and their descendants suffer from the effects of it, and on the other hand millions of men, women, and children are reduced to a life of continual poverty and misery through this very inequality that *we* permit. This in face of the fact that the demands of the people could be made for an economic and industrial *justice* in a manner so convincing and so compelling that no bodies or groups of men or families, however powerful they may be, however drunk with gain and influence, or however skilled in methods of manipulation, could do anything other than listen to and heed these demands.

Not hostility to the rich, a foolish as well as dangerous proceeding, but a fully prepared and determined and never-ending hostility to a political and industrial system that permits a few to become so excessively rich, and hence such unequal and such rapidly growing dangerous conditions. It is not their fault but ours if we permit these conditions to continue. They are doing only what large numbers of those who condemn them would do under similar circumstances.

It is a beautiful little village of 3,000 people. The public Common was a joy and a pleasure to all; rich in flowers, in grass, in trees, in birds and song. Sometime ago several influential families turned and now pasture their cows in it. The people through negligence permitted it. The owners of the cows are now using a great abundance of very rich cream. *But for the people the joy of the Common is gone.* Sometime the people will awake and the cows will be driven from the Common and forever. Their owners will never take them out of their own accord. They have grown to love cream dearly.

The *system* is now at fault, and must be changed even for the safety and perpetuity of the nation, as well as the welfare of the great mass of the people. As it is now the great proportion is simply a grist for the few.

Bishop Potter of New York has recently said: "The growth of wealth and of luxury, wicked, wasteful and wanton, as before God I declare that luxury to be, has been matched step by step by a deepening and deadening poverty, which has left whole neighbourhoods of people practically without hope and without aspiration."

In *The Churchman* of June 4, 1904, occurred the following paragraph: "Some startling facts were presented at the conference of the C. A. I. L. (The Church Association for the Advancement of the Interests of Labour) by its tenement-house committee. Out of 512 families investigated by Dr. Daniel, of the New York Infirmary for Women and Children, one in a little less than eight lived in rear houses, though these have been legally forbidden for years; two-thirds (377) lived in houses with dark halls; only forty in houses where the halls were really light. But one of the houses could be reported as in really good condition; 222 were in moderately good repair; 255 dirty and out of repair. The earnings of these families averaged $3.81 a week, and of this they paid almost exactly half, $1.85, for rent. The number of persons in a family averaged 4.26, so that there was left, after paying rent, forty-six cents for each person for food, clothing, heat, light and the rest."

We make poverty and then bountifully supply, or attempt to supply, relief for it to the sad, sad numbers who despite their most diligent and heroic efforts are cast into it. It is indeed a sort of "benevolent feudalism." It has been said and so truthfully, that the rich and powerful will do anything for the poor but get off their backs.

The munificence of our charities and relief works is in one sense a most beautiful feature of our country's civilization. In another sense it is one of the most horrible shames, in that it registers, and still countenances the great mass of the poverty among us, only a small fraction of which is necessary. We spend annually in charity and relief — public and private — over two hundred million dollars, and the demands are continually in advance of the ways of meeting them. The demand for relief always keeps considerable in advance of the supply — such is the testimony of Prof. Amos G. Warner in his able book "American Charities." But with it all we have not yet learned the far greater economy of *prevention* over cure, or attempted cure, in addition to the frightful amount of suffering and misery and degradation that such a system brings to such vast numbers. The following partial illustration may be suggestive. A few years ago in Glasgow there existed a frightful death rate among the people of a certain portion of the city. The municipal authorities, more quick to act for the people than in similar cases among us, examined into the conditions, found the causes, and demolished the houses in that immediate section and erected new tenements to take their places. The death rate was reduced from fifty-five per thousand to a little over fourteen per thousand. A slum immediately adjoining still had a death rate of fifty-three per thousand. Here stood two groups of dwellings housing practically the same class of people, one having a death rate of a little over fourteen to every thousand and the other a death rate almost four times as great. But for this common-sense action, this frightful and unnecessary death rate would have kept up year after year, and charity and relief would have been taxed both in money and in energy to a far greater extent than the amounts of money and energy that were required to make the surroundings of these people decent, and as becomes a civilized community.

The following paragraphs are filled with truth concerning this matter of charity and relief: "In its origin charity sprang from the noblest feeling — that sympathy with others which prompts us to relieve suffering. The impulse to feed the hungry, clothe the naked and shelter the homeless, is wholly creditable. But the modern machinery of public and private charities, supported by taxation or by private funds given out of a sense of obligation, is abominable.

"All statistics of charitable organizations show that

the real trouble with the great majority of the people who seek relief, is lack of work. At least 75 per cent of those who are assisted by private charity or public institutions are able and willing to work, if only they could find employment. And the remaining 25 per cent, including the children, the sick, etc., is indirectly the result of the same conditions of lack of work or low wages. Because of inability on the part of parents to make provision for their children, the orphan asylums and industrial homes are overflowing. Because of distress brought on by insufficient nourishment, or by living in unhealthy tenements, the hospitals are crowded. Because the sick are poor they must look for free medical attendance instead of employing a physician. So with practically all the objects of charity. Directly or indirectly the need for help arises from the fact that workers are not able to support themselves by their labour. . . . Those who have worked the hardest at charities know how hopelessly inefficient and insufficient they are. Charity fails, and always must fail to accomplish its aims, because it concerns itself with surface symptoms and not with fundamental causes.

"Since charity cannot stop anyone from shutting people out of work, it cannot do anything to alleviate or abolish the evils arising from want of work. When it pretends to do so, it is a fraud used to soothe the victims of partisan laws into silence.

"The rich are generally well aware of all this — so they charge their own indifference to their God, and say that Jesus said, 'The poor ye shall have always with you.' Jesus never said anything of the sort. He said, 'The poor ye have with you always and whensoever ye will ye may do them good' (Mark 14, 7); that is, may abolish their poverty and the causes of it, too. I commend to those religious persons the last four verses of Revelation."*

And while I think the author of these paragraphs is in the main right, I think he speaks somewhat too generally in regard to the motives that actuate many rich people who give to charity, for I know many are animated by motives of the highest and noblest type. And until they can see their way to spend a portion of their means and energy in a far wiser and more effective way — in an endeavour to bring about more just and equitable conditions in the social and industrial life of the country, may they not cease the good work they are doing.

Then so far as the practical effects of charity upon those who are its recipients, the following testimony of Mrs. Josephine Shaw Lowell, is quite thoroughly in keeping with the testimony of practically all experienced workers and observers in this field of charity. Mrs. Lowell says, "Whatever exception you may have encountered, you know that the rule is that those who receive relief are or soon become idle, intemperate, untruthful, vicious, or at least quite shiftless and improvident. You know that the more relief they have as a rule, the more they need. You knew that it is destructive to energy and industry, and that the taint

*From "Free America," by Bolton Hall.

passes from generation to generation and that a pauper family is more hopeless to reform than a criminal family."

Our efforts must be to deal not so much with charity and relief, as with the *causes* that make such vast amounts of charity and relief necessary. It is simply astounding, our willingness to let things go on as they are and then care for the unfortunate millions who fall in their struggles against such tremendous odds.

We allow our municipal and state representatives — who thereby become representatives of the great moneyed and corporate interests — to give over franchises for the use of great public utilities that should be used for the people and with millions upon millions in value, to the personal and private uses of little groups of men, without asking in most cases even a dollar in compensation and then we tamely accept poor service, high charges, many times disgusting and almost inhuman treatment. They give it. We accept it. We accept it even as if we did not know better and as if it were something we had to submit to, rather than because we choose to. Thus we make them increasingly rich and daring and unscrupulous, so that out of their enormous profits, wrung from the constantly increasing needs of the people, they are enabled to build up great corruption funds, to maintain strong and powerful lobbies to influence all legislation in their favour, to kill all that may be adverse, in other words all that may be for the interests of the people. In this way they have gone on and on, getting many times by direct purchase of the votes of the members of our city councils and of legislators, additional properties that by all laws of common-sense as well as the most crude laws of justice, should belong to, should be managed by and for the *people*. Some day, and before long now, we will wonder at the asinine qualities that we American people have displayed in this respect.

Little wonder then that the business and propertied classes have grabbed and are still grabbing everything in sight, as well as appropriating to themselves the machinery of government. They will continue to do this as long as the people permit it.

These agencies, eminently "respectable," though many times rheumatic and gouty, whence spring the greatest forces of corruption in the country, are already gnawing at the very vitals of the nation's welfare, as well as at its safety and perpetuity. The nation of freemen is already in danger. The mutterings of the great discontent are already most clearly audible even to the most indifferent and unconcerned. Of these all thinking men and women are most keenly aware. The nation cannot remain in safety, but must retrograde and this splendid example of free institutions and free men and women must be counted abortive unless a movement and a very pronounced and determined and unceasing movement is quickly made to beat back the advance of the sleek, cunning, conscienceless bands, whose motto is greed and whose method is corruption. It is carrying a blight, withering and deadening to free institutions, into every quarter that it touches.

"If the King of Mexico has any gold," said Cortez, as he and his followers stood clamouring at the gates of Montezuma, "let him send it out to us. For I and my companions have a disease of the heart which is cured by gold."

Sometime ago that very keen observer, matchless thinker, and great lover of justice and of men, hence, of his country's welfare, Henry George, gave utterance to the following most significant words:*

"The evils arising from the unjust and unequal distribution of wealth, which are becoming more and more apparent as modern civilization goes on, are not incidents of progress, but tendencies which must bring progress to a halt. . . .

"The poverty which in the midst of abundance pinches and imbrutes men, and all the manifold evils which flow from it, spring from a denial of justice. In permitting the monopolization of the opportunities which nature freely offers to all, we have ignored the fundamental law of justice — for, so far as we can see, when we view things upon a large scale, justice seems to be the supreme law of the universe. But by sweeping away this injustice and asserting the rights of all men to natural opportunities, we shall conform ourselves to the law — we shall remove the cause of unnatural inequality in the distribution of wealth and power. . . . substitute political strength for political weakness; and make tyranny and anarchy impossible. . . . Our primary social adjustment is a denial of justice. . . .

* "Progress and Poverty," p. 541 (1900).

It is this that turns the blessings of material progress into a curse. It is this that crowds human beings into noisome cellars and squalid tenement-houses; that fills prisons and brothels; that goads men with want and consumes them with greed; that robs women of the grace and beauty of perfect womanhood; that takes from little children the joy and innocence of life's morning.

"Civilization so based cannot continue. The eternal laws of the universe forbid it. Ruins of dead empires testify, and the witness that is in every soul answers, that it cannot be. It is something grander than Benevolence, something more august than Charity — it is Justice herself that demands of us to right this wrong. Justice that will not be denied; that cannot be put off — Justice that with the scales carries the sword.

"Can it be that the gifts of the Creator may be thus misappropriated with impunity? Is it a light thing that labour should be robbed of its earnings while greed rolls in wealth — that the many should want while the few are surfeited? Turn to history, and on every page may be read the lesson that such wrong never goes unpunished; that the Nemesis that follows injustice never falters nor sleeps! Look around to-day. Can this state of thing continue? May we even say, "After us the deluge!" Nay; the pillars of the state are trembling even now, and the very foundations of society begin to quiver with pent-up forces that glow underneath. The struggle that must either revivify, or convulse in ruin, is near at hand, if it be not already begun."

Thoughtful and fearless men are in increasingly

large numbers raising the warning voice. Shall we listen briefly to some types of these warnings? The following paragraph is from the editor of one of our prominent magazines:

"With the waning of religious faith comes the worship of wealth and the attendant evils of extravagance, ostentation, false pretence, envy, and wide-spread discontent. That nation is in a bad way, indeed, when it is notoriously true that the mass of its citizens will do almost anything to get money, and are able to do almost anything by means of money, to ignore or violate the laws, to laugh at decent opinion, to override popular rights, and to trample on the poor. The United States is not yet in such a lamentable case, our land still abounds in honest men and unspoiled women, but, with the unparalleled growth of private fortunes and the spirit of wanton display, with the increase, on the other hand, of misery and wretchedness, we are rapidly approaching the danger line where millions of our miserable poor may well cry out to thousands of our prodigal rich: — 'How comes it that you have so much while we have so little? How can you justify this shameful squandering of wealth when you see us, your brothers, toiling in factories and sweat-shops, starving in tenements, and wasted by disease?' "

The following is a type of recent independent pulpit utterance. Speaking first of the enormous sums expended annually in charity in the United States it continues:

"This colossal sum is about equally divided among public relief, private giving and the charities of the churches. How much good does it do? Is it merely an anæsthetic to benumb the poor, lest they cry too loud? Can wisdom and virtue eliminate the conditions that make charity necessary?

"The true philanthropist is the good steward — the man who labours, plans, executes the honourable business enterprises of this world. He who opens the doors of steady employment, pays an honest, living wage, by his foresight and skill frustrates 'panics,' 'depressions'— this is the true philanthropist. His business enterprises are a blessing to the community.

"Then, again, there are those whom Jesus lashes like scorpions — men who lay burdens on men's shoulders grievous to be borne, and do not as much as touch them with their little finger! There are those who, having a giant's strength, are using it like a tyrant — promoting monopolies that oppress the people, controlling the necessities of life — beef, sugar, oil, coal — and thus use their business positions as did the old barons their castles — places for plunder. This kind of social wrong makes poverty and prepares for social revolution. Jesus commends justice to all such. If parasites and plunderers were abolished, there would be very little need of philanthropy."

Said a well-known Bishop at a Chamber of Commerce dinner recently, at which many prominent millionaires were seated: "The people, the great common people, are suspicious that some great corporations and masses of wealth are protected, or their interests advanced in ways that are inconsistent with the rights of the people.

"They may have no material grounds for their suspicions, but they are suspicious, and so are many of you.

"I am not so afraid of the rich man in politics as I am of the poor and weak man in politics, and the rich man outside.

"Civilization cannot go on where there is mutual suspicion, and prosperity cannot go on long while the people feel or think that the reverence for law by which property is safeguarded is not upheld.

"The massing of great wealth in corporations has come to stay, but neither our sympathies, nor the risk to great properties, nor the curtailment or loss of our properties can reconcile us to any dallying with the rights and liberties of the people."

Sometime ago an able and well-known contributer to various English and Continental periodicals, one whose work has made his residence for sometime past in various capitals, and now residing in London, spoke as follows:

"What you have to deal with in America is snobbery. We have here in London a host of American women who have shaken the democratic dust of America off their feet forever, and who are nightly to be seen at the royal opera, their heads covered with tiaras and coronets, giving themselves all the airs and presumptions of sybaritic queens, and who think it a disgrace to talk of America. Yet their fortunes were made in the American mines and the American railroads, and without the American labourer they would this moment be living in the backwoods, on the remote plains, or on some obscure street of New York, unheard of, unobserved and unknown. Snobbery is undermining American institutions. . . . Within a short period of twenty years your rich American snobs have made of New York, Washington, and Chicago antechambers of London and Paris. . . . As for American women marrying English lords, I have this to say: the women who bring their fortunes here are bringing them to bolster up a decadent world. . . . I predict an invasion of broken-down lords of all grades in the near future, until at last there will not be a fortune left in America of any considerable size that will not pass to the favour of men residing in England or on the Continent. 'Come what may,' said an Englishman to me not long ago, 'we are bound to possess the wealth of the American millionaires in the long run, through the American women.' "

We have dwelt at great length upon the dark side of the picture, because it is so essential that we see this side fully and that we see it at once. But there is another side, and that not without a great deal of brightness. Were we in the condition of the people of Russia up to the present time for example — without a voice in the affairs of government — then we would indeed be in a bad way. With the forces we have been considering already so fully intrenched and so skilled in their methods, there would indeed be no hope. But the battles for political emancipation were waged and won, as King John and others, were they living, would so vividly recall, many years ago. We are a body of freemen with political rights, and the final deciders of what the conditions in the nation shall be. This gives us our hope and our power. With this we can gain and we shall gain, *industrial and economic* freedom, justice, and equality. This is the power with which we shall drive to the background, the forces that have been making a byword of freedom, equality and justice.

We have cause to be grateful by virtue of the newness and power of the country. What has been almost the cause of our undoing shall yet be the means by which we shall be saved. We have political freedom. We have full religious freedom, full independence of Church and State. We are free from the cast systems that constitute the bane of so many old world countries. We have it growing among us, but it is not fixed and can yet be broken by an aroused and determined people. Our reputation is somewhat sullied but in the main yet good. Labour is uniting, learning, growing; self-seeking and unscrupulous leaders are being discovered and thrown out. We have an educational system that is splendid in its quality, and that can yet be made to include all, even those that need it most, within its scope. The masses of the people of all types are becoming profoundly dissatisfied with present conditions. They are inquiring into their causes, and where this is, there is hope. It tells also much of the future outcome. A Roosevelt, a Folke, a La Follette is recognized in his ideas of and demands for a more equal justice, and is rewarded by the confidence of the people into a position of still greater responsibility.

The past several months even have witnessed a great stirring among the people — among others an examination into the infamous methods of the Gas Trusts in both New York and Philadelphia. So infamous had they become and so brazen in satisfying their ever increasing and insatiable appetites for larger and ever larger profits wrung from a great common need of the people, that public opinion was finally compelled to rise up and say, So far and no farther.

The people of another great city have registered their protest against the methods of another public service concern that has for years been taking millions upon millions of toll from them, and with a service in most respects the most abominable. They have asked why half-a-dozen or more men should every twelvemonth receive their millions, while the people should receive practical insult at their hands. They have voiced their protest so strongly and in such a common-sense and practical manner that the blood-sucking tentacles of the already over-fed and bloated creature are now being withdrawn. Other localities are taking lesson from this and are rising up against any further granting of enormous wealth-creating franchises to individuals, or if so, for nothing but *very short* periods, and then not without compensation full and complete.

Likewise revelations in connection with various other public and semi-public service concerns and the methods of still other large business concerns have been coming to us with startling import during even the past few months.

And just as soon as sufficient numbers of our people take enough interest in the public welfare,—which means always their own welfare to a far greater degree than many are given to realize, and thereby become conversant with the actual conditions that are fast crystallizing about us and the agencies that are at work in their sly and subtle manner bringing them about, then the forces will be engendered that will take the Republic to that eminent and true position, that by the grace of God and the awakened common-sense of the people, we believe it shall yet attain.

III

AS TIME DEALS WITH NATIONS

TIME has a strange way of dealing with nations and with men. Its great clock ticks unerringly on. It seems, in a sense, to be merely the sentinel of a great and immutable system of Law.

When the nation gets sufficiently sick and diseased it dies as does the individual. Its hour is struck off with an unerring precision. From that instant the process of disintegration sets in to crumble and consume the body, the structure that so shortly before held the spirit.

It would be useless and indeed foolish to say that there *seem* to be great immutable laws that govern and that determine the life, the ways, the fate of nations. If history means anything it means *this*, and he who will may read. These same laws exist to-day and as has occurred will occur again under like or similar conditions.

So clearly has history written her pages that he who will may go at once to her oft repeated forms, and read with a quickness and clearness that no man can misunderstand. It is always in substance — that great privilege and wealth and oppression have been the cause of the gradual undermining and the final fall and disintegration of all the earlier states that have flourished and that have passed. They failed to realize the immutability and the precision of the laws that govern men and nations. Moreover, no nation or no man has ever been rich enough or powerful enough to change or to escape the accuracy of their workings. There are those who thought it, and for a time their efforts have seemed to be successful, but at the right moment they have been crushed and powdered, even as the rock has crushed and has powdered the shell of the egg; and as long as time endures this story will be repeated in the life of every nation and every individual that does not stop to learn the writing.

"Every civilization," said the late Henry George, "That has been overwhelmed by barbarians has really perished from internal decay." Elaborating upon this, he has said:* "He would have been a rash man who, when Augustus was changing the Rome of brick to the Rome of marble, when wealth was augmenting and magnificence increasing, when victorious legions were extending the frontier, when manners were becoming more refined, language more polished, and literature rising to higher splendours — he would have been a rash man who then would have said that Rome was entering her decline. Yet such was the case.

"And whoever will look may see that, though our civilization is apparently advancing with greater rapidity than ever, the same cause which turned Roman progress into retrogression is operating now.

"What has destroyed every previous civilization has

* "Progress and Poverty," p. 525.

been the tendency to the unequal distribution of wealth and power. This same tendency, operating with increasing force, is observable in our civilization to-day. . . .

"To turn a republican government into a despotism the basest and most brutal, it is not necessary formally to change its constitution or abandon popular elections. It was centuries after Cæsar, before the absolute master of the Roman world pretended to rule other than by authority of a Senate, that trembled before him. . . .

"Where there is anything like an equal distribution of wealth — that is to say, where there is general patriotism, virtue, and intelligence — the more democratic the government the better it will be; but where there is gross inequality in the distribution of wealth, the more democratic the government the worse it will be; for, while rotten democracy may not in itself be worse than rotten autocracy, its effects upon national character will be worse. To give the suffrage to tramps, to paupers, to men to whom the chance to labour is a boon, to men who must beg, or steal, or starve, is to invoke destruction. To put political power in the hands of men embittered and degraded by poverty, is to tie firebrands to foxes and turn them loose amid the standing corn; it is to put out the eyes of a Samson and to twine his arms around the pillars of national life. . . .

"A corrupt democratic government must finally corrupt the people, and when a people become corrupt there is no resurrection. The life is gone, only the carcass remains; and it is left but for the plowshares of fate to bury it out of sight.

"Now this transformation of popular government into despotism of the vilest and most degrading kind, which must inevitably result from the unequal distribution of wealth, is not a thing of the far future. It has already begun in the United States, and is rapidly going on under our eyes.

"In theory we are intense democrats. The proposal to sacrifice swine in the temple would hardly have excited greater horror and indignation in Jerusalem of old than would among us that of conferring a distinction of rank upon our most eminent citizen. But is there not growing up among us a class who have all the power without any of the virtues of aristocracy? We have simple citizens who control thousands of miles of railroad, millions of acres of land, the means of livelihood of great numbers of men; who name the Governors of sovereign States as they name their clerks, choose Senators as they choose attorneys, and whose will is as supreme with Legislatures as that of a French King sitting in bed of justice. The undercurrents of the times seem to sweep us back again to the old conditions from which we dreamed we had escaped.

"Whence shall come the new barbarians? Go through the squalid quarters of great cities, and you may see, even now, their gathering hordes! How shall learning perish? Men will cease to read, and books will kindle fires and be turned into cartridges!

"Everywhere the increasing intensity of the struggle to

live, the increasing necessity for straining every nerve to prevent being thrown down and trodden under foot in the scramble for wealth, is draining the forces which gain and maintain improvements. . . .

"But as sure as the turning tide must soon run full ebb; as sure as the declining sun must bring darkness, so sure is it, that though knowledge yet increases and invention marches on, and new states are being settled, and cities still expand, yet civilization has begun to wane when, in proportion to population, we must build more and more prisons, more and more almshouses, more and more insane asylums. It is not from top to bottom that societies die; it is from bottom to top.

"But there are evidences far more palpable than any that can be given by statistics, of tendencies to the ebb of civilization. There is a vague but general feeling of disappointment; an increased bitterness among the working classes; a wide-spread feeling of unrest and brooding revolution. . . . What change may come, no mortal man can tell, but that some great change must come, thoughtful men begin to feel. The civilized world is trembling on the verge of a great movement. Either it must be a leap upward, which will open the way to advances yet undreamed of, or it must be a plunge downward, which will carry us back towards barbarism."

That very careful and able philosopher and economist, Professor Lange, has said: "We may show a hundred times that with the success of speculation and great capitalists the position of everybody else, step by step, improves; but so long as it is true that with every step of this improvement the difference in the position of individuals and in the means for further advancement also grows, so long will each step of this movement lead towards a turning point where the wealth and power of individuals break down all the barriers of law and morals and a degraded proletariat serves as a football to the passions of the few, until at last everything ends in a social earthquake which swallows up the artificial edifice of one-sided and selfish interests. . . . The state becomes venal. The hopelessly poor will just as easily hate the law as the over-rich despise it. Sparta perished when the whole land of the country belonged to a hundred families; Rome, when a proletariat of millions stood opposed to a few thousands of proprietors, whose resources were so enormous that Crassus considered no one rich who could not maintain an army at his own expense. . . . In mediæval Italy also popular freedom was lost through a moneyed oligarchy and a proletariat. . . . It is characteristic that in Florence the richest banker finally becomes an unlimited despot, and that contemporaneously in Genoa the Bank of St. George in a measure absorbed the state."

Again he says: "The present state of things has been frequently compared with that of the ancient world before its dissolution, and it cannot be denied that significant analogies present themselves. We have the immoderate growth of riches, we have the proletariat, we have the decay of morals and religion; the present forms of government all have their existence threatened, and the belief in a coming general and mighty revolution is widely spread and deeply rooted."

It was the eminent historian, the late Professor Mommsen, who said: "Riches and misery in close league drove the Italians out of Italy and filled the peninsula partly with swarms of slaves, partly with awful silence. It is a terrible picture, but not one peculiar to Italy; whenever the government of capitalists in a slave state has fully developed itself, it has desolated God's fair world in the same way. . . . All the arrant sins that capital has been guilty of against nation and civilization in the modern world remain as far inferior to the abomination of the ancient capitalist states as the free man, be he ever so poor, remains superior to the slave; and not until the dragon seed of North America ripens will the world have again similar fruits to reap."

Said Emerson: "As long as our civilization is one of property, of fences, of exclusiveness, it will be mocked by delusions. Our riches will leave us sick, there will be bitterness in our laughter, and our wine will burn our mouth. Only that good profits which we can taste with all doors open and which serves all men."

The eminent economist, Professor Smart, of Glasgow, makes a most suggestive statement in the following: "But when machinery is replacing man and doing the heavy work of industry, it is time to get rid of that ancient prejudice that man must work ten hours a day to keep the world up to the level of the comfort it has attained. Possibly, if we clear our minds of cant, we may see that the reason why we still wish the labourer to work ten hours a day is that we, the comfortable classes, may go on receiving the lion's share of the wealth these machines, iron and human, are turning out."

It is the great common people that has made and that has been the backbone of every nation, and as long as its interests are guarded and as long as the tendency is towards an ever greater equality of opportunities for all, so long is a nation safe. But as soon as extremes of wealth and poverty begin to manifest themselves, and privilege grows, resulting in still greater inequality in the distribution of wealth and power, that moment the destructive force begins its work — a force that grows by what it feeds upon, an evil that will never correct itself, and that, unless it be checked by the great common people, will carry the nation to destruction. Oppression and evil is its own destroyer.

It is the labourer with his vine-clad cottage, and sufficient of those things that make for peace and happiness and content in the life of a normal human being, it is a uniformly prosperous common people, that constitutes the really great nation, and not a few castles with their hordes of hirelings about them.

In addition to those nations that have been mentioned that have flourished, that have grown great and that have declined, we might mention still nation after nation. We might go back to Egypt, to Assyria, to Babylon, and to the other earlier civilizations, but we find the same cause in all. The law is immutable in its workings. Absolute, seems to be the word. The larger Justice will not be denied. She may seem to delay, she may seem even at times to take no account, but in her own good way and time she strikes, and when she strikes it is with a terrible vengeance. As she is with nations, so is she also with men.

How can we hope then that this civilization, this nation shall escape, any more than those that in their day were as great, as proud and apparently enduring, if by common consent the same forces are at work that in time spelled destruction to those that have preceded us?

IV

AS TO GOVERNMENT

THERE have been many able disquisitions on the theory and the functions of Government, and it would be interesting did space permit, to examine in detail into some of the best of these. Much, however, that has been said, though it might have pertained to a greater or less extent to the time or times in which it was said, does not pertain to our present time. It is the same with this as with a great deal of the earlier theological discussions, vast amounts of which have proved to be so inconsequential that we pay no attention to them at present and find that they have been of value only in a single respect — in that they have helped lead the way to the few real things that we are finding to-day constitute the basis of the true Religion.

It is also evident that a theory of Government that pertained to us Saxon people, say two hundred or three hundred years ago, and fitted the degree of evolution and life we had attained to then, is not a theory that would pertain to us, or that we would even for an instant think of accepting in total at the present time.

It can also be truthfully said that for a thinking, growing, aspiring people, some of the methods and principles in vogue in our own nation even fifty years ago we cannot, we should not, and as evidences on every hand indicate, we no longer honour nor do we countenance in the year 1906. A growing, progressive life demands that we keep ourselves up to the mark that is the truth of to-day, and that we be careful that old forms do not crystallize about us either in religion or in government, forms that will tend to make us satisfied with anything but the vivid, vital truth that will reveal itself to us to-day and to-morrow and to-morrow, if we are ever on the alert to recognize it.

It is so easy to hold on to the old shells, thinking that there is in them something of value, long after the life has departed from them and truth with all its goodly train has moved on, giving joy and blessings to those hat are keeping pace with her, while we fondly cling to the worthless thing.

The crying error of the time is that we stand in awe of government and forget that *we are government.* Everything that is enacted in the nation, or in any of at all similar constitution, is enacted by the people through their chosen representatives acting for their interests; or by the consent of the people, in that these representatives act for corporate and moneyed interests, through party machines and platforms and manipulators. Where the people should be supreme, manipulators and moneyed interests working through parties and through City Councils and Legislatures are supreme. Lobbies and manipulators and bribed or directly bought councilmen and legislators are only the tools of the moneyed interests. This is at the bottom, it is safe to say, of at least nine-tenths of all our present political corruption;

for the manipulator, the ward-heeler, the lobbyist, the saloon keeping councilman, the venal state legislator, are only the tools of these "interests." The latter are the principals, the former merely the agents through which they work to obtain the privileges — the natural rights and properties of the people — through which they make their royal millions.

It is a well-known fact that at those periods when corporations and private business has been most venal, political corruption, either municipal or state, has been the most open and brazen and black. Yet the principals have been our respectable business men, founders sometimes of our wealthiest and later on aristocratic and exclusive families. They, I repeat, have been the big thieves working through these agencies.

Lately the political corruption of some of our large cities has been traced and exposed by Lincoln Steffens in a series of articles in one of our leading magazines, and later republished in book form under the title, "The Shame of the Cities." In one of his articles entitled "Enemies of the Republic,"* Mr. Steffens has this to say:

"Every time I attempted to trace to its source the political corruption of a city ring, the stream of pollution branched off in the most unexpected directions. . . . It flowed out of the majority party into the minority; out of politics into vice and crime, out of business into politics, and back into business. . . . We are all of us on the wrong track. You can't reform a city by reforming a part of it. You can't reform a city alone. You can't re-

*McClure's Magazine for April, 1904.

form politics alone. . . . The corruption of our American politics is our American corruption, political, but financial and industrial too.

"Our political corruption is a system, a regularly established custom of the country, by which our political leaders are hired by bribery, by the license to loot, and by quiet moral support, to conduct the government of city, state, and nation, not for the common good, but for the special interests of private business. Not the politician, then, not the bribe taker, but the bribe giver, the man we are so proud of, our successful business man, he is the source and the sustenance of our bad government. The captain of industry is the man to catch. His is the trail to follow."

We as a nation would hold up our hands in horror even at the thought — we are so intensely democratic — of any titled person, and through such right, even though he be of the highest type and one imbued with the highest sense of public welfare and justice, ruling over us even for a limited time. But the large moneyed interests have gotten us so used to it that we seem to think nothing of having large and important portions of our public affairs in the hands of the lowest type of our citizenship, and allowing them to do most important portions of our governing for us. We seem to be fully satisfied that they be our rulers, for in some centres and at times it amounts to this. It is through them that we pass over annually the many millions of wealth that go to their principals, and accept in return, meagre and many times disgraceful and disgusting types of public service that many times, or to speak more accurately, that generally, give to the public.

Such has been the origin of the wealth of many of our enormously rich and well-known families, and they are now becoming so intrenched as to become a very distinct menace to the public welfare. It is only by a socialized people that their power can now be broken.

Of corruption in the government of our municipalities, Andrew D. White as ar back as 1890 had this to say: "Without the lightest exaggeration, we may assert that, with few exceptions, the city governments of the United States are the worst in Christendom, the most expensive, the most inefficient, and the most corrupt. No one who has any considerable knowledge of our own country and of other countries can deny this.

"The city halls of these larger towns are the acknowledged centres of the vilest corruption. They are absolutely demoralizing, not merely to those who live under their sway, but to the country at large. Such cities, like the decaying spots on ripe fruit, tend to corrupt the whole body politic. As a rule, the men who sit in the councils of our larger cities, dispensing comfort or discomfort, justice or injustice, beauty or deformity, health or disease, to this and to future generations, are men who in no other country would think of aspiring to such positions. Some of them, indeed, would think themselves lucky in keeping outside the prisons. Officials entrusted with the expenditure of the vast wealth of our citizens are frequently men whom no one would think of entrusting with the management of his private affairs, or, indeed, of employing in any capacity. Few have gained their positions by fitness or by public service; many have gained them by scoundrelism; some by crime."*

The same can be said of various members of our state legislatures. These are the types of men that most of our great corporate interests work through. Some are put there deliberately and directly for this purpose. Should anyone have any doubt of this, let him become thoroughly acquainted among other things with the history of the principal railroad in the states, say, Michigan, Pennsylvania, New York, Connecticut, Massachusetts.

The great common people have everything in their hands when they once fully realize it. They must come forward and make politicians and the moneyed interests know their power. They must take over and back to themselves the power that they have gradually allowed to be usurped by the politician, the political leader, for these enormously fat and gorged concerns and individuals.

A people with that great weapon of freedom — *the franchise* — are invincible in the expression of their preferences and their demands when they present an intelligent and united interest, if it be done before special privilege with its great accumulations of wealth and power has grown too great and too cunning and too corrupting. When we take into consideration how vastly

**The Forum*, December, 1890.

the great common working people out-number the privileged classes, something over a hundred to one, then we must wonder that greed and graft and vast and unscrupulous wealth have been able to attain to the proportions they have already attained in our midst. But the reason abounds; and later we shall consider it fully.

Certainly one of the great central facts of government, one of the greatest fundamental principles of a government of freedom and intelligence, is the insuring of *equal privileges for all and special privileges for none.* This we had nominally, at least in the nation, but in reality a very small fraction of this proposition is true to-day, and we are witnessing its departure from among us to-day more rapidly than ever before. If this continues at the rate it has been going on during the past twenty years or so, and at the rate it is going on at present it will be but a short time, and within the experience of many now living, until it will be that the " equal privileges and opportunities for all " will have been swallowed up completely by the special privileges and the consequent vast accumulations of the few.

Life in no country can be happy or prosperous or at all satisfying where special privilege reigns and one great class is produced that becomes simply a grist for another class. The loss to citizenship is so enormous, and its influences are so deadly that the entire nation becomes so thoroughly diseased politically and socially and its foundations are so quietly undermined, that before it is realized the nation is already in its decline, under the workings of the same mighty compelling laws that have never yet faltered nor delayed in decreeing the fate of nations. Each for all and all for each was the mandate that was written in the beginning, and as long even as time endures, it will brook no change nor will it permit the slightest modification.

V

A GREAT PEOPLE'S MOVEMENT

THE greater part of really important legislation is at present for the benefit of the great corporate and moneyed interests. Henceforth the greater part of it must be for the people — the great common people that has made this, and every country, and upon whose welfare ultimately all depends. We shall have the management of the nation's affairs in our own hands just as securely and just as quickly as we *really* so elect. There must be more of the people's men in our municipal, our state, and our national assemblies. A rich operator in Robert Owen's time, held, in connection with his fellows, that they could not afford to dispense with child labour because that would drive business out of England. The "maudlin sentimentalism of those who knew neither business nor human nature," they pronounced all legal interference with child labour. Yet he, according to his own admission, had been making in the cotton business 200 per cent in yearly profits. So the cries will go up to-day when the people begin to redeem the country and its resources for their own common use. The slightest movement that aims at checking the enormous profits that are being reaped from the resources that should belong to the people in common, is even now being met with that same cry. The number of labour disturbances during the past few years and to-day is in part, and among other things, the measure of dissatisfaction with the present monopolistic system. It does not bring justice to labour. This, all thinking and right-feeling men are realizing, and realizing all too keenly.

It was a great people's movement in connection with the "Corn Laws" in England, in Cobden's time, that brought about a peaceable revolution, in place of what would have easily been a revolution of another type.

We are to have among us a revolution, a great and a very clear-cut revolution, but a great people's movement insures that it will be an evolutionary revolution, a peaceable revolution, but no less marked and telling, in fact, far more telling than any blood revolution can possibly be.

In an intelligent and a determined political action on the part of the common people lies our safety; it is along this path that we must move. United labour is beginning to recognize this. It was but a short time ago that it was carefully avoided by organized labour, and its efforts were more along what is commonly known as mutual benefit lines, and this apart from all thought of any type of political action. And it is along these lines that the trust and combination and corporate interests wish even now it would be kept. What a power, *wisely directed*, this great and splendid body can become. It in itself, if sufficiently discreet and sufficiently patriotic in its desires and in its ways of voicing them, is sufficient, through the great balance of power that in a united form it can hold, to bring about practically any type of public administration it may desire. "In political action" is getting more and more to be the watchword of united labour. This, notwithstanding the fact that that part of the public press justly called the "capitalistic press," that endeavours to make the public believe otherwise, is the great good that is being accomplished by an intelligent Labour Party in Australia and New Zealand, and from there are coming many instructive lessons that we here can most profitably study. New Zealand has been described as a country without a millionaire, without a pauper, and without a strike. The common people, including labour, is simply compelling fair opportunities for all, a common-sense justice, and as a result a fairer share of those gifts and resources of the country that are intended for all. One of the best known of New Zealand's legislators, Hon. W. P. Reeves, in connection with their purposes has said: "It is the unconcealed object of our social legislation to make democracy consistent and possible — to create conditions out of which such threatening extremes of wealth-ownership cannot grow."

Money as a force in legislation, used as it is, sometimes almost like water by the great capitalistic concerns in their carefully studied direct and indirect ways, in the bribery and debauchery of public officials, is an evil of such a wide-spread nature that it *must* be corrected by the people. The complaint is now so frequently heard, that the people do not get a fair show. It is true; but it is also true that it is our own fault that we do not. If we look as carefully to elections and appointments as the great moneyed interests do, then that complaint will forever lose its force. This is a most vital fact for our great farming communities to learn, almost as much or even more, than any other portion of our people, because in some respects and in some sections conditions with them have at times become well-nigh intolerable. We must recognize once and for all the fact that government is always as good as the people demand it should be. "No King, no veriest tyrant ever ruled except by the will of the people. Because the popular will has been ignorant and evil, states have been evil." I think in the following paragraphs that clear-thinking and far-seeing statesman, the late Ex-Governor Altgeld of Illinois, has given us some wonderfully clear and thought-compelling statements along this line. In an address before the American Railway Trainmen, at Galesburg, Illinois, he said: "If our institutions are to undergo great change, it is vital that the men of America, and not the money, should direct the change. Money may be a blessing as a servant, but it is a curse as a master. Money never established republican institutions in the world. It has no natural affinity with them, and does not understand them. Money has neither soul nor sentiment. It does not know the meaning of liberty, and it sneers at the rights of man. It never bled on the battlefield in time of war, and it never voluntarily sought the public treasury in time of peace. . . . Men in time acquire the nature of those things which absorb their lives. Unconsciously and invisibly they undergo a change until those things which occupy their daily thoughts seem actually to circulate in their veins. Consequently in all countries, in all ages, and among all peoples, it has been found that as a rule the possessors of great wealth were not the patriots. On the contrary, they seemed to care little what flag floated over them, provided it was a flag that would give them a bayonet with which to protect their gold. The men who in the late war left their millions of hoarded treasure and shouldered a musket to fight for the Union were as scarce as the camels that have passed through the eye of the needle. The soldiers' cemeteries of patriotic dead are filled with men who when alive had to struggle for a living. It is the great masses of the people who defend the government in time of war, and who bear its burdens in time of peace, and these alone know the full value of free institutions. It is therefore important that the destinies of our government should be shaped by this class, and they can be relied upon to do justice to capital. They appreciate the fact that capital is not only a convenience, but may be of the greatest possible use to man when properly directed. While money may have done a great injustice to the masses, the masses have never done an injustice to money.

"Now, how will you meet these problems? Standing as individuals in the presence of mighty combinations you will be crushed and there will be no hope for you or your children. I can see no other course for you than to stand together, shoulder to shoulder, intelligently and patriotically. A great force never holds itself in check, whether in the phenomena of nature, in politics, in government, or in religion. Only a counter or resisting force will check it. If concentrated capital shall meet with no checking influence, or force, then republican institutions must come to an end, and we will have but two classes in this country, an exceedingly wealthy class on one hand, and a spiritless, crushed, poverty-striken labouring class on the other. The hope of the country depends upon having a number of forces that will counterbalance or check each other. And in this connection let me suggest to you that the world has progressed to a point where intelligence will always defeat brute force, and any method of contest that involves violence belongs to a bygone age. The modern methods of warfare in society are of an entirely different character. You complain sometimes that you do not get a fair show, that capital controls legislation, that by selecting the candidates for the judicial offices, it in many cases controls the courts and that the same is true in the execution of the laws. But you have yourselves largely to blame. . . .

It has happened frequently in the past in this State and in other States that you wanted legislation which you thought was necessary and just, and you supported men for the legislature whom you believed were honest, but who, as soon as they received their certificate of election, crept up the rear stairway to the office of some corporation and tendered their services in the hope of obtaining some financial or other advantage. Did you afterwards spot those men as being unworthy of your confidence? Not at all. Their chances for public preferment were just as good thereafter as they were before. Again, corporations have for many years looked after the matter of selecting judges, especially of the federal courts. They realized the fact that the construction of the laws is even more important than the making of laws, and to have a friend on the bench is much more important than to have a lawmaker at the capitol. It is asserted that for a quarter of a century no man has been appointed to the federal bench unless he was either a corporation lawyer or was known to hold views which made him satisfactory to those interests, and when these judges afterwards distorted the law and usurped powers to assist corporations and smite you, they were not necessarily corrupt. They were simply giving force to prejudices which they had imbibed during their former association with corporate influences. It has never happened in this country that you or any other organization of labour men or of farmers sent a delegation to wait upon the President in reference to the appointment or rejection of any particular man to any judicial office. You have not looked after your interests and you have no right to complain if you are discriminated against under these circumstances. Every man who seeks office in this country will need your support, and once let him understand that you are capable of acting intelligently and standing together, and that you insist on being honestly dealt with, and you will see a great change. Fall in with what is the spirit of the times. Practise intelligent combination. Move along the lines of law and of justice and practise foresight and you will be able to right almost any grievance.

"In conclusion let me say that you and the labouring men of this country are more interested in maintaining republican institutions than any other of our people. You are more interested in making the stripes and stars stand for free institutions than any other people in this country. Wealth has always courted aristocracy and bowed to monarchy. It is manhood alone that is interested in liberty and in maintaining those conditions under which the greatest possible opportunities are opened to every citizen of the commonwealth. You cannot leave your children millions to squander. It is therefore important for you to endeavour to leave them a country in which intelligent and honest effort will be properly rewarded and in which the labourer will not only be worthy of his hire, but will have open to him and to his posterity all of the fields of honour and the paths of glory."

A nation such as this depends solely, for its welfare as well as for its perpetuity, upon the hearts and minds and ambitions of its *people*. With these crushed and traduced by monopoly and the despoiler, the nation is doomed and even the corporate interests themselves will in time be torn to pieces,

To trace the long fight for political freedom which those before us had to undergo, shows us how hopeful and how advantageous our position is. Had we not political freedom and the right of the ballot in face of these rapidly growing concentrations of evil among us, our position would be well-nigh hopeless. As it is we cannot be other than masters of this critical situation if we come but speedily to a realization of the great forces that lie within our reach, and if we use them as intelligent freemen. The great battle that must now be waged is the battle for *economic* freedom, for equal opportunities, for justice in working conditions, for justice in legislation and administration.

He who owns or controls that upon which others depend owns and controls them. The fundemantal issue at stake is justice and equal opportunities, a more equal justice in the distribution of the results of labour, and a using for all the people o those great natural common resources that are now being grabbed and monopolized and used for the enrichment of the few.

How strange our position is, could be revealed by an estimate of the millions upon millions in the form of natural franchises that we allow to be taken from us each year, and that are making so enormously rich the few men and families that have become so self-conceited as they roll in this wealth, and then to make a comparison of the immense preponderance of the voting power of the people over this relatively small number — millions compared to the thousands. But they have been making this their business. Very quietly, while the masses of the people have been going about their own private affairs, they have been getting possession of and diverting to their own coffers these immensely valuable concessions, and which have grown more enormous in their profits as the country has grown in population and the needs of the people have increased. While the people have been farming the farms, this small privileged class, as an able writer has recently put it, has been "farming the farmers." They have acted upon the principle that he enunciates in speaking of their methods as follows — do not fool yourself while there are other people to fool. The way to succeed is not to work, but to work the workers; not to farm the farms, but to farm the farmers.

And how even now money is trying to blind the eyes of the people to prevent them from seeing clearly and taking back to themselves these great resources, can be seen on every hand. But the hour has struck and we are on the move. The day to hesitate or to delay is passed. Revelations have been coming so rapidly of late, and facts so momentous in their import are becoming so clear, that we could not turn back even if we would. Every law of human nature and human development cries out against it. And although concentrated wealth and power may exert every influence to climb and to stifle the idea of greater equality and justice, the thoughts and the voices of men of genius and insight are up, and the great common people are hearing them over and over again giving voice and sanction to their own thoughts and rapidly forming conclusions.

Attempts to do something for men by philanthropy to take the place of what is taken away from or what is denied them, will fail. And they ought to fail. No manipulations of this sort will ever take the place of *justice.* Justice is the absolute law, and it will compel obedience to itself sooner or later. The enlightened people — the people of the great nation want and will demand conditions of such a nature that they can build with the builder's satisfaction and pleasure their own art museums and libraries and institutions of learning. Not benefactions, but what *by right* belongs to one. What belongs to labour and the citizen by moral right shall be made so in fact by legal right. Nothing short of this in the end will satisfy.

"Social service," and schemes for "social betterment" are good, and praiseworthy in their place, but they will never be accepted as taking the place of those more essential things that are the rightful inheritance of the people, nor should they.

"The separation between the owners of fixed capital and the labourer has long been noted; but with vast federated plants, managed by hired intermediaries, it is unavoidable. There will be brave attempts to meet the difficulty by alluring philanthropies, by 'doing something for the workingmen.' If merely philanthropic, these will fail as they deserve. Benevolent schemes that bear the slightest taint of charity have at last got the contempt of the intelligent wage-earners.

"Importunate, and never again to be silenced, their demand is that they get their benefits, not as gifts or favours, but as recognized rights. Philanthropies are a dangerous substitute for honest wage payment, shorter working time, and increased influence over the conditions of the labour contract. What may be called the Great Bluff of our time is to put gratuities and benefactions in the place of justice. There is no donation, however gaudy, that can fill the place of justice. The attempt of the ruling class to do this is the oldest trick in history. It was the opinion of a Roman emperor, 'Magnificence in gifts may deceive even the gods.' The crowd could then be quieted by the brutalities of a pageant, the butcheries in the arena, by fleets of stolen grain scattered among the people, as a Tammany heeler scatters gifts and personal kindnesses before the election. We are at least civilized so far that we demand more decorum, and a certain humanizing of our largesses. They must bear the image of charity and good-will to men. They must be educational, artistic, and in all ways incentives to good morals and religion.

"Now it would be both untrue and offensive to deny that these later bounties are vast improvements upon the free circus of Caligula. No wise man would check a generous instinct of any multi-millionaire. The books, pictures, churches, and schools take their places among the welfare institutions of our time. They are influences which deserve the honest and grateful approval of the public.

"Yet when this tribute to good motive and good result has been paid, the story is not finished. We are hoodwinked, unless we see that there ought to be, and possibly may be, a still better way than this to acquire individual and social morality. The sturdy self-respect in any community that should build its own church, school, library, dispensary,— paying every honest bill as it goes,— would show an exhilarating superiority before which everyone of us would hasten to pay respect. We must be grateful to our princely givers, but the mistake would be fatal to accept this method of splendid subsidies as a finality. What we really want is the ability and the instructed will to pay our own bills, even if the pace of our civilization halts a little." * Excellent, and nothing in the quotation more suggestive so to speak, than the last phrase — "even if the pace of our civilization halts a little." Why should we be proud of mere largeness and rapidity? especially as it does not benefit the great masses of the people, but only the few, the very small fraction. But upon closer examination the fact will reveal itself, that excessive wealth is of real value to no man, and especially when gotten by means so manifestly unfair and so morally unjustifiable, as the great portion of *excessive wealth* is gotten to-day. Give me neither riches — great wealth — nor poverty, will ever be the desire of the truly wise, but give me that comfortable amount that is conducive to the highest, the noblest, the most useful, and consequently, the most happy life.

Justice, not gifts, not charity.

There is a spirit in the American people, in all Saxon people, that rebels against the proffer of gifts and charity as an equivalent for what rightly belongs to them. This spirit can be neither changed nor broken until at least the present unequal distribution of wealth grows to such an extent, that it results in the concentration of the greater portion of the wealth and resources of the nation in so few hands, that the poverty of the people becomes *so great*, that the spirit of freemen is

* "The Social Unrest," by John Graham Brooks, p. 203.

so broken that they sink to the position of paupers and public wards.

Said Mr. Lecky, recently, in speaking of the prosperity of nations and their causes as indicated by history: "Its foundation is laid in pure domestic life, in commercial integrity, in a high standard of moral worth, and of public spirit, in simple habits, in courage, uprightness, and a certain soundness and moderation of judgment which spring quite as much from character as from intellect. If you would form a wise judgment of the future of a nation, observe carefully whether these qualities are increasing or decaying. Observe especially what qualities count for most in public life. Is character becoming of greater or less importance? Are the men who obtain the highest posts in the nation, men of whom in private life, and irrespective of party, competent judges speak with genuine respect? Are they of sincere convictions, consistent lives, indisputable integrity? . . . It is by observing this moral current that you can best cast the horoscope of a nation."*

This social unrest that has been vaguely witnessed during the past few years, increasing yearly, has gradually brought the people to a definite point of view and to a definite knowledge of facts. Evolution indeed has been doing its work in spite of the rapid aggressions of the immensely rich, over against which has been set the slowly moving discernment of the people. For a long time there was unrest coupled with a sort of groping in the dark, a failure to understand the full significance,

* "The Political Value of History," by W. E. R. Lecky.

let alone the causes of this great unrest. Back of it all, however, has been *thought*, in addition to *feeling*, on the part of the people, quickened and intensified at times by most bitter experiences, until now a new mental activity is born, and it is being quickened by the possession of some clear-cut and wonderfully significant facts. A little time now spent in the careful study and elaboration of methods, and the great battle for social, industrial and economic freedom is fully on, and greater than this and one fraught with a greater moment, no battle has ever been waged perhaps in the entire history of civilization.

Says Benjamin Kidd, in the closing pages of his very able work, "Social Evolution": "We see that, under all the complex appearances our Western civilization presents, the central process working itself out in our midst is one which is ever tending to bring, for the first time in the history of the race, all the people into the competition of life on a footing of equality of opportunity. In this process the problem, with which society and legislators will be concerned for long into the future, will be how to secure to the fullest degree these conditions of equality, while at the same time retaining that degree of inequality which must result from offering prizes sufficiently attractive to keep up within the community that state of stress and exertion, without which no people can long continue in a high state of social efficiency. For in the vast process of change in progress it is always the conditions of social efficiency, and not those which individuals or classes may desire for themselves, that the unseen evolutionary forces at work amongst us are engaged in developing. . . .

"Nor is there any reason why the great social development proceeding in our civilization which has been but feebly and inadequately described in the preceding chapters, should be viewed with distrust by those of more conservative instincts amongst us who profess to have at heart the highest interests of humanity. The movement which is uplifting the people — necessarily to a large extent, at the expense of those above them — is but the final result of a long process of organic development. All anticipations and forebodings as to the future of the incoming democracy, founded upon comparisons with the past, are unreliable or worthless. For the world has never before witnessed a democracy of the kind that is now slowly assuming supreme power amongst the Western peoples. To compare it with democracies which held power under the ancient empires is to altogether misunderstand both the nature of our civilization and the character of the forces that have produced it. . . . The fact of our time which overshadows all others is the arrival of Democracy. But the preception of the fact is of relatively little importance if we do not also realize that it is a new Democracy. There are many who speak of the new ruler of nations as if he were the same idle Demos whose ears the dishonest courtiers have tickled from time immemorial. It is not so. Even those who attempt to lead him do not yet quite understand him. Those who think that he is about to bring chaos instead of order, do not rightly apprehend the nature of his strength. They do not perceive that his arrival is the crowning result of an ethical movement in which qualities and attributes, which we have been all taught to regard as the very highest of which human nature is capable, find the completest expression they have ever reached in the history of the race."

Such indeed is the opinion of many other clear and disinterested thinkers in addition to that of the able author of "Social Evolution." A great people's movement to bring back to the people the immense belongings that have been taken away from them, and to prevent a continuance of this from now on, is the supreme need of the time. Slowly and almost gropingly we have been leading up to it, but the incentive is on, the knowledge underlying its cause is increasing and never so rapidly as of late. There is no power now that can stop it or even materially hinder it any more than human power can hinder or prevent the workings of any of nature's great laws. It is indeed most glorious to be alive, to witness and to have a hand in the culmination of this new order of life that all the centuries have been leading up to.

VI

PUBLIC UTILITIES FOR THE PUBLIC GOOD

IT is strange how long and how heavily we allow ourselves to be fleeced, or robbed, by custom. Because we commence a thing in a certain way, is many times the reason we continue it in that way long after it could be changed to our great advantage. Because we began that way we are still living and acting under the delusion that great public utilities, the value of which is caused by all the people in common, instead of being managed by, and for the benefit of the people, should be managed for the private benefit and the enrichment of an individual or little groups of individuals called companies or corporations.

It is a delusion something akin to the belief, which, according to Charles Lamb, so long held sway among the Chinese when the savour of roast pork had been accidently discovered through the burning down of Ho-ti's hut, that, in order to cook a pig it was necessary to set fire to a house. By and by, however, they found that that method was not only crude and wasteful, but also uncertain in its results. But until a Chinese sage came forward and invented a rude type of gridiron which, according to Lamb's interesting dissertation, was the forerunner of the spit and the oven, no one had ever thought of a pig being roasted without the burning down of a hut, or were it for one better circumstanced, a house. They, therefore, had to follow the only method they knew. With us, however, in connection with the supplying of certain great common needs it is different; for there are other methods of which we already know, that indeed have been known and have been in successful operation in other countries far more progressive in this regard than we, for more than a score and in some cases, for more than two score of years. The only excuse I can see is that in having begun in a very crude and thoughtless and expensive way, we have not been bright enough, or energetic enough as yet, to find and adopt a more common-sense and satisfactory way.

At one period in the development of our national and municipal life there may have been a reason for allowing these common necessities to be dealt with by private individuals or private companies. There may have been a good or at least a satisfactory reason for this method when our proportions were small and our needs were not so great and not so complex, when it meant giving over to individuals not such vast amounts that should be used for the advantage of all the people, and when the opportunities for getting these great advantages away from the people through political corruption and debauchery were not so great as they are to-day. So there may have been a reason in the beginning, but the basis for that reason has now passed. This method may have been even right at one time — though this in common with many I question — it is no longer right now. And the fact that we are beginning now to think so rapidly along the lines of a saner and a better way indicates that the method in vogue so long has more than seen its day. Nevertheless, although our awakening has been tardy, our advance will be rapid.

It is the people — the people in common — that make valuable those enormously rich franchises that have been given over to individuals for their private enrichment, in the form, to deal first with the city — of light and heat and transportation and telephone privileges, not to mention the various other ones at present. It is not only the people, but to state it still more concretely, it is the very needs of the people that give them their enormous values, and it is through these that their enormous profits are secured. If this be true, why then should not these great interests be conducted by and for the benefit of the people, instead of by and for the enrichment of a few private individuals? Especially as under our system of enormously rich gifts to these individuals or groups of individuals, and their conducting these enterprises with no thought of the public welfare but with the one thought of the greatest amount of profit for themselves, first, last, and all the time, we have been having for years and are still having along these lines as poor a service with the highest costs, and the greatest amount of evil and abuses, as any country in the entire world.

As long, moreover, as any of the utilities that are public necessities and that from their very nature should be conducted by and in the interests of the people, are allowed to be run for private gain, this condition of affairs will continue to exist.

With all our progress along other lines, it is almost universally understood that the conduct of our municipal affairs in the United States has been among the most backward and costly and degraded and unsatisfactory of any in the entire civilized world.

In the conduct of these affairs we are far behind all such countries as Germany, England, France, Norway, Sweden, Belgium, not to go through almost the entire list of civilized and progressive nations. It seems to me clearly evident that from the very nature of the case we cannot do violence to the principle — "That which the people collectively create they should collectively own," without suffering this as a result. Moreover, we shall never reach the highest state in municipal or even in state or national administration, until we recognize and act upon the principle — what the people can do best for themselves, that, through their agent, the government, they should do. They should not, therefore, permit purely governmental functions to be seized and to be exploited by individuals and corporations.

There must, therefore, not only be blows struck that will forever put an end to the giving over to individuals of these great common properties of the people, but there must also be, to use the words of one of our foremost American editors,* "The recovery to the people of all franchises belonging to the people, but diverted from public to private uses, by the purchase of corporations and individuals, corruptly working through state and municipal legislatures."

* Henry Watterson — The Louisville *Courier Journal*.

To our present method is to be attributed the almost unbelievable amount of graft and bribery and corruption that has become so rampant among us of late and that has been steadily swelling in its volume during the passing of the years. "Nothing," says one editor of another of our foremost papers, "has conduced so greatly to graft and bribery in municipal and state affairs as the fact that franchises of enormous value for public utilities are to be obtained by favour of certain officials. Give the streets back to the city and this element of corruption is at once eliminated." Continuing — it was an editorial on the significance of the great and splendid vote recently given by the people of Chicago in their determination to drive from their midst all further domination on the part of the Rapid Transit Companies, their determination to come into complete possession of their transit facilities and to conduct them for their own benefit — the writer said:

"What Chicago has done New York can do, though on the very day the Western city scored its victory we of New York were called upon to face a defeat. The same agencies that waged war on Judge Dunne and what he stood for killed the Elsberg Bill in the New York Legislature; and though that measure — designed to prevent any more scandals such as the gift of the people's Subway to August Belmont — had the endorsement of every New York civic organization interested in the cause of good government, and was openly opposed only by the Belmont combination and the unrepresentative Rapid Transit Commission, it was beaten in the Senate at Albany.

"The triumph in Chicago and the disaster in New York simply mean that though a legislature may be influenced to favour special privilege at the expense of the people, the people themselves can neither be bought by a corrupt lobby nor driven by bosses working for their peculiar interests."

If we take entirely away from private gain those great public service utilities, then we at once strike the axe at the roots of the larger share of the source of our political corruption and debauchery for which, especially in municipal matters, we stand as the most notorious nation in the entire world. As lovers of free institutions and of ordinary public honesty and decency, *this end alone*, is of sufficient importance to demand of us such a course, to say nothing of the enormous gains otherwise. The fact that both city and state legislation is so dominated by great accumulated wealth and by corporations, *especially public service corporations*, indicates that our prevailing methods are not healthy, and that this great menace to free institutions, and to a government for and by the people, should be speedily removed.

A matter of such vital importance to the national and individual welfare as the public ownership and control of all *public utilities* is worthy of a most detailed consideration, more than we shall be able to give it in so limited a space. It is to become, as it is so rapidly beginning now, one of the paramount questions in the policies of the American nation.

I think there is perhaps no better way of proceeding to a consideration of the argument in favour of such a method of supplying our needs and necessities than by considering first, what has been accomplished in this line in the municipalities of other countrics, *and with what results.* Many times a long and detailed argument that a certain thing cannot be done, is best met by showing that it already has been or is being done, and most successfully.

On account of the general characteristics and conditions there being probably more nearly akin to our own, shall we look in the direction of Great Britain first.

I think we cannot do better at this point than consider some facts as presented by Mr. John Martin,* whose statistics in connection with Great Britain are vouched for by the British Imperial Board of Trade. These facts and figures I shall give exactly as they were presented by Mr. Martin himself.† After speaking of the various small beginnings along these lines that we have made here, he continues, "Driven to desperation by the cobra-like voracity of the lighting trust, New York is erecting a plant to light its streets and public buildings (nothing for private consumers yet), and so is beginning to toddle like a babe in those paths of business thrift in which we shall see that European cities have been running like athletes for decades.

* Mr. Martin was formerly a member of the Hackney Borough Council, London. He is now a resident of New York, where he is well-known as a writer and an authority on Municipal Problems, and as an effective worker along the lines of clean politics.

† Proceedings of the Annual Conference on Good City Government, held by the National Municipal League at New York, 1905.

"How different has been the record abroad! We are thirty years behind the cities of Great Britain and Germany. And from the beginning they were more businesslike than we are even now. To them it would seem the height of economic folly to forbid a city to supply electric light to householders and to allow a private monopoly to retain its extortionate prices for them while the municipality sought relief by multiplying wires and dynamos for itself. The 355 localities of the United Kingdom and the numerous German cities which own and run electric lighting plants, hold the monopoly in their districts. Competition being, in the nature of the case, impossible, the city holds the field.

"The same with the gas-works in the two countries. Thrifty business management requires that somebody shall hold a monopoly, and political sense requires that that somebody shall be the city itself. . . .

"No less that 260 cities — Great Britain — supply their whole population with gas-light and power. . . . They charge on an average, taking large and small, those distant from and those near to coal fields all together, sixty-four cents a thousand cubic feet for gas. Therefore the consumer is benefited, for the private companies, on an average, taken in the same way, charge a little over seventy cents. What they would charge were they not held in check by municipal competition Cousin Jonathan could tell John Bull.

"Has the taxpayer been mulcted to make up? No, indeed. The net revenue has been 7 per cent on the capital, and, if anything, the taxpayer had been too well cared for. In Manchester he received $350,000 last year to help to pay for the schools, etc., the price of gas being sixty cents; in Leicester he got $190,000 with gas at fifty-six cents, and in the other places lesser sums in proportion to their size and the success of the management.

"And the workman? He has not been forgotten; for everywhere he gets slightly higher wages than he would from a private corporation and somewhat more generous treatment with respect to hours and holidays.

"Electric lighting tells the same tale. While I am writing this there comes a return compiled by the London County Council showing that the fourteen local authorities in the metropolitan district which supply electric light, sell it at an average of slightly less than eight cents a kilowatt hour, nearly 20 per cent less than corporations charge in adjacent districts, and nearly half as much as submissive New Yorkers pay. And yet, after paying all expenses and the interest on the debt they had a surplus of $1,244,515. Clearly they understand the notion of thrift in production; they do not regard every city department as a spending agency.

"Space fails me to tell the details of the electric light works of the 323 local authorities in the United Kingdom with their approximate capital of $150,000,000, and of the numerous similar examples in Germany. Their success is sufficiently indicated by the fact that after the most virulent attacks have been made on them in the last four years, supported by a group of corporation representatives from America who went as kindly missionaries to point out to Britishers what a terribly wicked mistake their municipalities were making, after a long investigation by Parliament and a vigorous defence by the highest and most influential administrators in the Kingdom, not only has there been no cessation of municipal activity, but it is steadily increasing. Meanwhile the corps of anxious Americans who thought they could fool the slow-witted Britishers into the adoption of American ways, have been sent home routed and labelled 'Physician, heal thyself.'

"Still more remarkable, especially to those belted Spencerians who piously believe that a government is congenitally incapable of managing a business enterprise, must be the record of the street railway achievements abroad. For a change of air, let us leap the North Sea and travel to Berlin. . . .

"Berlin's most illuminating experience has been with her street railways. In 1898, in order to get the lines electrified, the city granted a charter for twenty-one years, with these provisions included: 1. Workmen to have a ten-hour day. 2. Waiting-rooms at transfer stations to be erected and to be kept warmed and lighted. 3. Uniform fare for the whole length of each line to be 2.38 cents. 4. Eight per cent of the gross profits, plus half the net profits over 12 per cent on the old capital and 6 per cent on the new capital, to be paid to the city. 5. At the end of the lease all the lines and the rolling stock to become the property of the city.

"Please bear in mind these terms, made by a government of taxpayers, when we consider, later, the action of the New York Rapid Transit Commission.

"Berlin's bureaucracy is as able and honest as any in the world, and it worked as well as officials ever can to keep the corporation to the terms of its bargain. In addition, an association of citizens was formed to watch and fight. But even then the trouble involved in protecting the citizens from the universal tendency of franchise corporations to evade their obligations was so harassing that after a few months this council of taxpayers decided that no more franchises should be granted, and that the city should enter the railway business. A short strategic line which happened to be obtainable was bought, other lines were built, and now the government is an active competitor and is ready to take advantage of every franchise as it expires. . . .

"No less than 162 localities in Britain have shown ability, enterprise and foresight enough to take over and manage their own street-car lines. Among them are London, Liverpool, Manchester, Glasgow, Birmingham, Hull, Newcastle, Nottingham, Halifax, Leeds, Sheffield, Aberdeen, Brighton, Dundee, Yarmouth, Belfast and Rochdale. All of them are so well satisfied with the results in lower fares for the passenger, better conditions for the workman and profits for the taxpayers, that no party is even in existence which advocates the re-surrender of any system to a private corporation. The mere whisper of such a proposal would be a request for political execution and burial. . . .

"London owns the surface lines both north and south of the Thames. Those on the north side, in a fit of lukewarmness, when for one term the Progressive and

Moderate parties were evenly balanced, and to the present regret of the population served by them, are leased for operation to a corporation on terms remunerative to the government, but obstructive to improvement. The city has electrified its lines; the corporation refuses to follow suit. So much for that superior corporation enterprise of which we hear *ad nauseam*.

"During the eight years of municipal ownership these returns have been secured. On the lines worked by the council, 44 per cent of the passengers pay one-cent fares, 43 per cent pay two cents, 8 per cent three cents, 4 per cent four cents, and, to compensate for the 99 per cent of the passengers who pay less than our straight five-cent rate, just one poor soul, who wishes to travel the whole length of the line, has to pay six cents.

"In those years, despite the increases of wages, the annual holidays and the day's rest per week given to employees, the street railways have contributed $1,465,-000 to the general city treasury, $1,670,000 in reduction of the debt on the lines, $330,000 as a renewal and reserve fund for the southern system, $450,000 for taxes on the southern system during the last six years, and $630,000 in reduction of debt from proceeds of sale of horses, etc."

In addition to the extremely low fares that are paid in German cities for street-car service, and with far better and cleaner and more up-to-date cars than we have — with a rare exception here and there — there is this noticeable difference. There the number of seats each car contains is posted in clear and artistic form in the interior, and each seat has its number just above it. As soon then as all seats are taken no more passengers are permitted to enter, but a sufficient number of cars is run to provide a seat — that which the payment of a fare always implies — for every man, woman and child. It makes a difference whether a matter is conducted for the comfort and convenience of its patrons or for the deliberate purpose of extracting from them the last possible penny, giving many times in return an accommodation that we, had we the civic pride and the sense of justice that we — and I had almost said, above all people — should have, would not put up with more than the number of days absolutely required to bring about the change.

Compare the German citizens' two-cent fare and his guaranteed seat and clean and artistic accommodations with our five-cent fare, even if for half a dozen blocks, with our many times rattling cars, sometimes even junk when they are bought, and our almost equal chances that for this excessive fare we will get in exchange a strap to hang onto in common with a number of people standing equal to or sometimes greater than the number that the management deigns to accommodate with seats, and all the discomfort this means on entering or leaving the car. Many times merely room to stand upon a platform is all they will permit us to have, and for a fare that is at least twice as high as it should be even for the best sitting accommodations.

They are thirsty leeches, these owners and managers of our public service corporations. But it is because we permit it. Their blood-sucking propensities seem never to be satisfied nor do they decrease, but by virtue of a great natural law they are ever on the increase. And again, because we permit and stand it.

There, one finds almost without exception, vestibuled cars for the protection and comfort of their motormen. This portion of their citizenship is looked after the same as all others. But here it is scarcely ever that the management of the roads adopts this plan voluntarily, and when the demand of ordinary decency and fairness takes a measure to the legislature compelling it, the company's representatives are there with their money and their lobby to defeat it in common with practically every measure looking to the comfort and welfare and safety of those the public service corporation is supposed to serve.

The winter just passed but one was a frightful one in the amount of suffering these men had to undergo, and who for the most effective service as well as for the public safety, should be kept always at their best. In New York City alone it caused the death or resulted in the undermining of the health of many a poor fellow. They are sometimes scorpions, these owners and managers of our public service corporations, for they sting to the death in their excessive and unchecked greed for gain. But we, the common citizens, are not free from guilt; for indirectly we also had a hand in this frightful amount of suffering that resulted more than once in death, and that brought sadness and want to those dependent upon their breadwinner; for we are dwellers in a country of democratic institutions where the people are responsible for the conditions that prevail among them.

In the matter of the municipal ownership and management of public utilities, we have heard much of late of Glasgow, and not without reason. The people of Glasgow have stood among the most fearless and the most successful in managing for themselves their public utilities. It has been a long time since the franchise grabber has been able to exploit the people there. The people of Glasgow, strange to say, prefer to keep for themselves the millions of dollars their public utilities return each year, instead of handing them over to a little group of capitalists, foreigners many times, and whose only interest is to take from the city the largest amount of tribute it can exact. For over thirty-five years, or since 1869, Glasgow has owned its own gas-works. As a result, its people pay fifty-three cents per thousand feet for gas. Its municipal electricity is supplied at five and one-half cents per kilowatt hour. All the markets are owned by the city. Private slaughter-houses were abolished many years ago and the city is now supplied by three central establishments. From Lake Katrine in the Trossachs it brings its splendid water supply. The Water Department also supplies hydraulic power.

In addition to its hospitals, its parks, its art galleries, museums, libraries, botanic gardens, art schools, technical schools, etc., it has also its winter gardens, its free concerts, facilities for golf and other games, gymnasia and playgrounds for the children. It has also homes for the children of widows and widowers; it has depots for the supply of sterilized milk to poor children. "It," says Robert Donald, editor of the London *Chronicle*, "was the persistency of Glasgow that broke down the private telephone monopoly in Great Britain, encouraged other municipalities to establish their own system, and has now led to the complete nationalization of the whole service."

Speaking of Glasgow's municipal tramways, Mr. Donald says: "It will be interesting to state the effect of municipal ownership, and to explain the policy which guided the City Council. The company — as all private enterprises must do — kept mainly in view immediate profits. Like most British companies, it pursued a narrow policy. The keynote of the municipal system was service, giving the best possible to the citizens. The municipality operated the roads in the interest of all. It greatly lowered the fares, banished all advertisements from the cars, made the names of the routes and destinations conspicuous, opened up new routes and linked up new districts. It also considered its employees. Without a contented staff there cannot be a perfect service. So the drivers and conductors were dressed in new uniforms, their wages were increased, their hours reduced. The citizens had the feeling of personal possession when they patronized the cars, which display the city's arms and its motto —'Let Glasgow Flourish.' Civic patriotism asserted itself later on, when the displaced franchise-holders started a competing service of omnibuses, which failed to get support and soon disappeared. . . .

"The fares in Glasgow are one cent for a stage of a

little over half a mile, and over 30 per cent of the passengers travel this short distance, and bring in nearly 17 per cent of the receipts. For an average of two and a third miles, the fares are two cents, and close on 61 per cent of the passengers travel this distance and contribute 66½ per cent of the receipts, so that 91 per cent of the total number carried pay two-cent or one-cent fares. Only 6.31 per cent travel for three cents. . . . Less than one per cent of the 189,000,000 passengers last year paid five cents or more. . . .

"The Glasgow tramways are managed by a Committee of the City Corporation, which holds frequent meetings and reports regularly to the City Council. It consists of twenty-eight members, who appoint sub-committees for supervising different departments. It obtains the sanction of the Council for its actions. The Council might be regarded as the legislative authority, and the Committee as the executive.

"From a financial point of view the Glasgow undertaking has been remarkably successful. . . . Last year's accounts indicate the healthy financial condition of the tramways. The total receipts, for instance, amounted to $3,624,255, the operating expenses to $1,684,100 — 49 per cent of the revenue. The net receipts showed a gross return on the capital outlay of 17.46 per cent. . . . The accounts of the department are examined and audited by independent professional accountants. The accounts are published with elaborate detail, showing the smallest item of expenditure worked out to percentages and comparisons with previous years.

"The Tramway Department, as I have indicated, generates its own electric power, the total cost of which is less than one cent per kilowatt hour.

"The Tramways Committee delegates considerable power to its general manager, who is responsible for the staff who form part of the permanent civil service in the city. Politics does not influence appointments, and promotion is by merit. . . .

"With liberal depreciation and reserve funds to meet renewals and obsolescence, with a redemption fund which liquidates the original capital of the undertaking in thirty years, which is at the same time maintained in an efficient condition out of revenue, the City Corporation is more than doing its duty to the next generation. Lower fares for long distances should be easily possible in the near future, and there is a prospect that the average fare will come down to one cent. A universal one-cent fare irrespective of distance could then be adopted."

Here then we have a municipal enterprise which after paying its annual interest, making its payments into the sinking fund for the redemption of its capital, allowing for depreciation and reserve fund, paying its local tax assessments — for it makes the same contribution to local taxation as if it were a private concern — and which although carrying over nine-tenths of its patrons for one-cent and two-cent fares, will at the end of thirty years — between nineteen and twenty years now, pay for itself entirely without one cent of cost to the people or to the municipality. Moreover, from the very beginning, it has been more up-to-date than any privately owned system.

There is indeed quite a contrast between the sturdy common sense and business sagacity of our Scotch brethren and the way we allow ourselves to be fleeced in connection with practically all of our public utilities and the type of service that even then we accept.

Is it any wonder then that so many thinking men among us are now realizing so keenly the stupid folly and lack of business management among us in this respect? And is it any wonder that at the close of the recent election in Chicago, resulting in the demand of her people for the municipalization of her transit systems, that a man of such business insight as Mr. Andrew Carnegie should send to the newly elected Mayor the following message as he is reported to have sent: Tell Judge Dunne not to stop until every public utility that can be made the subject of private monopoly has been placed under the control and operation of the city. Chicago is still in its infancy. It has scarcely yet begun to grow.

For some additional concrete facts shall we take a glance at Liverpool's transit systems. In this we have no less an authority than Mr. C. R. Bellamy, General Manager of the Municipal Street Railways of Liverpool. Some time ago Mr. Bellamy gave an address before the National Convention on Municipal Ownership and Public Franchises, held under the auspices of the New York Reform Club. In opening, he showed how the accommodations on his roads were doubled during the rush hours, and although he had a population of but

700,000 to deal with, the fan-shaped form of the city of Liverpool became, he said, terribly congested night and morning, and the traffic was quite as difficult to conduct as in any other city.

"In Great Britain," continued Mr. Bellamy, "the municipalities have largely concluded that local tramway management should be taken up in the common interest and worked entirely for the common good, treating it as a necessity in the same category with water and artificial light. . . .

"All objections to municipal trading are based on the surmise that it is fraught with danger to the community, and will end disastrously; but an ounce of fact is worth a pound of opinion.

"In 1897, a company rented the tramway lines which belonged to the municipality under an expired lease of seventeen years. The service was inadequate, the fares were high, and there were loud complaints as to the conditions of labour of the employees. It was felt that mechanical should supersede horse traction, that the system should be largely extended and fares reduced, and the company not being willing to make these changes, negotiations were opened resulting in the purchasing of the stock and shares of the company.

"It was at once arranged to scrap the entire undertaking and to adopt electric traction, and within three years of its acquirement the whole of the sixty-eight miles of track were reconstructed, together with forty miles of additional new track, which were equipped with 400 regular cars.

"The total carrying capacity was quadrupled, the fares reduced by nearly one-half, the wages of the employees largely increased and their hours of labour reduced, and they were all supplied with uniform clothing.

"It was a bold movement, and was considerably criticized, but the response of a grateful public to the facilities afforded made it at once evident that the success of the new scheme was assured."

Here, then, is a system which in addition to making its annual contribution to local taxation, putting by a regular fund for the redemption of its capital, allowing for depreciation, keeping itself in the highest state of efficiency, has nearly doubled its earning capacity within a period of five years, although raising its employees' wages and shortening their hours of work, and is giving its patrons a most up-to-date service and accommodations, charging a fare of two cents within the city limits, and a fare of four cents on beyond the city limits, and that in a few years will entirely pay for itself without one cent of expense to a single citizen or to the municipality. As soon as this period is up, then a still greater reduction of fares can, and in all probability will, be made; for such is the policy of these municipally owned and managed utilities. Another fact should be mentioned in connection with this system — one person, employee or passenger, was killed the previous year in every 13,000,000 people carried. They also, as in connection with all municipally owned and managed utilities, had no expensive legal and court proceedings to compel private owners to carry out their agreements with the city.

We could go into hundreds of other cities in Great Britain, in Germany, in Belgium and other continental countries, as well as into Australia and New Zealand; but in all we would find the same general facts and conditions, varying slightly in detail simply by reason of varying local conditions.

Now in all fairness I ask, if the people in the cities of these countries can save for themselves the returns from these wonderfully rich properties, aggregating hundreds of millions annually, instead of allowing these vast amounts to flow into the pockets of a few already overly rich individuals, why cannot we American people do the same? If we cannot then we must admit that we are less capable in business management and in the matter of self-government than they. This we can scarcely believe, especially when in some respects we have proved ourselves even more capable. I cannot believe that in these matters we are any less capable, or that we will show an inferior ability when we are sufficiently alert and determined.

The reply is made, if we had the honesty in municipal administration that they have in England, in Scotland, in Germany and the various other countries where such splendid municipal ownership results are obtained, then we could safely travel along the same lines. True, but the municipalities in these countries did not always have this characteristic, but they have attained it by simply going about it to attain it. They made the start which in a very definite way has led them to such splendid results. This is the stock argument presented against the municipal ownership and management of public utilities, and that it is a strong argument is held, and very honestly held, by large numbers of people. It *is* an argument, the only argument really worthy of consideration, but an argument not without an answer. We had better keep as we are lest we get into conditions still worse, it is said. But this latter is no argument, and it has no truth even as a statement; for taking it all in all it is absolutely impossible to have conditions in this respect worse than they are when we consider the uniformly excessively high charges and the generally poor and inadequate service, and the thousands of unnecessary killings and maimings that form the total for each year. With this must be combined the great amount of political corruption and debauchery that passes every year, and coupled with it all we must not refuse to take account of the yearly additions of the millions to the wealth of these little groups of already excessively rich men, many of whom are thoroughly unscrupulous in their dealings and in their entire outlook, as is all too clearly evidenced by the methods they have been and are continually using in furthering their ends, and in getting control of still larger amounts of the people's properties, so that they have become a menace to free institutions and to the welfare of every man, woman and child in the nation. Matters, I repeat, by no stretch of the imagination, could be any worse than they are, unless in connection with the taking over of these utilities for our common use, we cut loose from all common-sense in our methods of procedure and business management, which I am sure we are not liable to do.

The present amount of political corruption and graft in our city administration is, I am inclined to think, one very great argument, when we look at it in an all round way, for taking from private exploitation the management of these public utilities; for then the responsibilities at City Hall will become so great that we, the individual citizen, will be compelled to give the amount of time and study and attention to municipal affairs that we should be giving, for it is on account of this lack that these public service corporations have been able to have seated in our city councils the men that they have been able to make their deals with, and who, for consideration, have been handing over these public properties for their private enrichment. This is the great evil that we must now quickly face. It is the sore that has been gradually rotting and festering and gradually enveloping the very vitals of our entire social body. Men's abilities and real qualities assert themselves in the degree that responsibilities are placed upon them. So with something personal enough and large enough and inspiring enough for our splendid common citizenship to work for, as this great movement and all that it carries with it must be, and especially if we strike for it at once without delays or dickerings, and without any more millions being handed over or any further alienation of properties and rights, we would quickly make a splendid beginning in purging our social body of this rapidly growing and vigour-sapping disease. And when we begin to experience the direct personal results that will follow, then I am sure that we will never stop until we have put completely by the old, and into full and complete operation, the new.

Hand in hand with the extension of this movement must go the continual extending and perfecting of our Civil Service system, making it continually stronger in its requirements for admission, with perhaps continually greater leeway along the lines of dismissals for proven incompetency, and if the management in making removals cannot appoint except from the duly qualified lists, there will be but little chance for the political machine methods gaining control, or even extending themselves materially. By a wise and judicious extension of such a system, hand in hand with the growth of municipal ownership, the machine elements would be compelled gradually to disappear.

There can be no argument that the financial burden in connection with these undertakings would be too great for our cities to assume, because under wise and judicious management no additional burdens need be assumed, and these enterprises can be taken over and improved and extended just as they have been in the cities of Great Britain and of Germany already noted, and can be made to pay for themselves out of their own earnings without involving a burden of a single dollar upon any individuals or upon any municipality.

But this entire matter of municipal ownership is nothing new nor startling even with us; it is in fact merely an extension of the municipal ownership methods that we already have, including municipal water supplies — practically all of which are now or soon will be under complete municipal ownership and management. So our fire departments, our street-cleaning departments, our parks, and our public schools. Are these and others that could be mentioned not managed more economically and satisfactorily and more uniformly for the public welfare than if they were left to private enterprise? Who is there bold enough to say at all seriously, that any of these public utilities should be turned over to private enterprise? But to be supplied at satisfactory rates and in an all round satisfactory manner with lighting and heating facilities — gas and electricity — street-car and telephone facilities, etc., is just as important, for they are just as much necessities as those already mentioned.

And even in the matter of the now rapidly crystallizing municipal ownership movement, we are not without precedent and not without some very telling results. Chicago for example, for over fifteen years has owned and operated one of the largest electric lighting plants in the country, with which she lights her streets and public buildings. At one time she paid $125 a year for an arc-light. She is able to make her own light for about $54 per lamp. She has been doing this despite the fact that she has not been furnishing the private consumer with light. And on account of the fat-pursed private concerns, her city lighting plant, which has always been a menace to the private gas and electric companies, has been fought and hampered by them at every movement. Aldermen they have elected and Mayors they have controlled have crippled and starved it.

Notwithstanding this corporate hatred and intriguing and this official treachery, it has grown, has served the city splendidly, and has saved it large sums every year. It has therefore demonstrated what even under the most adverse circumstances can be done, and furnishes a basis upon which the city will now speedily build a true electric lighting system, which will supply all her people with light and so will save vast sums for them each year also. With the passing of the private concerns will pass the great amount of debauchery and corruption they have been responsible for in the city's municipal administration.

It should also be stated in connection with Chicago's lighting undertaking that, during the period it has been in operation, something over fifteen years, in addition to doing her municipal lighting for about one-half of what private concerns would demand, it has in this short period of time entirely paid for itself, is now the property of the city without any cost to it, and is now in position to reduce still lower the cost of its lighting. And a short time ago both houses of the Illinois legislature heard so plainly the demand of the people along the lines of the municipalizing of their public utilities, that a bill was passed allowing the city of Chicago to maintain gas and electric lighting plants, and to pay for them — whether bought or built — by issuing interest bearing certificates to be redeemed out of the earnings of the properties for which they pay, thus not affecting in the least the city's general revenues or rate of taxation. Chicago will be very proud in the coming years to have the honour of being sort of a forerunner in this great municipal ownership movement that will eventually include every city of importance in the land. And we can well afford to give her this honour, for by her example and experience other cities will be encouraged and helped.

When in addition to the few millions the street-car companies of Chicago have been taking from the people in profits each year, several millions in addition are saved to the people in their gas and electric lighting bills, they can well afford even financially to bear with becoming grace this honour.

But the best thing about it all is that we are now on the move. It has taken us a long, long time to get started. But we have another characteristic, that, when we once start we are capable of moving rapidly. When the time comes that all public utilities are managed by and for the benefit of those to whom they belong, as they will be, and sooner I am inclined to think than many of us even now realize, we will then wonder that our bump of common-sense and business insight in connection with these matters did not mature more early. The price we are paying for this delay is certainly something enormous.

So far as the question of right in the people's taking over and managing these utilities for their own benefit is concerned, it is scarcely worthy of consideration, for we all know that it exists. Almost a hundred forms of private ownership in the form of tolls, etc., have gone. We can proceed by way of direct purchase, mutual agreement in regard to price, if it is found advantageous to buy the private companies out. The more that can be done in this way the better. Then we can proceed by way of condemnation proceedings, through the right of eminent domain. It is a recognized principle in government that the right or desire of the individual is always subservient to the public good. If I own a particular piece of property and though I may think very highly of it, if a street is to be opened that will be for the public benefit, or if a railroad owned even by private individuals is to be constructed, or a public building erected, the portion of the property required is taken, or all, if all is necessary, and I am given compensation for it according to its real value, and not in accordance with whatever estimate of its value I may be pleased to place upon it. Here is something to be noted when these public properties are taken over to be managed for all the people — they will be taken at their real values, not at any fiat values, and a shrinking in values to the tune of many millions will be witnessed. The people are always pre-eminently fair in matters such as these. They will want to pay for every dollar of real value taken, but they will not pay the prices that the companies, almost without exception, will ask. The millions in watered stocks will be of no value to the people as they are of no value to them now, but on the contrary, are the cause of their parting with many a hard earning dollar. We will pay and willingly pay every dollar any property is worth, but we should not pay a dollar more than its real value calls for.

An instructive lesson along this line comes from London. Various water companies, some dating even from the Middle Ages, were able to retain their grip upon the city until, through the progressive action of the London County Council, to which the city owes much of its modern people's movement programme, determined to take them entirely out of private hands. The old companies were dispossessed and the entire water supply was put under the management of the Metropolitan Water Board. An arbitrating board was appointed, consisting of some of the ablest engineers in Great Britain. Their finding was that the city should pay a sum equal to about 60 per cent of the amount asked for them by the old companies. The result was the saving to the people of a little over $10,000,000. It will not be an impossible task for similar boards composed of skilled men who thoroughly understand the matters they are brought together to pass upon, to estimate in a similar manner the *real values* of the various utilities we shall be taking over here.

It seems scarcely necessary in view of the facts we have already considered pertaining to the results that have already been achieved along municipal ownership lines, to attempt to say anything further in its favour. The mere enumeration of some of the things already accomplished, with their splendid results to the people, should speak and does speak more loudly and persuasively than any array of arguments that could be gotten together.

It is not, fortunately, a matter of experimenting. We

know from what has already been done what the results under wise and careful management must be. The fact as we have already noted that all privately owned and managed companies are actuated by the one motive, the largest possible gain, makes it absolutely impossible for the people to be served and benefited as they should be; nor will they ever be until these public utilities are conducted primarily for the benefit of the people. An editorial in the *Boston Herald*, sometime ago, contained the following telling and true sentences: "No public benefit is ever to be expected of corporations organized for gain, which are so powerful that they feel able to make the law or to defy it. No good to the consumers of products can be hoped for from a monopoly which begins by the creation of fiat-capital. Having eliminated competition, it will certainly squeeze out of the people every dollar that can be extorted, regardless of justice and indifferent to suffering, even to the verge of provoking popular revolution. They will proceed to control, by means they well understand, legislation, administration and judicial tribunals. The people have no rights they feel bound to respect."

In view of these facts we have really no choice in the matter. It is purely a matter of justice, a clearly written duty — that which is intended to serve all the people in common should be so managed that all the people are served. As it is, the millions are exploited by the few hundreds, and worse, for in many cases they are plainly plundered by them. And all these years we have been quietly submitting to it and acting as if we knew no better. We have been learning very rapidly of late, however.

The issue is becoming so clear cut, and so many able and well-known men are now coming forward with ringing and inspiring declarations in favour of this great movement that is now on foot among us, that an entire volume could be quickly compiled from these declarations alone.

Note the following extract from a letter in response to an invitation recently sent out by the Municipal Ownership League of New York: "Unless, indeed, it be the fact that — as some have recently cynically intimated — 'New York is practically insane,' its citizens will soon quite irresistibly demand the definite adoption and the genuine execution of the policy of municipal ownership (and municipal operation) of all these conditions and instrumentalities, the efficient administration of which, in the general interest, is at once absolutely essential to the prosperity and safety of the city, and, not otherwise to be preserved from the abuses and perversion inevitably incident to their exploitations as the private property of a profit-mongering and stock-gambling monopoly."

The following also in response to a similar invitation: "New York voters have tired of the stock-jobbing gas combination which charges exorbitant rates for a miserable, inadequate service, and which boldly decrees that our streets shall be constantly torn up rather than allow the providing of pipe galleries in the subways, which might give opportunity for the rights of the public to be asserted. They are tired, too, of giving away scores of millions of the city's property to the Subway company to become a tax-free asset of the Rothschilds. . . . I believe that the great majority of our citizens hold the supplying of light and transportation to be as much public functions as the veins and arteries are functions of the body. For these public functions to be exercised as private interests and with private profits as their chief end is a condition of mediæval anarchy which no possible combination of politicians will, for much longer, be able to uphold."

So conservative and able a business man as ex-Governor Douglas of Massachusetts in one of his late messages to the Massachusetts Legislature, had this to say in regard to the matter we are considering: "I recommend legislation giving to cities and towns wider powers in the conduct of business which derives its profit from the necessities of the community. The powers already granted have proved the economy and wisdom of the conduct of such business by the community itself. . . .

"In many cases of privately owned public service corporations the rates, fares and prices charged are too high. The public is entitled to reasonable charges for the services of these monopolies. It will be far more likely to obtain service at reasonable prices if it has the right to do business on its own account.

"When a public service corporation is giving good service at fair rates it is not likely to be disturbed. When its rates and prices are unreasonable, it should, in the interest of the public welfare, be disturbed.

"It is not disputed that, as a rule, private corporations conduct their business more economically than do public corporations. It is, however, disputed that the public usually obtains the benefit of this economical management. In most cases, therefore, the publicly owned and operated waterworks, sewers, gas and electric lighting plants have given the public cheaper and better service than have the privately owned concerns.

"For these reasons, I ask the Legislature to give every reasonable facility to those municipalities which desire to conduct their own public service utilities.

"Appreciating the difficulties of obtaining good business management and economical production by municipalities, I urge you, when making laws for municipal ownership, to so frame them that the evils of political management will, so far as possible, be eliminated. With proper legislation it should be possible to obtain Most of the benefits without any of the evils of privately owned and operated public service corporations."

Of course, it is not to be expected that *at first* the results will in every case be all that are looked for by the most sanguine. Some mistakes will be made. But this is one of the ways in which greater ability in the conduct of these enterprises will be grown. And then we already have such splendid examples to learn from. It will undoubtedly require careful and wise business management to obtain in all cases the highest results.

I think another paragraph from ex-Governor Douglas's inaugural address may not be amiss here: "If, when guarded by as careful and wise legislation as is possible, certain municipalities should fail in their attempt to give better and cheaper service to the public, it will be because the citizens of these municipalities do not insist upon having their municipal plants conducted in a businesslike manner. The principle of municipal ownership is sound. In cases where unsatisfactory results are produced the fault is usually to be found in a laxity of administration. I believe that every such franchise taken over by the public relieves the people from possible exaction, practised for private profit. With the low rates at which municipalities can borrow and the elimination of dividends, the rates must be inevitably lowered, and the people become alone responsible for the efficiency of the service."

So far, in this part, we have dealt entirely with the matter of the public ownership and management of those utilities that pertain especially to our cities. The number of people is rapidly growing among us who are also asking why we should not have a national and state ownership and management or control of those public utilities that pertain to all the people, the same as this principle is being extended in Great Britain and various Continental countries, so as to include telegraph, express, telephone, railroad enterprises, and thus secure for the people better service and lower rates as the people in these other countries are enjoying. There is no reason why this should not to a judicious extent come about, and that it will, is as certain as that the principle of municipal ownership will eventually so grow and extend itself as practically to include every city in the nation.

The principle of state and national ownership and control will grow and extend itself a little more tardily, but its eventual growth and triumph is just as certain. The beginnings will be made in connection with the managing of the municipal utilities for the benefit of the people, and as it is seen what gains will result from these, the demand for its extension so as to include all the "natural monopolies" that are now operated purely for private gain will continually increase. If this can be done in other countries and so successfully, as is now being done, then it can be done here, unless again in this, we are willing to be classed as incompetents as compared with our British and Continental brethren. And if it can be done so successfully and to the great gain of the people in one line, then it can be done also successfully and to the gain of the people in lines of a more or a less kindred nature.

Here again, fortunately, we do not have to deal with any matters of theory or speculation merely. For years the United States Government has conducted a great public utility for its people, and during all the years it has been in operation it has given them a service incomparably better than that of any private company or companies even by the wildest stretch of the imagination would have been, and at prices a mere fraction of what we would be now paying as a necessary tribute to corporate greed. We can, through this splendid government service, send a message by postal card or a much longer one by letter to practically any portion of the entire world for a two-cent fee or a five-cent fee. Now, in all fairness I ask, what would be exacted for this service if this public necessity were under the control of private companies?

Judging from their charges in other things — express, telegraph, freight, can we reasonably expect that the one would be a fee of less than five cents, or the other less than ten? That is even for the shorter foreign services, with still an additional fee for the longer distances. In addition to the low fees we now pay, compared to what we would pay under private management, we get a service that is as prompt and efficient as it can reasonably be made. Dependent upon private concerns, our mail matter would be carried at their convenience. At first competition in connection with some of the routes would insure us against the worst of service, but later on when the various concerns through mutual self-interest had pooled their interests or had consolidated into one huge monopoly, then we would be practically at the mercy of this concern, the same as millions of people all over the country are at this very hour at the mercy of other concerns of a similar public nature. We appreciate too much our one-cent and two-cent fees for domestic postal card and letter, with the large leeway we have so far as amount is concerned in connection with the latter.

Then the conveniences we have for small merchandise many times allows us to save ourselves from the demands of the privately owned express companies when the element of distance enters. We should be paying them still more were it not for the benign and restraining influences the Post-Office Department exerts over their calculations. I have before me the report of the New York post-office for the year ending June 30,

1905. It shows a *net profit* for this period of twelvemonth, of a little more than $10,000,000. Quite a neat sum to go into the pockets of private individuals did we allow private concerns to attend to this necessity for us, the same as we allow them to attend to other necessities of a similar nature. This neat net profit would be much larger, however, for their charges would be in practically all cases higher than we are now paying. And by virtue of paying their employees less, and giving an inferior type of accommodation for the people, their operating expenses would be less, and therefore, their profits still greater.

In addition to this item of $10,000,000 in net profit for a single year, I think quite as significant a matter is the fact that on the day the report was made, twenty-six new sub-stations — for the people's greater convenience — were opened, one with a force numbering sixty-six. Private companies do not increase their operating expenses for the peoples' greater convenience, except as self-interest may dictate, that is, when a competing company makes additional accommodations for the convenience of the people a method of securing additional business. This also is interesting: "One hundred additional clerks who have served their time as substitutes were added to the regular staff to-day. . . . An additional hundred substitute clerks have also been appointed to take the places left vacant by those promoted. This makes two hundred appointed from the new eligible list."

All in all it is not a bad showing so far as clear-cut

and clean business methods are concerned, in addition to the neat business balance. Rather a stiff argument, isn't it, to present to the attention of those who argue that a great and complex service of this kind cannot be conducted as economically and as advantageously for the people by the government as by private concerns? I wonder how much of an extension of the free rural delivery service that is now coming to the convenience of millions in the country and rural districts, who especially, need greater conveniences, there would be if private concerns were fattening upon this great public utility, pardon me — were performing this service for us.

How about the revelations in connection with the irregularities and dishonesty in the Post-Office Department that came to the public knowledge some months ago, I hear it asked. There were irregularities and there was corruption. The very fact, however, that we heard so much of it and the fact that the perpetrators of it were arraigned and brought to justice, argues well for such government ownership and administration. Moreover, I venture this assertion, that the aggregate of losses sustained by the public through this agency, have not equalled *one thousandth part* of the amount of debauchery and corruption that would have resulted were this public service utility allowed to be in the hands of private individuals or companies, and therefore run from beginning to end for private gain. I also venture this statement, that all the losses sustained through dishonesty and fraud in our government Post-Office Department, from the first year of its operation down to the present time, have not equalled—to be conservative —one five thousandth part of the amounts that the profits of private management would have taken from us, to say nothing of the uniformly inferior type of service furnished, compared to that which we have been and are enjoying.

Can any one present what would be regarded as any reasonable argument, and one that would be accepted by any number of reasonable and thinking men, why the government cannot carry for us our express packages through the medium of a parcels post, and attend to our telegraph and telephone needs, as successfully as it now attends to our postal needs, and the same as other people through their central governments are having done for them with a better service and at much lower rates than they were able at any time to get from their former private companies? Certainly no one of these is as difficult and as complex as the service the government is already performing for us. And to take these over simply as extensions of the department already in operation would be by no means a difficult task. Those who are familiar with the parcels post in Great Britain for example, and its nominal "peoples" charges, compared to the tribute levied by our express companies, appreciate what this change will mean. The absurdity of a minimum express charge here being twenty-five cents! It would make an Englishman's or a German's or a Belgian's blood boil to have such a tribute levied upon him, with no other reason than for the purpose of lining the pockets of a few already wealthy company owners.

What would they say to such as this for example: A few weeks ago through the breaking of some minor parts of a cultivator I was compelled to send to the factory for new pieces. The cost of the parts was a dollar and twenty-five cents. The bulk was less than half a cubic foot, or perhaps equal to that of an ordinary pasteboard shoe box. The distance was about a hundred and fifty miles. The tariff levied by the express company was seventy-five cents. The time taken to bring the parcel was considerably more than twice the length of time it could have been carried and delivered in. The company or companies could have carried such a parcel for a charge of twelve to twenty cents and made a *handsome* profit.

And then when the service is poor or careless, in addition to being excessively high in its charges, there is no recourse for the people, for public service companies have no ethical sense that would lead them to any amicable settlement when the shipper suffers either great inconvenience or loss. He has no recourse except to take the matter into the courts, which does not pay unless the amount involved is large, and even then he is subjected to delays and dodges of almost every conceivable type. It is the policy of such corporations never to pay out a cent unless it is utterly impossible for them to find any way of avoiding it.

Here is another concrete example of a frequent type of private corporation methods. Some time ago I had sixteen hundred young fruit trees shipped from a point a few miles south of Rochester, New York, to a point thirty-four miles from New York City to the north. It was a lot of specially selected, high-grade trees. The nature of the goods was known to the railroad company. The cases were labelled — perishable, without delay, do not allow to freeze. It was in early November. The time in which they could have been carried handily with a service organized for the people's convenience and welfare would have been a period of not more than five or six days. They were on the way between fourteen and fifteen days. The last two or three days of their transit they encountered an intensely cold and stormy period. Though ready to plant them so as to have them in readiness for an early pushing out in the Spring, I was compelled to heal them into the ground for the winter, not knowing until Spring would tell, whether they would come out of the ground in a normal or in a damaged condition. Large numbers proved to be damaged and a block of several hundred had to be thrown out entirely. The various inconveniences and losses incident upon this were, after the lapse of several months, put into the form of a letter with an offer to accept a very reasonable settlement, provided it were made promptly, and sent to the claim agent of the railroad. The amount was considerably less, taking *all* things into consideration, than the damage really sustained. In the course of several months several letters passed. I finally received the announcement — final, the agent indicated — that a careful and thorough examination of the case had been made, and that they would decline my offer as they found themselves not liable, for another road into whose hands they had given the freight, had carried it, they found, as long a period as they. Though prefering otherwise, an effort to secure justice can now be had only by taking the matter into the courts. But this is simply an example of but one type of inconvenience and loss that thousands upon thousands of people are being put to every year, in addition to charges in practically every case higher than they should be, because we are sufficiently stupid as to continue to allow private concerns to get possession of and create many times into a monopoly, the public service that should be conducted by the people through their agent, the government, for the benefit of the people.

Another concrete case by way of a personal experience was that of another road in taking seventeen days to carry some goods from a point twelve miles out of Boston to the same destination — thirty-four miles north of New York City. I dare say there is scarcely a reader of these lines who has not had similar experiences with the privately owned corporations that abound in the country. I suppose if all could be chronicled, especially with all the adjectives and all the feelings that escaped at the time, books could be quickly compiled that would form a very large public library.

The people of other countries have for years been taking all these utilities, such as express, telegraph, telephone, railroads, etc., out of the hands of private control and monopoly and through their central governments are supplying themselves with these services in practically every case greatly to their advantage. We are at least a quarter of a century behind them. Outside of the United States over two-thirds of the railroad mileage of the world is owned and operated by the governments of the various countries. Ours is almost the only great country now in the world that does not own and operate the telegraph lines. Those who are acquainted with the telegraph service in Great Britain know and appreciate the fact that there they can send messages for twelve cents to any part of Great Britain, for which the charges here would in no case be less than twenty-five cents, and sometimes would reach as high as forty and fifty cents for the same distance covered. In addition to this one is furnished there with a much more convenient service both at the point of sending and in the matter of delivery, for it has all the conveniences of the Postal Department with which it is connected. The fact that our minimum telegraph charge is twenty-five cents is quite as ridiculous as that our minimum express charge is also twenty-five cents.

In Great Britain the history of the telegraph under government ownership has been one of continual enlargement and development with the thought of the widest and best possible service for all the people, and with the least possible charges. The result is that it has become a great public convenience serving all classes of the people. The charges here under private ownership are absolutely prohibitive for such uses as are made of it there by all the people in common.

There was a great fight made on the part of the private companies to retain their grip upon it when the telegraph service was taken over by the government. Many arguments were used, and similar to many encountered here, against the government doing the same in connection with these same general utilities. The private owners and those in any way allied with them and influenced by them, were fairly bursting with reasons why the government should not perform these services. Among them — It was not the government's business to telegraph; the rates would be higher; it would not be as progressive in its management as the private companies; there would be a deficit to be met; the use of the telegraph would be less; there would be less of a stimulus to invention, and hence, new improvements; it would be an arbitrary and unjust interference with private rights for the government to invade the field of private business, etc., etc. In spite of these and their arguments, and in spite of every effort made by the private companies to impede and to prevent the movement, the telegraph system of England was bought by the government and made a part of the postal system in 1870.

As to the results in this case, they have been formulated by a very able authority as follows:* "The immediate results of public ownership were: First, a reduction in rates of one-third to one-half; second, a vast increase of business and work done by the telegraph, doubling in the first year after the transfer; third, a great extension

* The late ex-Governor Altgeld, of Illinois, was a most competent and earnest advocate of the principle of both municipal and national ownership and control of all public service utilities and all "natural monopolies."

of lines into the less populous districts, so as to give the whole people the benefit of telegraphic communication; fourth, large additional facilities by opening more offices, locating offices more conveniently, and making every post-office a place where a telegram may be deposited; fifth, a considerable economy by placing the telegraph service with the mail service, under single control, thus avoiding useless duplications in offices, etc.; sixth, a marked improvement in the service, the aim of the post-office being good service, not dividends; seventh, a decided gain to employees in pay, in shorter hours and in tenure of office; eighth, in unprecedented advantages to the press for cheap and rapid transmission of news at the same time freeing it from the pressure of a power that claimed the right to dictate the views and opinions it should express; ninth, the development of business and strengthening of social ties, such as ties of kinship and friendship; tenth, the removal of a great antagonism and the cessation of the vexations and costly conflict it had caused between the companies and the people.

"These were the immediate results. Now, after a quarter of a century of use, the following further results are noticeable: First, a further reduction of nearly one-half in the average cost of a message; second, while the population increased only 25 per cent, the telegraph business has increased 1,000 per cent; third, a six-fold extension of lines and a fifty-fold increase of facilities; fourth, a steady policy of expanding and improving the service, adopting new inventions, putting underground hundreds of miles of wire that formerly ran over houses and streets, etc.; fifth, a systematic effort to elevate labour, resulting in a progressive amelioration of the condition of employees in respect to wages, hours, tenure, promotion, privileges, etc.; sixth, satisfaction with the telegraph service, even on the part of conservatives who objected to the change before it was made."

Gaining valuable knowledge and experience in connection with this great national public utility, Great Britain is taking under government ownership and management her entire telephone system — a portion of which was taken some years ago. The people are already great gainers, and I dare say the government will carry out the same plan of greatly extending and making more convenient for the people this great public utility also.

Can we not see a very great similarity between this government owned and administered utility — Great Britain's telegraph system — and our own government owned and administered postal system? Are not the constantly increasing facilities for the ever greater convenience and accommodation of the people, the successful business administration, the uniformly low charges in our system closely akin to the above detail of results in connection with Great Britain's national telegraph system?

And as important even as are these results is the fact that this makes one less great source of public bribery and corruption and debauchery; for the fact that privately owned companies have gained control of most of our public service utilities, and their efforts to retain and to continually increase the scope of their holdings is the greatest source of our notorious political corruption.

As has been the history and results of our government postal system, Great Britain's government telegraph system, so have been in a general way the history and results of the government owned and controlled railroads of Germany, Belgium, New Zealand, Australia, and many other countries that have brought or that are bringing under government ownership and management their railroads.

A recent number of *Officia Corre pondence* (Berlin) contained an important article in regard to present European policies of railway management. The movement is now determined toward nationalization of railways, especially in Germany; Austria is now aiming at the same consummation.

"Germany," says the writer, "which has the most extensive system o railways of all European countries, has decided at last upon making an end of the remnant of private railways. By the law of December 7, 1905, the purchase of the Palatinate railways, 450 miles in length, by the Kingdom of Bavaria, has been provided for. There now remains only the railway from Lubeck to Buchen, which is but seventy-five miles in length, and whose acquisition, for the sake of a unified system of railway management, is very desirable. Rumours relative to the purchase of this line have been afloat on the German stock exchanges during the past year, but they have been mostly devoid of foundation. . . .

"In Austria it is anticipated that in the near future

the oldest and most extensive private railway, the Kaiser Ferdinand Northern Railway, 1,036 miles in length, will be transformed into a line managed by the State. It is no longer any secret that the Austrian half of the Hapsburgian Empire is endeavouring to obtain a purely state system, such as already exists in the Hungarian half. Holland, Belgium, Switzerland, Denmark, Sweden, and Norway have already carried out the nationalization of their railways. The idea of a state system of railways has, however, met with most success during the past year in Italy. Twenty years ago public opinion was so strongly against the state management of railways that even the railways already belonging to the State were leased to private companies. In February and April, 1905, however, the Italian Parliament decided upon a system of state-railway management. Since July 1, 1905, over 6,300 miles have been taken over by the State. The purchase of further lines is being negotiated, especially the Adriatic network, but no result has yet been arrived at. After the experiences which Italy has gained, especially in the year 1905, of private railway management, there can be no doubt that the State will remain victor in the struggle for the possession of the lines."

No one agency, perhaps, has so contributed to the growth of corruption, lawlessness, and privilege, has stifled competition and all chance of justice as between dealers as well as justice to shippers and buyers of all types, and contributed to political corruption in both our state legislatures and in our national legislature as our privately owned and controlled railroad systems. For years we have been trying to get ahead of or to keep even with these abuses, and with what results, anyone familiar with the records of our Interstate Commerce Commission, or familiar with the powerful, and up to the present time, almost uniformly successful efforts on the part of the railroads to defeat and escape all public efforts to make them reasonably fair and just and to have them stop their open and villainous disregard of the laws, will fully comprehend.

If the same efforts that have been spent, and in great part vainly, in the various attempts to make the railroads of the country simply law abiding and decent in the conduct of their affairs and in their treatment of the public, if these efforts I repeat, had been spent in evolving plans in getting them into operation under government administration, we could to-day be standing at least *near* the point of advancement that other countries that are so far ahead of us have made.

Though it will perhaps be one of the last of our great public utilities to come completely under government ownership on account of the powerful private interests that will in every possible way oppose it, nevertheless it is one of the most important from the standpoint of the great common welfare. And while we have been spending time trying to regulate them and to secure some little measure of justice from them, to say nothing of our charges being higher than those in any other modern country in the world, other countries have solved this problem by going boldly forward and administering their railroads for the people's and for the great public benefit, the same as we shall find that we shall do eventually. And while at the present state of affairs it is well that still greater efforts at control and regulation be made, at the same time we shall lose much if in the meanwhile we are not putting forth efforts looking to the time when this great *public necessity utility* be taken under government ownership and conducted in the interests of all the people.

Announcement has recently been made that the Court* has approved of proposed additional subway routes in New York City, aggregating nineteen in number and costing some $450,000,000. It is to be seen whether the Rapid Transit Commission will again deliver the people's rights and tremendous future properties over to a band of traction financiers, agents of foreign capitalists, the Rothschilds, or whether they will have a sufficiently strudy stamina to resist these agencies, and will have the brains to find a method or methods whereby these can be built, owned, and controlled by the great city itself. The people have to considerable extent already been aroused to the iniquity perpetrated in connection with the subway already built, an iniquity that will reveal itself in greater proportions, as a rapidly increasing intelligence along these lines becomes more and more the possession of the people. I think, moreover, they will scarcely sit quietly and witness a repetition of such methods. Boards and Commissions of the same nature in the various and numerous cities of other

*The Appellate Division, the Supreme Court.

countries can find the brain power and a sufficient fertility of resources to hold such properties for the people, and some very legitimate questions will be asked, if it becomes apparent that they cannot be found by members of this commission, as also by similar commissions here. The decision of the Court approves the routes of the subway system as laid out on paper by the Rapid Transit Commission, but a legal point never suggested before, and "which," as a writer in a leading New York paper* says, "may upset the financial calculations of the Rapid Transit Commission," is pointed out by the Court in its opinion. Continuing, the writer of the article says: "the vote of the people in 1894 that subways should be constructed with public funds renders it questionable, say the judges, if it is 'permissible by law' to build them with private capital, as contemplated. 'Upon which question,' says the opinion significantly, 'because not before us, we express no opinion.' Chief Justice O'Brien, who writes the opinion, gives as one of the most weighty reasons for attaching a condition to the complete approval of the system, that such a course might preclude the possibility of building a municipally owned and operated system." Following are his own words:

"By the adoption of the proposed plan and the practical monopolizing of all the city's streets, wedded to a single scheme of transit construction or management, the people are practically forever excluded from asserting and exercising the right, which has much of reason and

* *New York American*, July 13, 1906.

argument in its support, to wit: to own and operate their municipal subways.

"It may be that in a year or a few years the vast majority of the people of this greater city, in their enlightened judgment, will demand the construction and operation of their own transportation facilities. . . ."

So free have public service corporations been in the use of money in bribing and corrupting public officials to get the people's public property into their own hands, that there comes a time when even they have to pay the penalty in having to part with a greater amount of their profits than they would voluntarily pay. They have created such a debauched condition in some city councils and state legislatures that their first offers of two thousand or five thousand dollars for votes in connection with some particular measures, have so emboldened the members as time has passed, that they have demanded as high as fifty thousand and even more, for votes in connection with other measures. Sometimes we hear the managers of corporations complaining that they are held up, blackmailed, by councilmen and legislators. Their methods have instituted such foulness and venality that sometimes in the end it does amount to this. They have themselves to blame. The more bold have been known at times to pay with checks; those more cautious and wary pay with money; the still more cautious and wary give dividend paying stocks in the company or some allied company, and pledge in addition their continued political safe keeping to the member, and others adopt still other methods.

There are those who get elected to our city councils and state legislatures for the sole purpose of making deals with these corporations, and getting out of the office in this way the largest amounts they can get. Corporations then again, have their own particular men elected, with whom they have made a deal before election, or with whom there is the understanding that they command their services after their election.

Some corporations are known to have in city councils and state legislatures a member whom they support and pay to look regularly after their interests. Sometimes to disarm suspicion a very good type of citizen — whom they judge weak on the itchy palm side — is induced to accept nomination, his election is secured by them, and he is then manipulated according to their interests. Political machines do the same. Once in a great while they get fooled by not rightly calculating their man. Such was the case when the machine in St. Louis promoted the selection of Joseph W. Folk for the office of Circuit Attorney. Mr. Folk at the time said substantially that if elected he must have a free hand, and that he would conduct the affairs of the office in his own way. They thought he was merely talking. Some, for their error in calculation in this case, are now serving good penitentiary time. While speaking of Mr. Folk, I think it may not be uninteresting to note some of his findings when the bills of the old score were one day finally presented for redemption. The following is from a public address delivered at an important centre of the state of which he is now Governor:

"For another franchise $250,000 in bribes was paid to the members of the preceding assembly. This franchise was afterward sold for $1,250,000, but the city received not a cent. Twenty-three of the twenty-eight members of the House of Delegates took bribes of $3,000 each for this franchise. Seven members of the council obtained from $10,000 to $17,500 each for their votes. One councilman was given $25,000 to vote against the franchise and afterward accepted $50,000 to vote in favour of it. He returned the $25,000 to the man who gave it to him, saying he did not believe he could 'honestly' keep it without 'earning' it by giving his vote in accordance with the terms of purchase. Upon reflection he likewise sent the $50,000 back, with the hope of getting more. He finally voted for the ordinance with the expectation and under promise of obtaining $100,000 for his vote. His friend, the promoter, disappointed him by leaving the city early the next day without paying him. More in sorrow than in anger the official tracked the promoter to New York, and after much difficulty succeeded in obtaining $5,000, but not until the promoter had him sign a certificate of character saying, 'I have heard rumours in St. Louis that you paid members of the assembly for their votes. I want to say that I am in a position to know, and I do know that you are as far above offering a bribe as I am above receiving one.' This was literally true, as the official had taken bribes right and left, and the promoter had boodled on a gigantic scale in getting his bill through the municipal assembly. Seven members of the council, elected to serve the people at a salary of $300 a year, were paid a regular salary of $5,000 yearly to represent corporate interests. A lighting bill was bribed through the House of Delegates for $47,500. The bargain was made right on the floor of the House. The money was given to one of the members, and after the meeting they met in the home of one of their number, where the 'pie' was cut and the money divided. . . . Nineteen members of another House of Delegates obtained $2,000 each as bribes for their votes on still another franchise.

"Men would run for a seat in the municipal assembly with the sole object of making money by the prostitution of their position. The scheme of corruption was systematic and far-reaching. The people were careless; the public conscience was asleep. These city legislators went on without hindrance. They devised a scheme of selling the water-works, which belonged to the city, for $15,000,000, the works being worth about $40,000,000. They planned to get $100,000 apiece for their votes on this. The proposed sale failed, because of a wise provision of the city charter forbidding unconditional alienation. Then their gloating eyes fell on the old court house with the gilded dome. They thought of selling that. They hoped to obtain $100,000 apiece for their votes on this. Then they concluded to sell the Union Market, but the market men had considerable political influence. With this and the sum of $20,000 they raised and paid the members they succeeded in stopping the sale. Then came the exposure. Now some of these representatives are fugitives from justice in foreign countries: others have turned State's evidence; the remainder have faced juries, and eighteen of these givers and takers of bribes have received sentences ranging from two years to seven years in the penitentiary. . . . These conditions are the outgrowth of the commercialism of our times."

Various public service corporations are known to contribute very liberally to one or the other political party in campaign funds. Usually it is the dominant party in either state or city according as their needs lie. Sometimes to be on the safe side they are large contributors to the campaign funds of both parties. Their profits taken directly from the people's pockets are generally so enormous that they can afford to do this, in addition to maintaining large corruption funds for definite action later on.

That there are others — and the numbers now are very large — who realize these facts is evidenced by the following expression from the editor of a leading magazine: "The chief agencies of corruption, bribery, and debauchery of the legislative, executive and judicial departments of government, as has been shown time and again, are found in the public service corporations which operate natural monopolies or those utilities in which all the people are interested. To destroy this fountain-head of political corruption and to give to all the people all the benefits flowing from the operation of public utilities or natural monopolies, the city, state and nation, or the people, should own and operate them for the good of the community at large."

This also even though longer, from one of the sanest and keenest observers of our social and political affairs, and formerly governor of one of our leading states: "Private monopolies furnish the hand that bribes by day and bribes by night, that pollutes everything it touches, and the existence of corruption in our cities and in our state and national governments furnishes the strongest argument in favour of wiping out all private monopolies, for it will give the people back their government. The great question in America to-day is how to restore republican government, which has been destroyed by the corporations. They control not only the local city governments, but they control the state governments and the national government. They decide what the Legislature may and may not do, what Congress may and may not do; they determine the policies of political parties, and they have destroyed the vitality of both political parties.

"Only a few weeks ago the *Chicago Inter-Ocean* and the *Chicago Record-Herald*, two of the most influential Republican papers in America, lamented the decadence of the House of Representatives at Washington and declared that Congress had practically abdicated its functions to the monopolies; that great public questions were no longer discussed upon their merits, but were decided arbitrarily by the majority, and the decision was not the result of investigation and discussion, but was the arbitrary dictation of the lobbyists.

"A mere change of party administration signifies nothing so long as the same slimy hands control the policy of government. We had two such changes, and their history was written with the dirty fingers of the exploiters. We need a change of policy. Instead of being owned the people must be the owners, instead of being lambs to be shorn they must be masters of the fold. Our industries and our great public utilities were built with the money and the industry and the genius of the American people, but they have passed out of the hands of the people who made them and are now controlled by manipulators, controlled by bankers, by brokers, by speculators.

"These men do not build railroads. They do not build factories; they do not build cities; they do not create anything; they simply grab what other people have created. As a rule, they are mere birds of prey, tearing the flesh of the men and women who work with their hands, eating the vitals of the men and women who do the work of the land and who made civilization possible on this earth.

"No republic can endure that remains in the clutches of these birds of prey; they use government as a convenience in the process of exploitation, extortion and robbery. It is among the newly made and corrupt rich that we find the spirit of snobbery and flunkeyism that apologizes for republican institutions. It is the monopolists who demand the restriction of free speech and of a free press. They not only plunder the people, but they would rob them of their liberties. . . .

"If there were no other reason why the people should own the monopolies than that it will give them back their government, that reason is in itself sufficient."

The difference in the policies and the management of the various public service utilities in those countries where they are moving, and so successfully, along the lines of public ownership and operation, or management, and the prevailing policies and methods of management among us should I think be noted. In case of the former, the best and the most up-to-date service, with a minimum of cost to the people is the policy. Not the making of large dividends, but using what would otherwise be larger profits for the greater convenience and better accommodation of the largest number of people at the lowest reasonable cost. In case of transit, for example, municipal or state, the opening up of sections and properties in new and outlying districts, thus affording desirable and real homes to large numbers of people who otherwise would be compelled to remain as tenants in the already densely populated portions, because unable economically to reach the districts where they can have real homes of which they may become owners. It is the welfare of the people, of the largest numbers of the people, that is continually sought after. And what do we find here? We find these utilities, with a minor exception here and there, organized and managed with an eye single to the largest dividends that can be extracted from the people, and many times large dividends even on stock watered to two, three and even four times its real value, a proceeding, in my judgment, criminal in its nature and that should not much longer be permitted. Then on top of all this, after giving the vast sums we are continually giving to those private individuals and companies by way of franchises and privileges, the use of streets, highways, etc., we are struggling continually to have them, deal not honourably and fairly with us, but to be even *decent* in their charges and service and general treatment of their patrons. We have many times to fight legally and against the ablest legal talent that our combined contributions enable them to employ, to secure the most elemental rights, and many times the most ordinary forms of decency in treatment. The above is true in regard to practically all public service corporations, true of all natural monopolies of municipal, state, or national character. How much better the public welfare could be served if these utilities were in the hands of the people moving always and directly along the lines of their own best interests.

There are exceptions. In numbers of our smaller places the service is all that could be expected from the profits received, that is, all that could be expected under private ownership. During the past year, a well-known citizen of Australia, President of the Federated Council of the Chamber of Commerce of Australia, in visiting Chicago, spoke quite at length concerning their own methods along these lines and the methods in other countries compared to our own methods. The following are two or three brief paragraphs from what he had to say concerning his observations:

"In Australia all public utilities are owned by the

state or municipality, that includes the telephones, the telegraphs, the railroads, the street railways and the water-works. Under public ownership we have constructed some of the greatest water-works in the world.

"We, in Australia, have become firmly convinced of the principle that municipal ownership of public utilities means their administration for the people with the simple object of securing the most benefits for the smallest price.

"The truth of our theories seems to be demonstrated here in Chicago, where the people have to ride in dog boxes that are a disgrace to humanity. Do you suppose that our people in Sydney, or any other Australian city, would stand for any such coops for a minute as Chicago folks are compelled to ride in? Why, if any attempt were made to run such cars along our streets, the people would be up in arms in an hour and jam mass meetings 50,000 strong."*

What he would say were he to speak in a similar manner of his observations and findings in New York, it is by no means difficult to imagine.

A right good concrete illustration of the point immediately in hand, comes f om Milan, Italy. Prior to 1897 the street railways were owned by a corporation which paid to the city a lump sum of $200,000 a year. "Fares were high, service was poor, employees were overworked and underpaid; and the public was treated pretty much as the New York public is treated — like cattle." But thanks to municipal ownership in con-

* *Chicago Record Herald,* October 26, 1905.

nection with this utility, the city owns the tracks and has a supervising control over its entire railway system. It now receives an annual income of $600,000, and onc of the most valuable lessons for us, perhaps, is the following: — During two hours each day the fare on the street railways is the equivalent of one cent; during the balance of the day it is the equivalent of two cents. And the operating company, which has a twenty year *contract*, is able to declare right good dividends from its share of the annual arnings of $1,500,000. Since the city has owned its street railways line, farcs have been reduced as above, service has been *vastly* improved, employees hours have been reduced and their time made more regular with a guaranteed rest of four days in each month, while at the same time their wages have been increased. Thus the people of Milan, the second city in the country, have the satisfaction of knowing that they have one of the best street railway systems of any city in the country — this satisfaction itself a valuable asset of the people. Isn't it really about time that we "progressive" American people began to sit up and take note?

The owners of these public service utilities find a way in spite of all efforts against it to make them monopolies, and the people are then at their mercy. A safe and sane principle is this, if in connection with anything there is a monopoly or the possibility of a monopoly, then the people should own and control that monopoly. It then becomes a benefit to all alike and an injury to none. It doesn't enrich the few while it helps economically to enslave the many, as at the same time it abounds in corruption and helps undermine and paralyze republican institutions. Why shouldn't the people, as many are asking now, through their agent, the government, own and develop the coal fields, upon the product of which practically all are dependent. Why shouldn't we get our coal cheaper, at a more uniform price, and free from the inconvenience and distress that result from the frequent disturbances between employer and employee? This is something that would influence in a very direct way the economic, and hence the entire welfare of every man, woman and child in the country. Isn't it a saner and a more common-sense principle that all be able to obtain this necessity at the great saving that it could be obtained at, and at a steady and uniform price, than that it be allowed to be monopolized by the few who have become already unduly rich, and who are free to exact from the people whatever tribute they may see fit, even to the extent of causing great suffering and not infrequently even death?

The principle that thoughtful men everywhere are beginning to recognize as a sound and common-sense principle is this, that *all natural monopolies* be brought under government ownership and control, municipal, state, or national, according to the nature of each, and so be administered for the direct benefit of all the people in common, in distinction from their being grabbed and cornered and through corruption and debauchery and venality monopolized for the over-enrichment of the few. Under the head of natural monopolies would fall such utilities as pertain to dwellers in the city, such as water, gas, electricity, transit, etc., and those that come under the head of state and national ownership and control, such as the postal service, the telegraph, the telephone, the express, the railroads, the coal fields. the oil fields, and mines of sufficiently important types. Can any argument, that will stand a thorough and all round examination, be put forth why these great *public necessity utilities* should not, in some way, be held and administered for the common good of all the people?

The principle of public ownership is sound — the ownership of those utilities, that from their nature become or may become monopolies, or of those utilities that from their nature derive their values from the common needs of the people.

Whether now or as time passes it may be practicable or advisable that *all* such utilities come under public ownership and control, is something that can be determined only by the people in a reckoning with the conditions in each particular locality and in each particular case. But there is a principle thoroughly safe as well as sound that should be put into immediate operation in every state, namely, that each locality have the right — by statute, as it has the natural moral right — to purchase, or to construct and own, and to operate or control such of its utilities, as at any time *it* may decide upon. And any legislator who sees fit to oppose, or who dares record his vote against any *enabling measure* of this nature, gives evidence, with possibly a rare exception, of his subserviency to certain agencies that do not represent the people, or of his anticipation of such subserviency, and these are the men who, as we get a little more stamina in the recognition of and the performance of our duties as citizens of a progressive and advancing nation, will be quickly read out of public life.

If a private company is giving a good service at a reasonable cost, and is decent and honourable in its methods and in its dealings with the public, there may be no reason, and in large numbers of cases there will be found no reason for interfering with it. But, where such is not the case the city should have the right even for the protection to say nothing of the welfare of its people, either to bring such concern to terms, or to throw it out of business entirely. The fact of the city having such right, will, of itself act as a tremendous protection, and the chances are that such right would have to be exercised only now and then as occasion might demand. In regard to this principle I think all fair and unbiassed minds cannot fail to agree. Numerous examples could be given of how this principle has already worked. Following is a case of how it works when there is an actual worker behind the works. I quote from a recent issue of a leading New York paper,* an editorial with the heading, "Cleveland's Lesson to New York."

"What an intelligent Mayor can do with a traction monopoly is illustrated by the news from Cleveland. Cleveland had a merger of a number of street-car companies with a watered capitalization like that of the Interborough-Metropolitan. But Cleveland also had a

* *The New York World*, July 21, 1906.

Mayor, Tom Johnson, who had been in the street-railroad business and knew all about its costs, possibilities and profits.

"Instead of doing business with himself in his dual capacity of Mayor and railroad man, Tom Johnson acted only for the people of Cleveland. He threatened that if the traction monopoly did not make better terms with the people he would have their routes paralleled with three-cent-fare lines. Rather than fight the municipality the traction monopoly now offers to sell seven tickets for a quarter, to give universal transfers and to build what extensions Mayor Johnson may direct.

"The way to simmer down a monopoly is to threaten it with competition at a reasonable price and to bring it thus to terms. That is the opportunity New York has with its new subways. One subway with a three-cent fare would force the traction monopoly to reduce its fares or to lose all competitive business. If this new subway had branches to Queens County and Brooklyn it would compel the Brooklyn Rapid Transit and the Interborough merger to exchange free transfers or they would lose the Interborough business."

This shows what can be done by a man who has actually at heart the interests of his fellow-men, who has in his brain structure a certain quality we designate by the term stamina, and who is honest and straightforward in his general make-up. Moreover, a man who thus serves his city in a fearless and an honourable way, serves not it alone, but his example is an inspiration whose bounds may know no end.

The fact that practically all of our cities, and even our larger ones, are still in their infancy, shows how careful and how zealous their people should be in the disposition of their public utilities, for the values of these will, as time passes, increase to tremendous proportions.

On account of these natural monopolies being grabbed and monopolized for the enrichment of the few, and therefore not administered for the common good of all the people, the two greatest evils among us as a nation have gradually come about. The one lies in the great inequality in the distribution of the wealth of the country, in that we have the few thousands of the overly and sometimes criminally rich, over against the millions of the poor and resulting in the almost unbelievable conditions we have already noted. If you will search carefully you will find that practically all the great fortunes now held by individuals or families have been built up through the ownership and control, or the monopoly, of these public service utilities or these great natural monopolies. Look carefully and see if this is not true. Once in a while you will find an exception, a minor exception, but so rarely that the other becomes pre-eminently the rule.

To these as the new generation comes along, we owe our continually increasing numbers of the "idle rich," some of whom — both men and women — have never been known to do an honest day's work in their lives. They live and fare sumptuously, they roll in wealth, and all the time, as John Steward Mill has pointed out, they are being supported by the daily toil of others.

It is they who become in time eligible to the lists of the 400. Gradually they come to believe that they are made of a different type of clay from those about them, that they were made to be served and supported by others, and so also their children. In this way many become "smart" and foolish and gradually prepare the way for their decendents either immediate or remote, to become degenerates or linked with degenerates, through whom the ability to live longer through the support of others, becomes dissipated. It is they who lose the respect of the great common people, and when this is once lost something is lost that no amount of wealth or supposed station will ever compensate for. This is true as every sane person will realize, not of all, by any means, but it is true of very many.

The second great evil lies in the vast amount of bribery and corruption and debauchery that has come about in public and political life, the riding over the rights of the people that these agencies have brought about, and that will eventually mark the downfall of our very institutions if not speedily checked and eradicated. It is in this way that the liberties of the people in all nations that have flourished and then either perished or degenerated, have been undermined. Civilizations perish through internal decay, not through outside agencies. Such has been the rule with scarcely an exception.

A detail of the political intrigues of the companies and corporations in their manipulations of the people's representatives in city councils and in state and national legislatures for their own private business ends, would fill volume after volume. Most people are now familiar with it in some form or another. We can see how handicapped are the forces for reform and for representative government in struggling against company and corporation rule and its accompanying corruption. The fact that great private wealth so dominates legislators is proof in itself that it is not healthy. When, therefore, these great sources of private wealth that belong by right to the people are taken possession of and run in the interests of the people, we shall then witness a gradual letting go of the grip of this monster. Those industries gigantic in monopoly should be taken first, and the others as they become so.

The way organized labour has been of late turning to this government ownership idea and also to political action, argues well for the strides we shall soon be making along this line.

We must get away from the idea that we are to be governed. The people must govern. It is not only their right, but their *duty*. If the people do not govern, then the exploitation of the many by and for the gain of the few will inevitably follow even as it is going on to-day, and as has always happened when the people themselves have not ruled. Not only as a common-sense principle of self-interest, but a sense of safety for the common-wealth, *pure patriotism itself*, demands that without undue delay these great public service utilities and these great natural monopolies be owned and controlled in the only way they should be, for the interests of all the people in common.

The wealth that is created by the common needs of the people or by the continually growing life of all the people should belong to all the people. By moral right it belongs to them, and without undue delay *that which belongs to the people morally must be made to belong to them legally and by custom.*

As this movement increases among us, "commissions" will be appointed by those interested in retaining their grip on the properties from which they are deriving their annual millions, to go abroad to "study," and "investigate," the municipal and State ownership movement in other countries. They will be sent to those countries where the people are gaining so much and are so continually extending their operations along these lines. They will be so selected that the "majority reports" will be unfavourable to the public ownership methods as applied to the United States. Men more or less prominent will also be sent or will go as individuals and will cable back, or will send back, for publicity purposes, similar opinions. As time passes we will probably witness much along this line. My suggestion is, in each case make a little investigation of the matter in order to find what connection the authors of such reports and such messages have with certain interests, or, note the life of the authors of such reports and such messages, and see what influences have shaped or are shaping his prevailing trend of thought.

VII

LABOUR AND ITS UNITING POWER

A GREAT people's movement is now the only power that will save and redeem the nation. I think there is no more significant factor in the getting ready for this great purpose than the splendid companies of men that are bringing themselves together in our Labour Unions and Brotherhoods and Federations. And among them is, it must be said, some of our princely citizenship.

I know that there are various opinions held in regard to the purposes and even the good of our labour unions. This can be said, however, and without any fear of successful contradiction, that those who know most of them and what they have accomplished, and most of the business and labour world in general, realize the splended results they have already achieved and the equally important work that is yet before them. Certainly upon their *wise and intelligent growth and development* depends much that will make for the highest welfare of our coming institutions.

I know that there are those who have doubted even the right of labour combining in this way, to say nothing of the expediency of it. It is not only right and expedient, as I view it, that labour should so organize, but it is also absolutely necessary that it do so, necessary not only for its own good and welfare, but also for the good and the welfare of the very nation itself.

It has been the history of labour that what it has gained for itself — and it has gained much — it has gained entirely through its own efforts.

Those who are at all acquainted with the conditions of labour in times past, and especially prior to the present century, know out of what a condition of bondage it has gradually lifted itself. It was at one time in that condition in which it had literally no rights that were considered as belonging to human beings. Before considering the matter farther it is interesting to note that in the industrial world, the captains of industry — the employers, had this same fight for liberty and for justice, and they are now, mark you, not such a great ways ahead of that larger class called wage-workers.

Concerning this an eminent authority has said: "In ancient times, particularly in the Roman and the mediæval world, a manufacturer or merchant, though his ships might cover the inland seas, though thousands of men might be doing his bidding, yet he had no voice in the government, was not considered fit for a gentleman and patrician to associate with, had no voice in making the laws that should govern him, nor in determining what taxes he should pay; he was plundered indirectly by means of taxation, and when this did not suit the purpose of dissipated and rapacious officialism, he was plundered directly. To be born a patrician, to be a member of the priesthood, or a successful military chieftain, entitled a man to rule. The man who supplied the world with necessaries had no social or political standing, and this continued to be so throughout the Middle Ages — continued to be so in most all Europe till toward the end of the last century, and is to a great extent still the case in Russia and in the Turkish provinces of Europe. . . . In England the employer acquired his rights earlier, and has for sometime had a voice in the government. But even in England the much praised Magna Charta was not for the benefit of either employer or workman, but simply of the nobility — the idle, who, by reason of the accident of birth, were enabled to appropriate the labour of others."

Continuing and speaking also of the early conditions of the wage-workers, he says: "But, upon the whole, the employer in his struggles for justice is not a century in advance of the class we to-day call the wage-workers, and they, the labourers, were in ancient and later times practically all slaves. To be sure, we catch here and there, in ancient literature, a phrase about the labourer being worthy of his hire, but when we examine into the actual condition of the toiling masses we are forced to treat such utterances as the emanations of fancy, for not only was the labour of the mass at the absolute disposal of the master, but practically, and in every-day experience, their lives were also. True, there was in most countries a law providing that the master should not kill his slave, but if the master did so he generally went unwhipped of justice. This continued to be the condition, with slight exceptions, throughout all Europe down to near the beginning of this century. For unnumbered centuries they were absolute slaves, belonging to individuals; then they belonged, as it were, to the soil, and were known as serfs and, in time, in England they may be said to have belonged to the county or shire. . . . It is true there were in some European cities organizations of skilled workmen, who enjoyed not only their freedom, but some advantages that may be said to have been ahead of their time; but, as compared with the great mass of the common people, they were so insignificant in number, and their situation was so exceptional that we need not consider them further than to call attention to the fact that they developed the technical skill of their members, and enforced sobriety and honourable conduct, while by means of their meetings and discussions they became, in a measure, educated, and thereby reached a much higher plane than was otherwise possible, and they thus wielded a powerful influence for good. . . .

"In 1360, during the reign of Edward III, it was provided by law that if a labourer refused to work for the wages fixed by law or by the justices of the county, or if he went outside of the county he was to be brought back by the sheriff, was to be imprisoned, and was to have the letter 'F' branded with a hot iron upon his forehead in token of his falsity. If he sought by any manner to increase the rate of wages, he was to be imprisoned. . . . From that time on, for four centuries, the legislation in England is of uniform kind, prohibiting by imprisonment all meetings of workmen, and providing that the justice should fix the wages to be paid in their county; that if any labourer refused to work for the wages fixed by the justices, he was to be put in the stocks; if any labourer was found idle and did not apply himself to work, he was to have the letter 'V' branded with a hot iron upon his cheek, and was to be sold into slavery for two years, his children likewise to be sold, and if either he or they ran away they were to have the letter 'S' branded on the cheek with a hot iron, and were to be sold into slavery for life, and were to be fed on bread and water, and it was provided by law that they were to be made to work by beating, by chaining, etc., and if they ran away again they were to suffer death. Children that had worked at husbandry till they were twelve years old, were forbidden ever to attempt to do anything else; other children were required to follow the occupation of their parents or be imprisoned. It is hard to conceive of a condition of the labouring classes that could be much worse than that of the English during these centuries."

And so far as the length of the work-day was concerned, during the reign of Queen Elizabeth, in 1562, the following statute was enacted: "All artificers and labourers being hired for wages by the day or week shall betwixt the midst of the months of March and September be and continue at their work at or before five of the clock in the morning and continue at work and not depart until betwixt seven and eight of the clock at night, except it be in the time of breakfast, dinner, or drinking; and all such artificers and labourers between the midst of September and the midst of March shall be and continue at their work from the spring of the day in the morning until the night of the same day, except in the time of breakfast and dinner."

So much then for the early conditions of both employer and wage-worker. We come on down then to our own time. As the employer class became fully emancipated they began to take matters into their own hands, and in their relations with those who worked for them and who were the absolutely essential factor in their business and who helped make their profits, they had the entire say. They paid what wages they chose. They laid down the conditions under which those working for them did their work. The labourer had practically nothing to say regarding anything. The employers were organizing among themselves; they were getting stronger, and as a rule, it can be truthfully said, more dictatorial. The wage-workers then began to take heed. They began to see what was to be gained through organization, through co-operation. They realized that they had grievances of various types, that they were not getting as a rule a fair share in the profits of the enterprise in which they were as necessary a factor as the element of capital and its management. They also realized that *as individuals* they had absolutely no way of making any of their wants or grievances known, and that for individuals to act in these matters was not only futile but unsafe for the one or ones so acting. Then organization and the uniting of the wage-workers in the form of the labour union came into being.

In reply to the question, "What originally were the

conditions and facts which seemed to make necessary the combinations of workmen called 'labour unions,' and which justify their present existence?" an officer of one of our larger labour organizations gave the following reply: "To describe accurately such conditions and facts would require many volumes dealing with social conditions, social injustice, special privilege, all over the world. The specific fact which made labour unions necessary was this: Wealth was produced as a result of a combination of labour and of intelligent direction. The direction, otherwise the employer, was in absolute control, fixed wages, treated the employee as he saw fit. The employers were also united in their social relationships, their mutual interests and in other ways. The employees, the workers, were isolated; they had no union, working from dawn till dark made social intercourse impossible. The unions of workers were formed for the same reason that the union of States in this country was formed — namely, to give to the individuals forming the union the greater strength that comes from united action, to give them the dignity that comes with escape from a servile condition, to give them the power enabling them to obtain for themselves fair wages, involving comfort and education for their families and leisure for mental improvement for themselves."

Said the President of the American Federation of Labour in a recent address before the New York Board of Trade and Transportation: "The very concentration of wealth and its possession is potent organization, and unless the wage-earners, the workers, combined their efforts in unions of labour, their condition to-day would be such as to shock the mind even in contemplation. That any hope for material improvement, moral advancement, or higher ethical consideration is possible without the organizations of labour, few now seriously believe."

This is quite in keeping with an utterance of former Governor Washburn, of Massachusetts, when he spoke as follows: "The fact that there is unrest and dissatisfaction when man is confined to unremitting toil is one of the brightest and most healthy omens of the times. It is an indication that his better nature is struggling for emancipation; it is a hopeful sign of finer and nobler manhood in the future. Such efforts for improvement should never be discouraged, but always encouraged."

So much then for the right, the expediency, and the necessity of the wage-worker organizing and uniting for protection and for mutual self-help.

The labour unions have committed errors of course, they are committing them to-day, and plenty of them. Counts of many various types can be made against them. Enemies of or those unfriendly to union labour could, I dare say, compile very long lists of errors and excesses of various kinds. Friends of and those sympathetic to union labour could compile also a similar list. But this is only natural, for in the early and formative days of any movement this is practically always true; there is indeed scarcely an exception. No movement or system, especially one involving such complex and such difficult matters to deal with and men in such various stages of development, can start in a fully perfected form, nor is it to be expected. Once it was urged in England that men should not be given their political freedom until they were fully prepared to use it rightly, and until there was no danger of their ever abusing it. This course seemed plausible and reasonable to those advocating it; to it Lord Macaulay replied, "If men are to wait for freedom until they have become good and wise in slavery, they will wait forever."

In a similar vein and speaking directly of organized labour, the *Springfield Republican* has said: "Viewed philosophically, it is inevitable that a riot of inexperience and inefficiency should characterize the early stages of labour's organization. No state of society is ever inaugurated with people already perfected for its coming. . . . Republican institutions were not deferred on earth until a people were found entirely capable of running perfect republics. Democracy did not await the advent of a population already fully trained in the arts of self-government. All these things come, and the people most concerned have to develop up to them. Such is the lesson of history. Labour-unionism came also, and, in the same way, its adherents have had to discipline themselves by experience in the best methods of organization and conservative management. On the whole, taking into consideration the enormous increase of unionism, it is no more than fair to say that it is constantly gaining in equilibrium and sanity."

The unions and their leaders have been learning rapidly in these matters. Generally speaking, the older the union the more conservative and quiet and at the same time firm and effective is it in its methods and its dealings. In other countries, in England for example, where the unions are a great deal older, they have even long ago worked through and out of the rash and tempestuous stages, the stages where so many counts could be made against them, and have reached the position that the unions in America have been gradually working their way towards. Here, as there, it has been a long, hard road to travel, it has meant fight and defeat, and at times apparent rout along with the battles won, the experience gained, the advancement made — the present priceless possession. It has meant brave sufferings many times not only on the part of the wage-workers, but also on the part of their families. It has meant at times, the facing of great uncertainty.

I think it should be said that from the managers of capital, labour has learned some of its worse features and excesses. I think it can be truthfully said that with all the excesses and violations of law on the part of union labour in times passed it has never, taking it all in all, equalled the amount of disregard for and violation of law that organized capital has been guilty of. It has been more open and awkward in its methods, perhaps, while organized capital in addition to being in many cases also glaringly open, has worked in a subtile and silent way under cover. The latter is more skilled, it may be said, and hence more apt in these matters.

But out of this long and at times apparently clumsy struggle, union labour in this country is also attaining a position where it is exerting a great and powerful good, not only for its own and for the public welfare, but also for organized capital, if the latter is wise enough to openly and freely recognize its power and its purposes.

In connection with the final settlement of the great strike in the anthracite fields some time ago, there were among others two utterances to me very significant and worthy of a wide reproduction. Judge Gray, chairman of the Arbitration Commission, said: "Unless my judgment is at fault and my faith unfounded, the labour unions will soon have passed through their period of trial and tribulation and will emerge on a bright and sunlit plain, where true American character, the fruit of American liberty, will illustrate the worth of our institutions. Purging themselves of every anti-social and unworthy element, recognizing in others the rights they claim for themselves, with malice towards none and charity towards all, subordinate to law, with a full sense of their appeal to the public opinion of the country, as our fathers made their appeal, they will be unheld in the time to come by employers, as powerful coadjusters, in the maintenance of American ideals of free government among men."

Much of the energy of labour unions up to the present time has been directed towards the securing of a larger wage and of a shorter workday, and in some cases towards both. It is quite natural that at first this should be true. But with this gained to a greater or less extent, there comes a time and it has now come, when it must push out into a larger and more general field. These gained, and with more time for council and intercourse, and with a greater recognition of its power and its standing, it is more able now to move upon a broader and still more telling plain. The union and the federation has also been an excellent means of training in reason as against crankery, in moderation as against rashness and hot-headness, in short for a broader and more substantial and effective citizenship. A very discriminating writer, in speaking along this line, has said: "If we omit certain unions in the more corrupt cities, where the leaders learn bad habits by imitation, and are too frequently bought and sold, there is at the present moment in this country no more powerful influence to train men for citizenship than the influences at work in the best and strongest labour organizations. This is true of the Federation; it is true of separate unions like the printers, trainmen, iron-moulders; many of the longshoremen, and cigar-makers.

"But especially do these older and stronger unions learn to check dangerous and revolutionary opinions. . . . As the trade union strengthens, its influence against turbulent and revolutionary projects steadily increases. The only agency that will prevent the spread of this conservatism is the fatuous obstinacy which insists upon defeating completer labour organization."*

The time has come it seems to me when organized and federated labour must move, and move in a very effective and telling way along the lines of political action. Not that the union or the federation as such, as an organiza-

* John Graham Brooks in "The Social Unrest" Chap. xii.

tion, must so act, for this all along it has steadily avoided and undoubtedly most wisely. There would be pitfalls innumerable for it, did it adopt or attempt to adopt such a course. Nor would anyone of judgment advocate the membership of the union or federation as such affiliating with any par icular party. To be *independent in party action,* here as in the rest of our citizenship should be, as it is getting more and more to be, the great fact; then for organized labour to work along the lines of educating its membership in the lines of policy and legislation that gives or that keeps for the great common people, of which the wage-worker is such a large and powerful factor, larger rights and fairer opportunities and more just conditions, as distinguished from the privileged classes by whom the chief portion of the machinery of government is now dominated and controlled, and in whose interests the larger share of legislation is now enacted. And so far as the immediate demands and the welfare of organized labour is concerned, it seems to me that the time has now come when this is the effective and the telling method of work, also the orderly and the peaceable, hence, the most satisfactory.

It is undoubtedly in the matter of strikes and the almost innumerable things that accompany them that union labour has suffered most in its reputation, and to a greater or less extent in its standing. Whether this part of its life could have been lived better or not is of no importance so far as the present consideration is concerned. The one concern at present is — the lessons that are to be learned from the past use of this weapon. Undoubtedly there are many and very important lessons to be learned; undoubtedly many have been learned. That strikes have been too frequently called, and especially the sympathetic strike, that others have been called rashly and without sufficient preparation, and without a sufficient consideration of the chances of success beforehand, that others have been too frequently called under a poor or ineffective, or self-seeking leadership, is undoubtedly true. The abler leaders and the better and more intelligent members have now come to the position where they recognize that the strike and its attendant circumstances is to be considered only as a weapon of last resort. The disposition, reached partly through very great losses, is now to conciliate, to adjust grievances and differences if any possible way can be found without a resort to the strike. The history of strikes, those lost as well as those won, has brought home to the intelligent and capable and unself-centred leader and union member some very clear-cut facts such as the following: that a strike should not be allowed to be called by a walking-delegate, or by any power outside of a full and complete vote of the union; that the union should move slowly and with every possible degree of fairness; that it should be thoroughly organized and ready for the strike; that it be under the direction of a thoroughly able and honest and *proven* leader; that it be sure that its demands or its grievances are thoroughly just and sufficiently important to pay this price for their attainment or their adjustment;

that it has come to pass that public opinion is the court or the power that finally decides whether the strike be successful or whether it end in failure; therefore, in addition to the necessity that the demands be thoroughly just ones, that there be no violence or rioting. True, owners and managers of capital — as well as sympathizers — have provoked or have deliberately planned violence and rioting, as they probably will in other cases yet to come, but by forbearance and patience the public can in practically all cases eventually be shown its source, and it will render its verdict accordingly. The very fact that this method has sometimes been deliberately resorted to, to help weaken or break a strike, is itself a powerful and quiet commentary upon the influence and the power of public opinion as the determining factor in a strike.

How keen the really able labour leader is in regard to the importance of no violence emanating from the organization in time of strike is shown partly by the following words of John Mitchell, spoken in connection with the anthracite coal strike, and not for its effect upon the public but in earnest council to the miners: "If you want to spoil your own cause and lose every sacrifice you have made for yourself and your families, give way to your temper and commit some violence. Just a few outbreaks like this and the public good-will, to which we must look in last resort, will fail us and we shall deserve to lose it." A leader of the keen insight of John Mitchell, understands all too thoroughly what the element of violence, emanating from the organization at a critical period of the strike, would mean in its effect upon public opinion. This, however, is not exceptional council, but it has grown to be that which is common on the part of the able, experienced, and efficient labour leaders.

The very large number of strikes that are prevented through the influence and the clearer councils of the abler leader and his subordinates, is probably not realized by the one not intimately acquainted with organized labour. The following letter by the very able general secretary of the Garment Worker's Union, Henry White, is also indicative of much that is going on at present:

"Mr. — foreman of — informs me that your only reason for calling out the men was that he refused to continue in his employ two men laid off for incompetent work, and that even your business agent admitted that the work of the men was imperfect. If such is the case, your action in withdrawing the men was not justified. This office, as well as the National Union, is opposed to forcing upon an employer men whose work is not suitable. It is just that sort of thing that creates needless opposition to the union, and causes no end of trouble. Your union is the only one that would make such a demand. Where members are made to believe that they cannot be discharged, no matter what they do, they become careless, and the poor workman falls back upon the protection of the union. The employer has got to sell the goods, and he assumes the risk, consequently he alone can be the judge as to the quality of work. As long as he pays the union scale and does not discriminate against active members, that is all you can expect of him.

"Now I trust you will not place us in a position where the General Executive Board will have to decide against you."

I know there are employers who have become very bitter against organized labour. I know also that some, at times have had to meet some very exasperating things from the unions. This I think is owing in great part to two causes: the feeling of power that has come to labour since the unions have become a force that must be reckoned with; and again on account of the sort of transitional period through which both employer and worker has been passing, where we have reached the end of the period where the employer has had practically everything to say in connection with the works and the conditions of labour, and where he is now loath to admit that the portion of his establishment, the portion as necessary as his capital, his management, and his machinery — the workmen — can have anything to say regarding any feature of his works. But the day has come when the wise owner or manager is he who openly and even cheerfully recognizes this. There are those who have taken this view of the matter, have acted accordingly, and are even now glad that this changed condition has come about. They are managing in such a way that great good is resulting to them as well as to their workmen.

The day of "my business" has passed; the day of "our

business" has arrived. The new industrial era that we are now entering upon is the one in which there shall be more consultation and more friendly co-operation between employer and employee; and where if this method is entered upon freely and with a fuller and more sympathetic recognition of each other's rights, and of the amenities due from each to the other, very great mutual gains will be made.

The one important factor that must now be looked for by owners of large enterprises and by companies, is men as managers who are keen enough to recognize the advent of this new era, and who are large enough to meet and to deal with labour upon this new basis. It is after all but an indication of the possession of a good degree of *modern* business ability. Speaking along this line a very able Eastern railroad president said some time ago: "To assume that we have got to go on spasmodically fighting the unions, is tactless and unintelligent. The truth is that the kind of man who is not strong enough to work with organized labour has not the qualification for his position. It is silly for powerful corporations to say, 'We will deal with the individuals, not with representatives of unions.' Organization of labour has got to be recognized as such, and dealt with as such, and the problem now is to get men with the qualities and capacities to do this."

Mr. Darrow, one of the miners' counsel, in speaking before the anthracite commission, spoke possibly more strongly though not more truly in the following. Mr. Henry D. Lloyd, also counsel, had just pointed out the fact that the commission could hope to bring no peace to the anthracite fields that could be in any way permanent unless it provided for agreements with the union. Mr. Darrow, speaking in regard to the recognition of the union, said: "You can do just as you please about recognizing the union. If you do not recognize it, it is because you are blind and you want to bump up against it some more; that is all. It is here. It is here to stay, and the burden is on you and not upon us. There is neither the power nor the disposition in this court, I take it, to destroy the union. It would not accomplish it if it could, and it certainly could not if it would. And if these wise business men, with the combined wisdom of business gentlemen and the agents of the Almighty, cannot see the union, they had better blunder along still a few more years, and possibly after a while they will know it is here and recognize it themselves."

I know there is still a great deal of unsettled opinion regarding strikes and lockouts, regarding arbitration, and especially compulsory arbitration. All who are familiar with it, however, are agreed that there is one form of arbitration that is unique in that it leads all other forms. It is what has come to be known as the "joint agreement." It might be more accurately spoken of as a form of conciliation than as a form of arbitration; or still more accurately, perhaps, as a form of working agreement between employer and employed. Its basis is, that once so often, according to agreement, accredited representatives of both employer and workmen meet in a joint session to consider, to discuss, and to draw up a set of agreements that shall be the basis of the year's or the period's work. The very fact that labor is organized and is capable of sending responsible representatives to such a meeting makes the "joint agreement" possible. Otherwise it would not be possible. The "joint agreement" is pre-eminently the highest type of arbitration, for it is arbitration from within. The features that mark its high value are many. First are its educational features, in that it makes both employer and employed acquainted with each other's points of view, with each other's needs as well as desires; it leads to a better understanding between employer and workmen, *probably the greatest need in our modern industrial world.* And if entered into heartily it has the tendency of creating an active sympathy between the two. This in itself will in time lead to a continually increasing mutual respect and mutual helpfulness. Again, agreements thus voluntarily made are far more apt to be kept, and more easily and conscientiously than in case of conditions imposed from without, and which in almost every case are bound to contain some features distasteful and onerous to one party or the other. Again, it is simply a recognition of a purely common-sense and practical method that is recognized and used in practically every other avenue in the business world. Finally, I think it can be said, that there can be no effective relations and no lasting peace between employer and workmen until the agreement is recognized as the common-sense and fair method of procedure, and is entered into in a whole-souled manner and with the purpose and intention on the part of both interested parties of living fully up to the agreement.

The "joint agreement" is not a new method of conciliation or a new method of procedure as between employer and employed, but in some fields it has been used for many years, and in most all cases with thoroughly satisfactory results. It can therefore be spoken of from the standpoint of its actual achivements. It is of later years, however, that it has been coming into a more general and into a continually increasing use. This fact is undoubtedly an evidence of its effectiveness and value.

There is so much testimony to be had in regard to its effective and satisfactory results that it would be interesting to consider much of it did space permit. The manager of one of the largest stove manufactories in the country has said of the agreement: "We have tried it a dozen years and it has settled all questions on this subject for us. Its best trait is that, as it works, it trains the men to see the limits within which they can get advantages. It makes the men more conservative and it makes us more considerate."

Mr. John Graham Brooks, in "The Social Unrest" has dealt with the joint agreement in a very effective way. At one place he says: "To keep agreements voluntarily, is a much higher discipline than to do it under force. For many years unions have actually kept contracts when employers have genuinely and heartily co-operated with the joint agreement.

"There is no such convincing proof of this as the

fifteen years' trial between masters and men in the Boston Building Trades. The agent of the employers, W. H. Sayward, who brought about this agreement, conducting it with growing success for eighteen years, allows me to say that under it scores of strikes have been prevented, millions of money saved, and the most delicate questions, like the limitation of output and apprentices, the use of the boycott, the conflicts between different unions, and the sympathetic strike, are now so far understood as a result of this education that they are no longer feared."

Mr. Sayward's testimony, in part, is as follows: "My experience has convinced me that labour thoroughly organized and honestly recognized *is even more important for the employer than for the workmen.* It makes possible a working method between the two parties which removes one by one the most dangerous elements of conflict and misunderstanding." Speaking farther, Mr. Sayward said: "that either for the building trades or other lines of work, these intricate and involved matters will not take care of themselves; they cannot safely be intrusted to *one* of the interested parties alone; *both* parties must have equal concern, must act *jointly,* not only in their own interests, but, in effect, in the interests of the community."

If at anytime differences do arise under the joint agreement, or if they arise when it is not in use and trouble seems iminent, then conciliation or voluntary arbitration is the next sensible step. It is safe to say that there is scarcely a case where the strike or the lockout need be resorted to if there is an eminent spirit of fairness on *both* sides. Conciliation and fairness. A looking at the matter from the standpoint of the other, a pocketing of pride to gain something larger and fairer and more satisfactory in the end. A getting away from pure fool obstinacy and allowing a spirit of openness and fairness to assert itself and lead to what will prove to be a wiser course and a better end. The workmen to be fair and to be sure they are making no unjust demands, not hasty but considerate of the probable difficulties that lie in the employer's way. Employer to pass rapidly beyond the foolish and inane period where "this is my business and I will conduct it absolutely to suit myself," "I will not be dictated to"; "there is nothing to arbitrate." The public is pretty well tired now of "there is nothing to arbitrate," and popular disapproval will soon call a halt upon this puerile obstinancy unless owner or manager finds sense enough to abandon it himself. All that is needed to prevent precipitated labour troubles — strikes and lockouts — is for the men in overalls and the owners or managers of industry to grow sufficiently large as to enable them to throw away their prejudices and meet as they meet in other things, on the common-sense platform of fraternity and humanity. Each must manifest the spirit of open fairness, and the more fully this is done the more smoothly and pleasantly and satisfactorily will the negotiations run. President John Mitchell has given this bit of testimony: "I have never seen in my experience a strike that could not have been averted if the employers and the men who work had met in conference before the strike was started.

"I have said on many occasions that I was opposed to strikes, opposed to lockouts, opposed to industrial turmoil; that I favoured peace, but always with the qualification that it must be an honourable peace. There will never be peace between the men who work and those who employ men to work unless that peace guarantees to each side that which is its proper due."

Herman Justi, Commissioner, Illinois Coal Operators' Association, has said: "With scarcely an exception, every strike that has taken place in our time, even where there has been bloodshed and destruction of property, has finally been settled in friendly council."

Speaking then of the plan of the Coal Operators' Association in their method of joint agreements with their men which have been in operation for a great many years, Mr. Justi says: "Our plan is to prevent these senseless and costly strikes, and the many differences and disputes arising between master and men which seem to place them in the attitude of enemies to each other, are settled in the same manner in which the most destructive strikes are finally settled, viz: by meeting in friendly council, where we try self-control long enough to enable us to say: 'Come, let us reason together.' This is, practically, all there is of the plan pursued in the coal mining industry of Illinois, and of this plan to prevent strikes and to promote harmony and good feeling it can be said, at least, that it is the fairest thus far offered."

But what a commentary upon the experience of the past twenty or twenty-five years to know that finally practically all strikes are settled by the very means that could have prevented their ever occurring had more real ability or, to speak more plainly, more plain ordinary common-sense prevailed on one side or the other, or on both.

As soon as it becomes apparent that employer and workmen are unable to adjust their differences through conciliation or voluntary arbitration, then by the ordinary course, the strike on the part of the one, or the lockout on the part of the other, is resorted to. What the results sometimes are, when this method assumes control, all are thoroughly conversant with. Upon the public the chief burden is then thrown. It has always seemed to me that right at this point it is the privilege and the duty of the public to have its say. I know that many labour men, and among them some eminent labour leaders, hold a different view. To deprive labour of the power to strike they believe, and honestly, would be to take from it one of its most effective weapons. I would not deprive labour of its power to strike; and the more thoroughly and closely labour is organized the greater does this ability become. There is probably no one who believes more thoroughly in the good that is to result both to worker and employer, as well as to the public at large, from a continually growing and developing organization of labour. But the larger good must always be kept in mind, and when the calling of a strike or the instituting of a lockout becomes the *supreme* necessity, then the principle of compulsory arbitration is undoubtedly a sound one, even as it has proven so completely to be, much that we hear to the contrary notwithstanding, in New Zealand, in Australia, for example.

Were employer and workmen the only ones concerned in the matter of compulsory arbitration then it would present a somewhat, in fact an entirely, different aspect. But even then I should thoroughly believe in the principle, when the strike or the lockout would appear the only way of adjusting the differences. Men or groups of men in the mad, the fighting condition, are not as capable of adjusting difficulties as fairly — and there can be no lasting peace unless mutual fairness enters — as an able and impartial body of men selected for this purpose. And the enormous losses entailed upon both sides when the strike is at all long drawn out, are, it seems to me, thoroughly ill-advised. The ability to strike enables the workers to bring their difficulties or grievances to the point where, were it not strong enough to possess this ability, it would be in a most deplorable condition.

Two men have a difference. The time was when, worked up by rage into a fury — thoroughly mad, one species of temporary insanity — they took their bludgeons and pounded away at the skulls of each other. We have grown. When two men have a difference they are not allowed to go into the street and bludgeon one another, or deal with one another in the manner of even the modern fisticuff manner. The public has long ago decreed that they take their differences in an orderly and common-sense way before a man or a body of men, more calm and reasoning, and hence more capable of determining the right of the matter at issue. This is our method, the method that we have found far better than the former brute method. There is no one of average intelligence who would even think of appearing in public to advocate a return to the earlier methods. In this, however, the public is scarcely disturbed, or at most but a few persons, and then for but a few moments at most. Fisticuffs are ordinarily not lengthly affairs. Is there not a thousand times more reason for compelling this same sane, common-sense method when it comes to the disputes not of two men, but of two groups of men that may last for days or even for many weeks, and where the entire community is endangered as to life or limb, where it is inconvenienced, and all of its natural and normal relations demoralized, where it is subjected at times to tremendous losses, and where sometimes for weeks it is compelled simply to remain quiet and look on at these two groups struggling without reason because each is animated by the desire for the questionable glory of saying "we beat"? I am not saying that "we beat" is always the animating principle on the part of the contending parties. That in some cases it is, that in many cases it is, is all too evident, and sometimes when a struggle of this kind has been entered upon, with the greatest of reasons, it has frequently occurred that as the the conflict became extended the "we beat" business became the controlling principle. The strike or the lockout is too much a matter of vital public concern to enable it to be used upon the slightest pretext on the part of groups of hot-headed men. I say hot-headed advisedly because, were it not true of one side or the other or of both, then a less crude and bungling and a more common-sense method of settlement not only could, but would be found.

There was perhaps a justification, or at least a reason for the bludgeon and the pommeling method of settlement of differences between the two men. In order to reach the period of the "reason method," this period had to be passed through. There *was* also the same justification or reason for the strike and lockout method in the disputes between two groups of men. This crude method was also at first natural. We have too much common-sense in other matters, and in matters of a very kindred nature to allow it farther to be said that this method is any longer necessary or even natural. We become so accustomed to certain conditions that at times we do not move on as rapidly as is well for us.

I beg to repeat the statement that when the strike or the lockout is resorted to, there is a distinct threefold loss, to the worker, to the employer, to the public. Am I right? Some months ago witnessed a strike in Chicago, and it terminated rather to the disadvantage, if anything, of the side that called it. Here are a few facts taken at random from a general summary made immediately after by the *Chicago Tribune:* Duration in days, a hundred and five; number of garment workers originally involved, seventeen; total number of teamsters eventually involved, four thousand six hundred and twenty; persons killed in strike violence, twenty-one; persons injured (reported by police), four hundred and fifteen; police and deputy sheriffs on strike duty, five thousand seven hundred; cost to city and county for extra police and extra deputy sheriff protection, four hundred and six thousand five hundred dollars; loss to teamsters in wages, and cost to unions for strike benefits, one million fifty thousand dollars; cost to employers, (wages and lodging of strike-breakers and protection of wagons), two million dollars; shrinkage in wholesale, retail and freight business (estimated), six million dollars. Here then the cost to the unions was a trifle over a million dollars, to the employers, two million, while the public had to pay to the tune of between six and seven million dollars, besides shouldering all the exasperating inconveniences and a compulsory witnessing of all the diabolical happenings that were thrown in its way.

If this virtual defeat for the unions was caused, as it is claimed, by incompetent or self-seeking leadership, so much the worse for the unions that permitted such leadership to hold sway and to lead them into such positions where defeat was almost a foregone conclusion. How long will it take organized labour to learn its lessons along this score?

You will recall that in the summer of 1900 there was a street-car strike in St. Louis. The side in error, the side chiefly to blame in this strike, was the company, and when it was ended the chief defeat was also on its side. In this strike the loss to the men in wages was a trifle less than half a million dollars; the loss to the company in fares, in operating, and in damage to cars and plant was two million dollars; the loss to the city in *business alone*, to say nothing of loss in extra police and deputy sheriff needs, was thirty million dollars; there were fourteen killed, seventy injured by bullets, a hundred and fifty injured otherwise. Here then is a loss — in money alone of thirty million dollars on the part of the public compared to a combined loss of a little less then two and a half million dollars on the part of the company and its workmen. Who shall say that the right or even the duty on the part of the public in this case is not of a very clear-cut and certain nature. Under the head "The St. Louis Strike Folly" an editorial in the Boston *Daily Globe* at the conclusion of the strike spoke as follows: "This strike was begun innocently enough on May 8th. On that day 3,500 men stopped work. It was a fight on the part of the company to destroy the labour union, and because the company has succeeded in compelling 300 union men to go back to work and leave the union, and moreover succeeded in importing more than 3,000 men to run its cars day and night, it calls this a 'victory.' A few such 'victories' as this scattered over this continent would create a general civil war, in which victory would finally poise at the point of the federal bayonet. For a corporation to call a settlement forced by such conditions 'victory' is a libel on the English language. Yet the unions, animated by the same spirit that possesses the company, claim a 'victory,' too.

"No, this is not 'victory,' in this day when reason and the moral sense are supposed to have superseded the gun and the bludgeon. It is defeat, dismal defeat for both the company and the men. The only victory is found in the agreement of both sides to resume their old relations, forgive and forget old scores and begin all over again to be reasonable human beings. If anybody can conceive a victory after such disgraceful proceedings, where does it come in for the 700,000 people of the town who have been inconvenienced for nearly two months and whose losses in business are reckoned at $30,000,000? How many taxpayers of St. Louis will feel like calling this a victory by and by, when the costs have to be settled?

"This strike has had some features that are liable to sadly demoralize the calculations of corporations who fancy that the victory is won as soon as they succeed in hiring men to take the places of the strikers. This was the case in St. Louis. The company has 'broken the back' of the strike, but in breaking that back it was at the same time depleting its treasury so rapidly that it was forced to make an agreement with the strikers in order to save itself from impending ruin.

"Such a strike as this ought never again to be possible in this country. It cost the company over $1,500,000 in fares alone for its 'victory.' It cost the men $500,000 in wages. It brought disgrace upon a supposed civilized American city. The fierce boycott has been the cause of cowardly murders and assaults upon women. It has engendered bitterness among families and friends that will rankle for many years to come. And all for what? In order that somebody might finally be able to boast of a victory. Now both parties have fought to a standstill, and both, maimed, crippled and disgraced, have been forced to an agreement which each calls a 'victory?' How childish and how unworthy of intelligent men! Arbitration could have easily settled all this when it began. Now nothing is settled, except the fact that both sides have virtually been defeated. When will men ever learn anything from these sad experiences?"

To say that it is advisable longer to allow two groups of men to engage in such a disruption of public order and decency, throwing this enormous expense upon the shoulders of the general public, simply because one party or the other, and generally the one least in the right, is so bull-headed, or so lacking in ordinary brain capacity as well as in business insight as to be incapable of adjusting these difficulties without a resort to such clumsy and brutal methods, seems to me to be almost an insult to the most ordinary degree of public intelligence. I don't think there is an average of one person in fifty who, cognizant of all the facts, really believes that it is either advisable or possessing even the qualities of ordinary common-sense. What a commentary then upon the lack of initiative or movement on our part to allow this method with all its attendant horrors, and with practically nothing in its justification, still to be employed. Especially is this true when there is already a clearly demonstrated better method.

Sometime ago Carroll D. Wright, then United States Commissioner of Labour, in an article in the *North American Review* gave some of his findings in connection with an investigation of the matter of strikes in the

United States since 1880. Between 1881 and 1900 there were about twenty-three thousand strikes, which would be an average of more than a thousand a year. Nearly fifty-one per cent of all these strikes were successful, thirteen per cent succeeded partly, while the remaining thirty-six per cent failed. Over six million employees were involved and were out of work for a longer or a shorter period. Their loss owing to idleness was nearly two hundred and fifty-eight million dollars. The loss to their employers was about a hundred and twenty-three million dollars, or a little less than one-half the loss to them.

I have given just the losses from a monetary standpoint, and to the two parties engaged in these industrial wars. The still greater losses to the public at large, not only from a monetary standpoint, but in almost innumerable ways otherwise, can be imagined by the aid of the detailed statistics relating to the two strikes already mentioned.

One of the concluding observations by Mr. Wright in this article is abundantly worthy of notice: "It is recognized now that labour conflicts grow out of increasing intelligence. The avoidance or adjustment of such conflicts must be the result of increased intelligence. Fools do not strike; it is only men who have intelligence enough to recognize their condition that make use of this last resort. With increased intelligence they will look back upon the strike period as one of development; and when they shall have accommodated themselves to the new conditions, and when employers shall have recognized the increased intelligence of their employees, these matters will be handled in such a way as to prevent in the future a repetition of incidents like those which are chronicled in the statistical history of the strikes of the last twenty years."

It is generally the case, in the majority of strikes always the case, that the loss to the workers, who are far less able to stand it, is considerably greater than that sustained by the employers. The latter, moreover, have a way of making the public finally pay their losses, in addition to the still heavier losses that are always thrown upon it. Certainly the word *dense* is quite applicable to the public unless we take some lessons from this great array of happenings that has come to pass, and unless we now move speedily along the path of an insistence upon compulsory arbitration in that class of cases where no other method of settlement but open industrial warfare is able to be reached by employer and workmen. It seems to me there can be no shadow of a doubt in regard to this when it comes to strikes in connection with any public service industry, or anything where the inconvenience or loss to the public is specially great.

I think there is no better way of terminating this very brief examination of the points that seem to favour a compulsory arbitration plan in those cases that are not or that apparently cannot be settled through mutual concessions or by conciliation, with the result that the matter is thrown onto the public in the form of an open warfare, than by a very brief consideration of New Zealand's arbitration court methods. From that portion of the world we got our Australian ballot-system that has proved to be better than anything we had to compare with it. We can get still other things of good value there, the same as still older nations are from time to time getting things of good value from us.

The New Zealand law was drawn up by Hon. William P. Reeves, former Minister of Labour, after a most careful study of the arbitration methods of various other countries. It was passed after considerable discussion and not without opposition, on its merits, something more than ten years ago. Organization is, it might be said, the keynote to the working of the law. Employers and workmen are expected to form organizations on the assumption that all interests are best promoted by the organization of labour. The act, therefore, cannot be invoked by or against workmen not organized in unions, though employers may be sued singly. Very briefly summarized the chief points of the law are, "First, the privilege of securing voluntary arbitration quietly; and, second, voluntary arbitration failing, the law forces publicity and compels reference to a conciliation board and obedience to the law's awards. The parties in dispute go first before the local board of conciliation, there being six of such boards in all, and from there, if unsettled, the appeal can be made to the final court of arbitration sitting for the whole country. . . . The boards and court are composed equally of chosen representatives of both employer and employed. A guarantee of ability, experience, dignity and entire disinterestedness is expected to be secured by the appointment of a judge of the Supreme Court as president of the court of arbitration. It is a suggestive fact that every precaution is taken that the proceedings shall be cheap, expeditious and non-technical. Its immediate value inheres in the fact that the industry goes on uninterruptedly while proceedings are pending."

In a letter which appeared in the *New York Evening Post* sometime ago, Mr. Edward Tregear, then Secretary for Labour in New Zealand, in reviewing various statements that have gained circulation here regarding the failure of this arbitration court method in New Zealand, says: "Compulsory arbitration (as it has been nicknamed) is so far from being a disastrous failure that it is here considered a pronounced success. Only a revolution could displace it. Last session an amending act was passed whereby the Boards of Conciliation (which have no power of enforcing their recommendations) were practically set aside in favour of the Court of Arbitration that can enforce its awards with all the powers of the Supreme Court. . . . Here, then, as answer to calumnies set abroad by interested persons, we have the spectacle of the people of a colony, after seven years' experience of compulsory arbitration, approving and reapproving its principle. Our nearest colonial neighbour, New South Wales, sent one of its leading judges across to us to investigate the working of our act on the spot. As a result, that colony has just passed a compulsory arbitration act of a more drastic character than ours, for there are no Boards of Conciliation provided for New South Wales. South Australia and Western Australia have similar legislation on our model. Strange that, if we have failed, our near neighbours are so blind as to follow us into the pit into which we floundered in 1894. . . .

"In regard to the relations between employer and employee being strained, may I ask whether good feeling is promoted by strikes, lockouts, picketing, Pinkerton's detectives, etc.? Compulsory arbitration certainly has not strained this feeling. Last session of Parliament the Right Hon. Mr. Seddon, who is Minister for Labour, as well as Premier, declared to the House of Representatives: 'There has never been a better feeling between employers and employed than at the present moment, . . . So far as my power of observation goes, class bitterness is almost unknown in New Zealand, and most kindly feelings exist between employer and employed."

He then proceeds to consider the general outlook of the country, also the fact that years ago they were told that the effect of labour legislation would be to "drive capital out of the country." In answer to this he shows that during the period between 1894 and 1902 for example, capital instead of spreading its wings for flight, had extended its operations so that the number of men employed had more than doubled, and that the total trade of New Zealand during this period had *nearly* doubled in volume.

Organized labour stands at one of the most critical periods in its history at the present time, in this country at least. And, although I believe it is coming through successfully, it nevertheless will receive some strong knocks and will suffer some severe and entirely unnecessary set backs, unless some of its worst practices, or rather those of some of its members and sections, are quickly eradicated. Flushed with pride undoubtedly in attaining to the degree of power and recognition it has so far attained to, the members of *some groups* of organized labour, especially in the larger cities, are already showing marked symptoms of severe attacks of the "swelled head," and their conception of their rights is getting so fine that the rights of those employing them and of the general public, are now so minimized that they have become of almost microscopic proportions. Especially is this true in those lines of work where the public is concerned rather than the employer of labour in works. And, when organized labour, "The Union" becomes a shield for incompetent or shirking workmen, or backs them in giving a wholly inadequate day's work for a good high wage, or in carelessness of the rights and amenities due to others, or a reasonable care of their belongings, or when it becomes too technical, or too fine in its rules and its methods and its general programme, then it will alienate an intelligent and otherwise sympathetic public, so that its losses will quickly begin to balance its gains, and it will by its own foolhardiness, set a limitation to its advance and progress, that otherwise could not be set. If the animating motive is continual getting, with thoughts only of "us" and "ours" with no adequate return, and no sense of its relationship with the great *public welfare*, then it will soon fall into the pit of arrogance and pure self-seeking without due consideration of the rights of others, rebellion against which was the very thing that brought the labour organization into existence. A permanent organization or institution cannot be built upon any such basis.

A "labour trust" is just as obnoxious to the great common people, as is a capitalistic trust and they will stand for one no more than they will stand for the other, and moreover they will in time find a method of putting down and out of business the one, the same as they surely will the other. And again, if browbeating becomes too dominant a factor, if terrorism, and murder, and kindred villianous methods become too frequent or habitual, and too fully condoned by organized labour in efforts to coerce other equally honest and worthy men who cannot see their way to sanction all their methods, or still others who are too brave or too manly to sit idly by and see their families driven and pinched by want, then also a suicidal blow will be struck that will be a tremendous hindrance to what would otherwise be a more gradual but a permanent growth. The methods of the brute are used only where brains are not equal to the task it is desired to accomplish. In this way many of the strongest and best men in the labour ranks will be turned against it, and will in time become a most powerful element backed by the great public sympathy to be reckoned with. Better grow a little more slowly, and in accordance with just and righteous laws, and hence more surely and permanently, than to try the short-cut methods, for in this way many get swamped and tremendously delayed, while others never "arrive." Those of the policies and methods above described become a sore upon the great body of splendid, honourable labour, which can illy afford to condone or stand for such methods; and personally, I don't believe it will very much longer, nor even countenance them.

Does this seem like plain speaking? The only excuse to be offered, if indeed any excuse were necessary, is that it is spoken by one of the truest friends that labour has, and friends don't snivel, neither do they fawn and having no ulterior ends to gain, there is no need for reticence in relation to truth, nor for lying.

I believe the time is rapidly approaching, and it may be indeed immediately upon us as some signs seem to indicate, when labour is going to push squarely into the sphere of political action, even as the great masses of the people are moving along the lines of political action, unhampered as never before, because of more open vision, by political machines, or dictated to by notorious old hacks as party bosses.

The day has already arrived for this in England; and to-day — the results of the late election — we see a splendid body of over fifty labour members in Parliament, and if even fairly wise and discreet in their actions, as I fully believe they will be, their numbers will continue to increase, and there will be a strong party right in Parliament thinking and working *directly* for the interests of the great common people, not so hopelessly impotent, so far as actual accomplishment is concerned, as have been most of the political parties there during the last decade or more. I have long thought, looking at the numbers of the one and of the other, that the time had nearly come in Great Britain for the doing away of the House of Lords, and substituting in its place shall we say, a House of Labour. But, things move sometimes in a most indirect way, and it may be that through this the beginning of a long needed labour and people's movement, this result in effect would be brought about.

Who knows but that one of its greatest needs, perhaps the greatest need it has to-day, will be served by this new movement — that England and Scotland and Ireland will more rapidly be freed from the centuries old curse of landlordism, and that the land now so held will be nationalized or in some wise method be brought back to the use of the people. The Labour Party in co-operation with the progressive wing of the Liberal Party, should be able to bring about this sorely and long needed end.

And then if, speaking along general good lines, this combination could give to Great Britain a new, a better and broader universal public-school system, something, I do not hesitate to say, akin to our own, or better still, then they would at once be dealing with one of its greatest delinquencies and one of its greatest and most pressing needs. In this way numbers of other ailments, resulting directly from one or the other of these, or from both, would begin to be healed without any other special direct treatment. The excessive amount of drinking among the working classes, and among both men and women, the bane and the curse of this phase of British life to-day, and now almost universally recognized as such, would begin at once to be on the decrease. It comes primarily from the vacancy, the hopelessness, the want and the despair in the lives of these vast numbers of Britain's population that have been induced directly or indirectly by these two causes, probably as much or more than by all other causes combined. And, speaking along the same line, who knows but that the splendid Socialist body in the German Parliament to-day, already numbering between seventy and eighty members, and steadily increasing in numbers and in influence, will have as its essential or primary mission, the freeing of Germany of what royal and the privileged classes have evidently neither the brains nor the inclination to throw off, even for the relief of millions of people, the monstrous military system, under which it labours year after year.

I think this new Labour Party in England as it grows will give its aid also in dealing more humanely, honourably and hence in a more statesman-like-ship manner with India.

And to labour in politics in this country I would say, remember a fact accentuated by the fact of Britain's high and enviable position as regards cleanliness in politics, that we of the United States, notwithstanding our inclination to think otherwise, are among the lowest of the low in this respect, especially in our municipal politics. And remember that this condition has come about because we as a people have so allowed commercialism and large moneyed interests to take from us and convert to themselves such valuable properties that their greed for more has become so insatiable that no man who fills public office to-day, municipal, state, or national, is sure to escape their blighting and benumbing influences. Hence, be careful in your nominees and in men to whom you give your political support. A direct or an indirect gift, depending upon whether at any particular centre these agencies composed of our "successful" and "respectable" fellow citizens, are bold and brazen in their methods, or very plausible and smooth and cunning — a direct or an indirect gift, to repeat, of fifty thousand or a hundred thousand or more dollars, is a very sore temptation to a man in moderate circumstances, or to a poor man. The essential thing is to have men of *known and proven integrity*. Better a man of less culture, or even more liable to errors in judgment, than one subject to the money bags of the "successful" and "respectable" despoiler, the arch enemy of American institutions and of American citizenship to-day.

Another point I will suggest, hoping it will be received in the spirit in which it is given: Be not displeased or dissatisfied, if those you elect, or those to whom you give your support, do not vote favourably for *every labour bill* that is proposed. Labour's welfare, and the welfare of any class or portion, must be always subservient to the general welfare. Class legislation is always in time unsatisfactory and destructive in its results. Class legislation emanating from labour alone, would be but slightly preferable if any to that emanating from capital alone. Only as the general good is guarded and fostered and advanced will that of any class or portion be really and permanently conserved. Here is an inestimable service that lies in the power, if it lies in the heart, of labour to render itself and the nation.

There is indeed a prophetic insight in the words of the "Good Gray Bard of Democracy," words that were written by Walt Whitman nearly forty years ago: "I expect to see the day when the like of the present personnel of the governments — Federal, State, municipal, military and naval — will be looked upon with derision, and when qualified mechanics and young men will reach Congress and other official stations, sent in their working costumes, fresh from their benches and tools and returning to them again with dignity. The young fellows must prepare to do credit to this destiny, for the stuff is in them."

The following are a few characteristic words from a speech to his constituency by an able member of the British Labour Party, who has served with great ability in Parliament before, and who in spite of much strenuous opposition was re-elected at the recent election by a majority of something upwards of ten thousand votes. "The working class, professional men and shopkeepers are all struggling — some few to make a competence, but the great majority to earn a livelihood. Millions are steeped in poverty whilst millions more are but one degree removed from it. While the useful classes toil and suffer, the owners of land and capital, and the schemers and gamblers of the Stock Exchange, are heaping up untold wealth. Whilst the poor die for lack of the barest necessaries of life, the rich revel in a riot of excess. Great accumulations of wealth menace our liberties, control the great London organs of the press, lead us into wars abroad, and poison the wells of public life at home. Landlordism and capitalism are the upper and nether millstones between which the life of the common people is being ground to dust.

"My one object in politics is to aid in creating the public opinion which will sweep away the *causes* which produce poverty, vice, crime, drunkenness and immorality, and introduce an era of freedom, fraternity and equality. This ideal state cannot be reached at one step, but much can be done to mitigate some of the graver evils arising out of our present system of wealth production. The immediate object of the Labour Party is to create a driving force in politics which will overcome the inertia of politicians in regard to social reforms, and give the nation a strong, true lead along the paths which make for national righteousness. To see that children are properly fed and cared for, that the able are given an opportunity to work, and that comfort is brought into the life of the aged, are objects worth striving for. These things lie outside the domain of ordinary party politics, but they must be attended to if the nation is to be saved from decay; and should I again be returned as your representative, it will be my main concern to see that they are attended to.

"As a Democrat, I am opposed to every form of hereditary rule, and in favour of conferring full and unfettered powers upon the common people. In this connection I include women as well as men."

I think it is peculiarly fitting that an utteranec of Lincoln close this part:*

"In my present position I could scarcely be justified were I to omit raising a warning voice against the approach of returning despotisms. It is not needed nor fitting here that a general argument should be made in favour of popular institutions, but there is one point not so hackneyed to which I ask a brief attention. It is the effort to place capital on an equal footing with, if not above, labour in the structure of government It is assumed that labour is available only in connection with capital; that nobody labours unless somebody else owning capital somehow by the use of it induces him to labour. But capital is the fruit of labour and could never have existed if labour had not first existed. Labour is the superior of capital and deserves much the higher consideration. No men living are more worthy to be trusted than those who toil up from poverty; none less inclined to take or touch aught which they have not honestly earned. Let them beware of surrendering a political power which they already possess, and which, if surrendered, will surely be used to close the door of advancement against such as they and to fix new disabilities and burden upon them until all of liberty shall be lost."

Prophetic words, spoken of all who labour, and also words which show Lincoln's matchless faith in the

* In Message to Congress, December 3, 1861.

great common people. He came from them, he knew them, and he loved them. Can anyone have a doubt as to where he would stand in connection with the great and pressing questions that are immediately before us?

VIII

METHODS WHEREBY WE SHALL SECURE THE PEOPLE'S GREATEST GOOD

HOW can we, as a people, get the machinery of government back into our own hands? How can we meet and battle with and defeat the combination which great moneyed, corporate interests have made with the political machine, the combination that has already well-nigh throttled democratic or representative government in the nation? We have seen by illustrations perhaps almost too prolific, how the people's will is thwarted, how their desires are disregarded, and how they have literally to fight their chosen representatives in order to prevent them from selling out their interests completely to the agencies already mentioned.

We need now a new and more comprehensive application of the term, *traitor*, so that it includes in its scope, the one who, as a chosen and supposed representative of the people and hence of the country, for gold or for whatever gain, conspires with the enemies of his people, and sells to them his people's interests, as hundreds of our representatives, municipal, state, national have done in *one form or another* the past twelve months, the same as for many years that are gone. They will continue to do so and in greater numbers and to greater extent as each year passes, unless we as a people begin in some effective and common-sense way to attend diligently to our own affairs in government. This is not a mere putting together of words, nor a false charge, nor an idle, thoughtless statement, but a hard, cold, though exceedingly unwelcome, fact.

We must take it out of the power of men to make traitors in civil life, which are far more destructive and disastrous to the people's and therefore to the nation's welfare, than the occasional traitor that appears in time of war. I had almost said this *tendency* must be checked, but the hard, cold facts demand one instead to say, *this condition that is actually among us*, sucking the very life-blood from the body of freemen, must be speedily checked and driven from out the land, or the dissolution of the nation is to be the inevitable result, in addition to the humiliation attendant upon this condition, and also the great losses we have already sustained and will sustain to a continually increasing degree.

Our governmental institutions to-day, not in theory perhaps, but as they actually exist, are neither democratic nor representative. This no thoughtful, clear-seeing man at all acquainted with existing conditions will even attempt to deny, however great may be his desire to do so. It is not necessary here to ask, Why is this so? This we have gone into both directly and indirectly, to almost a wearying extent already. The question is, How shall we get back in fact, and in actual practice and results, to what government among us is in theory — the government and institutions upon which we so pride ourselves?

A serious shortcoming in our institutions has developed itself, a shortcoming which could scarcely be foreseen in the beginning. We must halt now to make the necessary changes and repairs, or the entire machinery will be wrecked, adding another huge junk pile to the wrecked and worn-out machinery of nations that once were great, but whose people were unable or illy inclined to see and grasp the meaning of new times and conditions, and arouse themselves sufficiently to master them instead of suffering themselves to be brought to a gradual ruin by them. A change now is essential, a repairing of the machinery.

We must take a long step and get back to, or move forward to, *actual representative government.* Representative, is here a better word perhaps than democratic. The New England town-meeting still in active operation in hundreds of New England towns and villages, and a similar method in vogue in many of our newer western states, is perhaps the best concrete example of the latter. You who have had part in or who have attended such a meeting or meetings, know how each year the voters of the town or village meet at the duly appointed time and place, and initiate, discuss, vote upon and adopt such measures, make such appropriations, select such men to carry out their programme as they decide is necessary or advisable for the coming year. You appreciate most fully how impossible it is with such a method to sell out the interests of the people of the village or town, because the people are there to attend to their own business and to look after their own interests. This method works just as effectively and as safely now for the interests of the people as it did a hundred years ago, or when it was first instituted, and the reason is apparent on the face of it. Those who are acquainted with its effective workings, would like to see it extended to all our villages and towns throughout the country, the same as it is being adopted here and there in various parts of our thriving newer western states. Because it has such a thorough common-sense basis, it works as well in practice as in theory. It is better than representative government. It is pure democratic government.

It is the principle upon which the institutions of a great nation can most safely be built. But when it comes to the larger units, the large city, the state, the nation, then its application becomes more difficult, if not entirely out of the question. As nearly as we can approach to it, however, is the best government; and in these larger units we have in theory an ideal system, in that we select men *to represent us at seats of government*, municipal, state, and national. We, however, have not completed the system. The result is that our theoretical representative government has become in practice thoroughly and notoriously — with a proper allowance of exceptions of course — misrepresentative. In other words our system has developed, or has given evidence of some most serious shortcomings, and I admit, shortcomings such as could not fully be foreseen in the beginning, but such as have made it what it has become, in some respects, the laughing stock of countries whose machinery of government is supposed to be far less representative than our own. And what we of this generation and those of the generation rapidly coming upon the stage of action are called upon to do, is to recognize the exigencies of the time and amend or complete what to-day is far from what it must be made to be.

Let the State Legislature be an example of both municipal and national legislative bodies. The chief failure or weakness of any particular session of any legislature is that it fails to do certain things that the interests of the people require, and it does various other things that are diametrically opposed to the interests of the people, whose representatives, its members are chosen nominally to be. Now the chief reason that is at the bottom of this two-fold failure has been gone into so fully in previous pages that it is unnecessary to make useless repetition here. But the point is, that in connection with the acts of these nominal representatives of the people, the people have practically no recourse, in other words *they are absolutely at the mercy of their agents.* We act in a way that no business man, even for an instant, would think of acting in connection with his agents, or in a way that if he did so act, his business would be irrevocably ruined and in many cases in less time that it would take to describe the process.

Now, one feature in connection with which it is essential that we immediately repair the machinery of our government is, that we have the power, and the quick and ready power to initiate whatever measures a sufficient number of people feel the public interests require. Another feature is, that we have the power to veto whatever measures our chosen representatives, or supposed representatives, may enact, that a sufficient number of the people feel are opposed to the public welfare. These are two principles, fundamentally common-sense and essential in order to perfect the running machinery of our government.

In our system of representative government as it has worked out to the present time, the people — the source of power and in whose hands all power should reside — have lost, to all intents and purposes, the ability of having their desires or wishes put into force. We delegate power to men and hold them in no way responsible to us for the use of that power, and with the tremendous prices large corporations, many of them fattened off of the people's properties, are able to and do pay, we expect men, many of them entirely irresponsible because chosen by these interests for the direct furtherance of their ends, to work for our interests and for the public welfare.

We do what no business management would consent to or even think of doing, unless he were deliberately inviting the disruption or the certain annihilation of his business; and it requires only the most ordinary course of reasoning and especially when reinforced by the lessons that are in such vast numbers being thrust into our faces, to know that the continuance of our representative system without a safeguard for retention of power on the part of the principals, will mean continued unsatisfactory and humiliating conditions and tremendous losses, and the eventual dissolution of every semblance of desirable government. In other words we have come to a weakness, a breakdown in our machinery of government, which could not be fully anticipated by those who gave us our splendid beginnings of government; and which, let it be said, if we have but half the wisdom they displayed, we will, without delay and at whatever cost be about repairing or remodelling, and we will bring it up to the development and to the needs of the times.

Now in what simple practical manner can we bring these two essential provisions into our respective spheres of government? Fortunately we do not have to theorize in regard to the matter at all; a system has already been initiated and has been in effective use for many years already. From a nation that of all nations has the most ideally representative government, because the most democratic in its essence, Switzerland, we have a system that has been in successful operation for many years, hence thoroughly tested, and that has worked equally well in other countries where it has been put into operation, as also in several commonwealths in our own country.

It is through the principle of Direct Legislation, by means of the Initiative and Referendum, that we can get the machinery of government back into our own hands, and establish a *truly* representative system of government among us.

"The Referendum started in 1830 in the Canton of St. Gall, the Initiative in 1845 in the Canton of Vaud. Since those dates the two institutions have marched in a triumphal tour through the Swiss Republic until they have been adopted in the Federal Constitution. It is not too much to say that within these few years, Switzerland has been converted from a nest of oligarchies, entrenched behind vested interests, into the model Democratic Republic."

The Initiative means the proposal of a law or statute by the petition of a certain percentage of voters.

The Referendum means a vote by the people on any law passed by the legislature, or on a law proposed by the Initiative.

The two are referred to many times under the term Direct Legislation, or sometimes characterized as "guarded representative government."

As a thoughtful writer has said: "Direct Legislation is simply an application of the fundamental principles of agency recognized in every court of law in the civilized world, *viz*: That an agent must hold himself at all times subject to the command and approval of his principal. One employing an agent to manage his business expects him to do as he is directed in its conduct. If he is not willing to do this he may be discharged by the principal. The employer retains the power of instant veto, not having to wait until the end of a specified term, during which his property might be mortgaged, sold or given away."

In reply to the question — What is the Popular

Initiative? in an able Symposium in *The Arena** the answer is:

"The Popular Initiative is the right of a certain percentage of the voters, usually five or ten per cent, to propose a law, ordinance or constitutional amendment for action by the legislature or decision at the polls, or both.

"Under what is considered by many as the preferable form, the measure which is petitioned by the requisite number of voters, goes to the proper legislative body, which may adopt or reject it, amend it, pass a substitute, or refrain from any action in reference to it. If the legislative body does not enact the measure as petitioned for, or if it takes adverse action in any form, the said measure together with the amendment, substitute or other action of the legislative body goes to the electorate for final decision at the polls.

"In Oregon a somewhat different form is in use. Here, on the petition of eight per cent of the voters filed with the Secretary of State, the bill or constitutional amendment included in the petition is submitted to the people at the next general election, and if the majority of those voting on the question vote Yes, the Governor announces that fact by proclamation, and

* *The Arena Magazine* has taken a very great and commendable interest in the matter of Direct Legislation. Its able editor has had a body of well-known men, also interested in the same matter, prepare for the June number (1906) a Symposium on the Initiative, and for the May number (1906) a like Symposium on the Referendum. Knowing its policies, that it is a magazine with a purpose, and that these articles have been prepared for the purpose of the greatest publicity and influence, the author feels free to quote somewhat fully from them.

from that date it is the law of the state without further question."

In answer to the question, as to why the Initiative is needed now to preserve a government of, for and by the people in the United States? the answer is: "Without the Initiative the legislature can block the will of the people by refusing to act. By the Referendum the people can veto legislative action when it goes wrong. When through timidity, conservatism, corruption or the pressure of private interest in any form, the legislative body neglects or refuses to pass a law or ordinance desired by the public, action may be secured through the Initiative.

"In many other instances during recent years the people have expressed their desire for legislation and their representatives have made anti-election pledges, but after they were elected they came under the influence of the lobbyists and the representatives of public-service corporations and other privileged interests, when they have been false to their trust and have deliberately violated their pledges. By the Popular Initiative the people can secure needed legislation in a peaceful and orderly way, in spite of corrupt influences that have thwarted the voters and defeated the interests of the community."

In reply then to the question, What is meant by the Referendum? *

"The Referendum means the referring of a law or ordinance or any specific question to the people for decision at the polls. A vote on a law or ordinance may

* *The Arena* May, 1906.

be taken, not for the purpose of decision, but merely to secure an accurate and definite expression of public opinion. This is a quasi-Referendum or public-opinion vote, such as is in use in Illinois; also in some cities, such as Chicago and Detroit. The Referendum also means the right of the people to demand the submission of an enactment or measure to the voters for decision; and it is also used to designate a statute or constitutional amendment securing this right. In Switzerland, during the greater portion of the last fifty years, the Referendum has been a part of the constitutional law of the republic. When a law is passed, if a certain per cent of the voters, say five, eight or ten per cent, within sixty or ninety days of the passage of the law petition that the people have the right to pass on the measure, the enactment is held in abeyance until the electorate has voted on the question."

In answer to the question — Does it take from the people's representatives any just rights that belong to them, or in any way limit their legitimate exercise of power, and also to the question — Would legislators be expected to oppose the Referendum? The reply is:

"The Referendum takes from the people's representatives no power that justly belongs to them. The legislators are the agents and servants of the people, not their masters. No true representative has a right or a desire to do anything his principal does not wish to have done, or to refuse to do anything his principal desires to have done. The Referendum merely prevents the representatives from becoming misrepresentatives by doing, through ignorance or dereliction, what the people do not want, or neglecting to do what the people do want.

"A legislative body may depart from the people's will because it does not know what the people's will is or because the pressure of private or personal interest, contrary to the public interest, overcomes the legislators' allegiance to the people's will. In either case the Referendum is the remedy and the only complete remedy; the only means whereby real government by the people may be made continuous and effective.

"No reason exists why any honest legislator should oppose it. But legislators who put the interest of corporations or other private interest above the public interest might naturally be expected to oppose the Referendum. . . . All legislators who have been corrupted or who desire to be corrupted by public-service corporations and privileged wealth will oppose the Referendum. All legislators who are looking for graft and who are ready to sell out or betray their constituents will oppose the Referendum, for it takes from them the power to effectively rob the people and sacrifice the interests of the public for private gain or the power and place that corrupt wealth is ever ready to aid its own tools in securing. These false or misrepresentatives of the people and persons who do not believe in a popular or truly democratic government are opposed to the Referendum."

In answer to the question as to why it is imperatively demanded to-day? the article concludes:

"The Referendum is imperatively demanded because there has arisen in our midst in recent years a powerful plutocracy composed of the great public-service magnates, the trust chieftains and other princes of privilege who have succeeded in placing in positions of leadership political bosses that are susceptible to the influence of corrupt wealth. . . . . In this manner the government has become largely a government of privileged wealth, for privileged interests, by the lawlessness of the privileged ones and their tools, with the result that the people are continually exploited and corruption is steadily spreading throughout all the ramifications of political life. Against these evils the Referendum is a powerful weapon. It brings the government back to the people, destroying corruption and the mastership of the many by the few.

"The Referendum is the surest and swiftest method of checking the aggressions of the great corporate interests that have captured our legislative bodies, from city council to national Congress. It is the fundamental reform before the American people."

Here is a simple, an effective and a fully demonstrated weapon with which we can strike the necessary blows. It is a practicable and attainable method because it cannot be made an issue of parties and politics. It cannot be made a football of political parties, because it is something in connection with which all men really agree. It is a principle that is almost axiomatic in its truth, and such principles are not subject to dispute. And moreover, so far as dominant parties at least are concerned, no Republican who believes with Lincoln, in "a government of the people, by the people, and for the people," will dispute its wisdom or oppose its adoption and use. And no Democrat who believes with Jefferson that "governments are Republican only in proportion as they embody the will of the people and execute it," and "government is more or less republican in proportion as it has in its possession more or less of this ingredient of the *direct action* of the citizens." And as is evident, no new party that has arisen or that may arise, working for the people's greater interests than they are able to be persuaded the two dominant parties as at present constituted are working for, will oppose the adoption and application of such a principle. Moreover, there is no leader (no party) sufficiently foolish, however great his natural desire might be to do otherwise, as to array himself against such an axiomatically sound principle of truly representative government as to oppose it, when its advocates once get it squarely before the people as an issue to be acted upon.

It seems to me also that those who have various desires and plans for the betterment of governmental institutions, however ideal their conceptions and plans may be, can and will unite upon such a common-sense and practical agency through which effective strides can be made that will pave the way, and that in time will lead to the realization of such hopes and such plans.

From the very nature of the principle of direct or guarded legislation that we are considering, it would almost seem that specific arguments in its favour were unnecessary. It may not come amiss, however, to give briefly an enumeration of some of those most evident, or a sort of summary, of those suggested or hinted at in the foregoing pages of this chapter.

First and foremost as must be evident to all who have more or less of an intimate knowledge of conditions as they actually exist among us to-day, is the fact that as a matter of pure self-preservation of our form of government, and thereby our interests, this amending, this completing of our political system is necessary. It has become essential to the proper working of representative government. Without this power held in reserve by the people, we make our chosen representatives who would otherwise be honourable men, intent and determined upon the people's interests, the prey of these same nefarious influences for all time to come, or, on the other hand, we make these supposed chosen representatives whose candidacy is managed by these same interests and who have us elect these, their own agents, for them, practically masters of all our common possessions, with a free hand to betray our welfare into the hands of these interests. In other words, Direct Legislation is essential to representative government in complex or large communities, essential to the realization of anything approaching true democracy. "It is simply a *common-sense* application of the principles of agency, affording the principal his proper rights of veto, construction, control and discharge. Direct Legislation means control of your servants instead of letting your servants control you."

From this, then, follows naturally the fact that bribery and the corrupt and venal lobby will, to a great extent, be done away with, or they will be so diluted that the results will be practically the same. Where $50,000 would buy the necessary number of councilmen, or legislators to buy the passage of a measure, the briber, the agent of the "interests" could not with this amount or any amount buy 50,000, or 5,000, or any large number of citizen voters to vote for or to pass a measure against their own interests. Such a thing is scarcely conceivable. The "interests" then are not going to pay their good money to men who cannot "deliver the goods," and under this system they cannot deliver the goods, because they would not have the final say in regard to the matter at issue. Rings and bosses will lose their hold and their business. Franchise grabs and blackmailing bills will in time disappear because in case of the former, the people will be able to see to it that their properties are retained for their own use and welfare, and in case of the latter the people can always be appealed to with the assurance that justice will be compelled. The following paragraph from a former distinguished Judge and a man who knew well the methods of the boss, the machine, and the "interests," is most appropriate here:

"The fierce commercialism of the age, which has tended to enthrone the dollar and enslave the man, has lowered the standards and has covered the land with corruption until corrupt concentrations of money, wielded by unscrupulous men, have acquired such a complete control of the governments, national, state and municipal, that the people are almost helpless. Laws destructive to their interests are passed through bribery, and laws necessary for their protection are kept off the statute book by bribery. To meet this new and unfortunate condition it is necessary that the people be given the power in certain emergencies to legislate direct, either by a popular vote to put specific acts upon the statute book, or to declare certain specific acts already on the statute book to be null and void. This would destroy the business of bribery, because it would render the fruits of bribery worthless. No corporation would buy a legislature or a city council if the acts of that legislature or council could be nullified by the people.

"This system has worked marvellously well where it has been tried. . . . It is not a question to speculate about. It is not a chimerical idea. It is simply a question of self-preservation."

And the following from Governor Folk when the people of Missouri were finally aroused and determined to free themselves from most debasing and well-nigh intolerable conditions, is more than suggestive.

"Vote for the Initiative and Referendum, a system that will be the death blow to corruption, and the only true remedy for bribery. Why elect me unless I am given the proper tools?"

While on the one hand the application of the Initiative and Referendum * would have a very telling effect

* Ellweed Pomeroy, President of the National Direct Legislation League, is one of the highest authorities in the country on this subject. He has made an exhaustive study of its workings in the Swiss

upon the party boss and the machine, upon the star chamber, "arranging" methods through which almost every phase of legislation must pass, it would also on the other hand call into public life in many cases a higher grade of men, for the higher the plane politics are upon, the better the men that are naturally attracted to it. This is the general rule; the exception occurs in case of the occasional brave and earnest man who sees the well-nigh intolerable conditions in political affairs around him, and who without thought of self and without counting the cost, sets about in an endeavour to end them.

It will promote thought and discussion and a greater intelligence on the part of all people in connection with all public measures. As it is, the average citizen, good citizen if you please, has no part in the discussion nor in the forming of conclusions in legislative matters; he has no method except in some cumbersome and roundabout and generally ineffective

government, and has been a most indefatigable worker for its adoption here. He has during the past ten years or so discussed its merits before popular gatherings in many different states, before schools and colleges and before many educational and civic bodies; and it is perhaps no more than just to say at no small loss to himself, for he is a business man and for most business men their time is money. He has at no period been more deeply interested in the movement for which he has stood than he is to-day.

In a biographical sketch of him by the editor of one of our current exchanges, the writer says: "He belongs to a group of thoughtful young Americans and to a band of thoughtful workers who reflect the spirit of altruism, or co-operation and brotherhood, as opposed to the spirit of commercialism, greed, and egoism that is struggling to establish an oligarchy or plutocracy under the mantle of republican institutions, as the di Medici family subverted free institutions and established a despotism under the garb of a republic in Florence during the Renaissance."

His address is Ellweed Pomeroy, A.M., East Orange, N. J.

way of making his desires or his protests regarding matters of legislation known. With this simple and effective direct instrument in the hands of good citizens, their interest in good government and in all measures of public concern and welfare would revive, and by reason of the healthy stimulation it would receive, it would give birth to a new type of patriotism that would redeem and carry our institutions long strides towards what they are yet to be. And its influence upon the youth of the land, as they in turn come into the field of action, it is easy to forsee.

It would strengthen our respect for law, instead of our growing disrespect for it, because then its enactment would emanate "from the mind, the conscience, the abiding will of the sovereign people," instead of legislators, "some of whom," says an editorial in the New York *Independent*, "are wise men, some of whom are good men, many of whom are fools, and not a few of whom are scoundrels."

It will separate issues from men, thereby fostering intelligent discussion and keeping real issues fairly before the people. As important a feature as any in its favour is the fact that it is the remedy, the reform, the amending, the completing of our governmental institutions *along the lines of least resistance*, which is a most important feature in connection with practical politics and in connection with political growth and continual higher political attainment.

We have considered, though in very brief form, the reasons or arguments in favour of direct or guarded legislation. What are the arguments against it? I have never seen more than two that are really worthy of consideration. One is, that the people will make mistakes. The other is that they will abuse this power.

As to the former, we will readily grant the truth of the assertion. The people will make occasional mistakes, and they will be apt to make more mistakes at first than they will later on with more experience and with such increased intelligence in connection with matters of public policy as this educative process will bring about. That no system is wholly perfect will be most readily admitted by all. But the real, the vital question is, will the people make as many mistakes working directly for their own interests, as the mistakes made — and that mistakes are sometimes made by the people's representatives will be admitted and freely perhaps by all — by these representatives, combined with the frightful wrongs and injustices that are frequently perpetrated under our present irresponsible representative system, where bribery and graft and public debauchery have become so widespread and so general on account of this weakness in our system, as to make us the laughing stock of practically every other civilized country in the world, Russia possibly excepted. The people know their own desires and aims and their own business better than it can be known by any number of representatives, even though they might be uniformly wise and honest.

The man who is afraid to trust the people when it comes to attending to their own affairs, has something radically wrong in his mental make-up, or has something under cover that will not stand the scrutiny of honest and honourable men. Watch him.

We must, moreover, get over the idea that matters of government are deep and intricate and complex matters. When it comes to attending to their own affairs on the part of the people, there is nothing intricate or complex, or there is nothing as intricate and complex as would at first thought seem. But things are made or are made to seem, intricate or complex, by the professional politician, by the paid agents, and at times the paid attorneys of thieving or stock juggling corporations or privilege seeking or law defying corporations, combines and agencies of the various types that are continually at work.

So much then for the argument that the people will make mistakes.

As to the other argument above noted — that the people will abuse this power, the testimony in an overwhelming abundance is, that it is entirely unfounded, that it has no basis in actually demonstrated fact. This argument that the people will abuse this power which is not borne out by the facts, but which has on the contrary been wholly disproved by such facts as we have up to the present time, brings us to the enunciation of one of the strongest possible reasons for the Initiative and Referendum, namely, that the very fact of the people having this power reserved in their own hands and without having to have recourse to it at all, prevents in many cases, questionable or baneful legislation, and on the other hand compels legislation that would not many times be enacted were it not that the people hold this compelling power. The holding of this power indicates, and makes all too plainly evident to the people's representatives and to those who would debauch and buy them, that the people hold in their own hands the final power, and their legislators cannot be bought successfully without the buying of the people, which on the very face of it is impossible.

Direct Legislation amendments have already become a part of the constitutions of several of our progressive newer western states. One state has had the Referendum as a direct constitutional amendment since 1898. It has never yet, however, been driven to the necessity of making use of it. "It remains, just the same, a 'flaming sword' in the hands of the people, constantly reminding the unscrupulous lobby and the designing 'boss' that there is a reserve power which, when the occasion demands, can and will be brought into requisition." Where the proposal of Direct Legislation has been brought squarely before the people to receive their sanction or their veto, it has in almost every case been adopted by an overwhelming vote. It was adopted in one state by a vote of over five to one. It has been made part of the charter law already in a few cities, and in every case so far — state and municipal — it has given good results; in many cases results that could not possibly be accomplished in any other way, or by any other at present known way.

A Direct Legislation Amendment went before the people of the State of Oregon at the general election of 1902, and was adopted by an overwhelming majority. This was just ten years from the time agitation for it was first begun. The essence of this new provision may be said to be as follows, contained in the opening sentence of Article IV, Section I: "The legislative authority of the State shall be vested in a Legislative Assembly, consisting of a Senate and a House of Representatives, but the people reserve to themselves power to propose laws and amendments to the constitution, and to enact or reject the same at the polls, independent of the Legislative Assembly, and also reserve at their option the power to approve or reject at the polls any act of the Legislative Assembly." As to the numbers required to make effective this power held in reserve by the people, eight per cent of the legal voters of the State have the power to propose or initiate laws, constitutional amendments, etc., and five per cent may demand a referendum on any act or acts passed by the Legislature when their petitions are filed within ninety days after the adjournment of the Session during which they were enacted.

During even the comparatively short time that the people of the State of Oregon have had this amendment incorporated into their constitution as has been well said, "it has proved a field of dragons teeth to the Oregon machine politician." Through the possession of this they have already secured that now essential measure for political decency and political progress, a Direct Primary Election Law, than which there is nothing more effective to put political bosses and machine politicians out of business. In a late number of *The Review of Reviews* is a very suggestive article by a resident of the State of Oregon, giving a review of the methods used to bring this amendment about and some of the results already evident.* The following brief paragraphs are taken from it:

"The initiative and referendum amendment was not an end in itself, but a means to an end. It provided, first of all, a way by which the constitution could be amended in any particular within a reasonable time by the people acting in their legislative capacity. Those who were responsible for bringing forward the amendment had in mind several important reforms whose enactment into law they believed would be made possible only by this means.

"One of the reforms for which the amendment was intended to prepare the way was a primary-election system of nominating State, county, and local officers. So strong was the demand for this reform that in the campaign of 1902 both of the leading political parties pledged themselves to secure its enactment by the Legislature. The question of the popular election of United States Senators was also a most practical one in Oregon, in view of the various legislative "hold-ups" chargeable to the old constitutional method of choosing Senators, and as early as 1901 a bill was passed providing for a popular vote for United States Senator. The People's

*Oregon as a "Political Experiment Station," by Joseph Shafer, *The Review of Reviews*, August, 1906.

Power League, however, which had fathered the initiative and referendum, resolved upon the enactment of a thoroughgoing primary law that should include, as an organic feature, the nomination and election of Senatorial candidates. So a bill was drawn up and presented to the people at the general election in June, 1904, which was passed by a great majority.

"On the 20th day of April, 1906, the primary law was employed for the first time in nominating candidates to be voted on at the regular election in June, and it is not too much to say that by its means political methods in Oregon have been revolutionized. To a remarkable extent, old political leaders who had shown undue devotion to private or corporation interests were eliminated, while the great parties vied with each other in the effort to bring out candidates whom the public could trust.

"The way in which this formidable list of subjects was dealt with is highly creditable to the Oregon electorate. . . . In no case was there indifference; everything points to the fact that the ordinary voter studied the questions proposed, made up his mind before going to the polls, and voted independently on all the propositions placed before him. The measures have provoked a vast deal of discussion; indeed, it may be said that for a number of months past the people of Oregon have all been more or less actively engaged in the business of legislation. The educational benefits incident to the system are bound to be very important. With a change in the initiative law perfecting the method of distributing copies of proposed measures to the voters, there is no reason why every farmers' club, labour union, and lyceum in the State cannot become in effect a miniature legislative assembly. In this way the interests of all sections and all classes of the people are bound to receive attention; measures will be proposed for submission to the local representatives and others to go before the people at the general elections.

"But, with all this political activity, there is no evidence of dangerously radical tendencies. The people want to make their government as perfect as possible, but are not disposed to hurry the process unduly. The recent election, indeed, revealed in a striking manner their conservative disposition.

"In conclusion, we remark among the Oregon people a genuine joy at the discovery of their political capabilities. Representative government is good, but there is an exhilaration in direct participation in law-making, the interest is sharpened, the intelligence is quickened moral susceptibilities are aroused. The Oregon people are convinced that in the double form of government, partly representative and partly direct, they have discovered the true solution of the problem of self-government in our American States."

Another agency that is going to tell strongly in the redemption of our present political methods is, independence in party action. The time has about passed when a sort of blind, senseless, fanatical allegiance to party is going to dominate men as it has in the past. Thoughtful men everywhere are beginning to realize the stupid and more, the moral criminality, of *such* allegiance. One reason that the low party machines, as well as those of the higher grade, have been able to be built up with all their damnable characteristics, is that good men and thoughtful men and patriotic men have not in sufficient numbers rebuked their party managers and defeated them in their questionable and dishonourable doings, and have not rebuked the selection of questionable or venal or notoriously unfit men by defeating them at the polls, thereby pushing home a lesson to the party boss or party managers that would be of telling effect, that would be of real service to the party. And when a sufficiently large number of men make it clearly understood that they will give unqualified support to that party which in every case puts up the best man for public office, and which stands honestly and squarely for measures of the best public policy, then we will see a great difference in the standards of men nominated for public office, and in the methods of political party management.

"In our country we fool the people with some pretended differences between one party called the Republican and another called the Democratic." So says an American writer in dealing with the agencies that have made the governments of Australia and New Zealand so truly representative of the people's welfare.

This cry to loyalty to party is generally an emanation from some old hack of a party boss many times dissolute and dishonest and criminal, both at heart and in practice — an emanation, directly from him, or through some of his equally dissolute lieutenants, to hoodwink and to hold the members to the party under his or their joint domination, in order that at the right time they may deliver the goods — the people's interests — to those with whom they are in league. That the people have not seen through this method and have not recognized this fact in such larger numbers long before this, is a most astounding fact. But eyes are now open, and minds are now alert and discriminating, and the death knell of those parasites upon the body politic, of these scorpions in their deadly sting, and the methods of the moneyed interests in their dealings with them, are being understood more clearly every day and every month

Says a writer in *The Springfield Republican:* "Independent voters, after all, are every year more numerous in this country. In Massachusetts and Rhode Island there were some 50,000 men who, after voting for a Republican candidate for president, were capable of voting for a Democratic candidate for governor. In Minnesota there were at least 50,000 more of the same sort, and they did business on election day. It is discrimination of this sort that will make the republic live forever, if anything will."

Let us see how it sometimes works as it now exists. An election is approaching and nominations for certain offices are to be made. The directing officers or the agents of certain leading public service corporations, etc., want always to be on the safe side and want to be sure that "safe, sane, and conservative" men are nominated. At the appointed time and place a conference is held between them and the party boss or the party managers, — the party that is dominant or that seems the more likely to carry the particular election. Then if there is doubt in regard to this, the party boss or the party managers of both parties are "seen," and arranged with. The "interests" care no more whether the men to be elected are members of one party or members of another party than they care whether they belong to one or another religious denomination.

If the business interests that are liable to be affected have nothing of special importance before them just then, they in turn are "seen" by the party boss or party managers to ascertain if the candidates about to be selected are agreeable to them, in order that the party have their support, etc., etc., and the ticket is made accordingly. If it is a locality where this type of machine politics has been in operation for some time and where the party managers are of the ordinarily low type and have a sufficiently certain hold on affairs, then men of like character are the natural nominees, those whose subserviency is a matter not open to question. If conditions are different, then a very respectable type of man, but always "safe, sane, and conservative," such as we find for *some reason* watching out most carefully for the "interests" business for them, is the natural type of candidate. But whichever the type selected according to the exigencies of the case, as the campaign advances the "loyalty to party" cry is continually to be heard through the various agencies and methods employed and with which we are now so familiar. Then on election day we march up to the polls to be plucked by this machine management that will sell us and our interests out at the first opportunity, or by this contemptible combination of machine politics with the "interests." I do not say this is true in every case. In many of our smaller towns and villages there may be simply traces of this, in some cases none at all. But wherever it is of sufficient importance you may be sure that matters are "taken care of." Moreover, there is not a city of any considerable size in the country, and there is not a state where this has not been, or is not now going on. This is the combination that has brought the corruption and bribery and debauchery into politics that is now undermining our very institutions of government.

And what are we going to do about it? I'll tell you what we are going to do about it. We are going to change our method of nominations, and change it in such a way, that the boss, the machine, in their combination with the "interests" are going to have their feet knocked from under them. A system of direct nominations by the people whereby they can ballot for their own candidates after much the same plan as they now ballot at regular elections, will soon enable us to select our own candidates for public office, thus making it harder for the combinations to be made whereby we are continually being sold out, sometimes so openly and so brazenly, or in cases where it is not this, then making it harder for combines and trusts and public service corporations to secure such favouring legislation as enables them to become monopolies, stifling all honest competition, ruining thousands of businesses, moving up and keeping up prices of necessities to suit their own advantage, and always in advance of whatever advance comes in wages to the wage-earner, the professional man, and to all outside the combination.

The caucus and the nominating convention *as it has become to-day*, is the starting point of all that is corrupt and venal and vile in our American politics.

It is the stronghold of the boss and with this in his possession he controls elections and legislation, spreads corruption as suits his ends, and makes merchandise of government. Through it he has well-nigh destroyed popular rule, and through him the people have at each election, with an occasional exception here and there, been given merely the choice of two evils. It is only through the destruction of the present system that the power of the boss and his machine can be destroyed, for it is through it that he thrives and carries on his impudent business.

Several states have already enacted tentative, or more or less effective, primary election laws, not perfect, but being amended and made better as each opportunity for betterment manifests itself. Minnesota, Wisconsin, and Illinois are among these states. As they have so far worked out the following may be said to contain the chief details:

"Hold the primaries of all parties on the same day, under the control of the regular election officials. Do all the voting at primaries from the regular registration lists. Let candidates for office get their names on the primary ballots by petition only — five or ten per cent of the voters in the district of the office-seeker belonging to his party. Let each man vote for the ticket he chooses, and let him vote for but one ticket. Require each candidate to set forth in his petition for a place on the primary ballot his policy as to the office he expects to fill and as to no other office. Let the candidate of each party who receives a plurality of the votes cast by his party in the primary for the position which he seeks, be the party nominee for this position. As a matter of right, let his name go on the official ballots for the general election."

With such a system it is evident that no party boss could dictate nominations, and without this power he could control neither patronage nor subsequent legislative action, for he is able to dictate these solely through the dependence of candidates upon him. Newly elected officers could then look to the people for their instructions and not be compelled to receive their directions from the party boss and his machine. And so far as the voters are concerned, "each voter would have set up before him in every primary election, and later at the general election, definite, intelligent statements as to the policies which would be carried out in this or that office by the candidates who sought his suffrage. National, state and local issues would not be mixed together. If such a system were in force no people would have to submit to the shame of accepting the marionette of one boss or another. No machine could fatten on officially protected vice, or on the sale of legislation. The government would be as good as the people, no better, no worse."

Here then is a simple, a practical, and an effective way whereby we can battle with, undermine and wrest the control of government from this combination that has been steadily and systematically perverting all our forms of government for years.

Direct Nominations by the people, and direct legislation by the people through the Initiative and Referendum will give us back our government.

They are not ends, merely means of ends. But they are the weapons, the strategic weapons, if you please, that must be gained in order to fight successfully the great battles that are now on, for almost before we have realized it the revolution has already begun.

As it is, fighting with these forces of mammon and corruption, or this combination between the two, it is like an army, a large army, if you please, moving out with wooden swords and wooden guns against opposing forces, much smaller it is true and but a small fraction in numerical strength when compared to the greater army, but entrenched behind fortresses of great strength and of systematic building and every individual armed with the most up-to-date patterns of machine guns, with which the entire oncoming army can be mowed down before it can get even to their entrenchments. We must have these weapons or lose in the great fight. How shall we secure them? for they constitute the key to the whole situation. Clearly they will not come to us through the initiative action of any political party as such, that is until forced by the people. We will secure these measures, these weapons, through the action of groups of determined men throughout all our states, who will band themselves together in Leagues, known as Direct Nomination, Direct Legislation, People's Power Leagues, or whatever name or names they may see fit to work under. They will formulate the issues, with no small expense both as to time and as to means, they will carry on an educational campaign, and later, reinforced by the support of the people, they will take their bills to the various legislatures. They will compel whatever members may choose or whatever members may dare to oppose them to show their colors, that the people may know who their natural enemies, their betrayers are. If then a sufficient number of members is bought off by the combination in the first meeting of the Legislature before which their bills are brought, they will profit by the knowledge of the methods employed to defeat them, they will go back to their campaigns and to the people with a renewed energy until the voice of the people will speak in such uncertain tones that even the lowest of the combination tools will not dare do anything but listen. Thus reinforced they will go back to the next meeting of the Legislature into which they have in the meantime put men who will fight from within, and after another hard fight, or possibly even another in some cases, these weapons will be secured and put into the hands of the people.

We can spend years in desultory warfare with ineffective or inadequate weapons. With these weapons we can make an effective, a telling, and a conquering fight, taking one after another the citadels of the entrenched interests opposed to the public and the people's welfare, the citadels of monopoly and of corporation greed, all of them resulting from the combination of the "interests" with the political boss and the political machine. With these weapons we will be moving and continually moving, not merely marking time. With power in our own hands through the possession of these weapons, instead of a much talked of and boasted power that has become merely an empty shell, while the real power is in the hands of the almost insignificantly small numbers who are using it for their own purposes, we will stand as a body of freemen holding the franchise in their own hands, should stand.

Now here is a programme, simple and effective it seems to me, that we can begin at once to put into operation to bring to an end this intolerable situation that has gradually come about among us. If anyone has a better, simpler, more effective programme, I am willing to yield at every point where its really superior features can be established. I do not mean for some ideal state in the bye and bye, but I mean as a force to set into operation in a practical and telling way *now*, that we may be up and doing those things that will lead to the ideal state that will be established by our doing now, to-day, what there is to do, and to-morrow the same, and to-morrow. I am an "opportunist" in that I believe that the way to attain is to take hold with the clearest insight we can command, of the thing that needs to be done and that can be done to-day, letting that lead to the next thing that will in turn develop itself from it, and this into the next, until in time the foreseen goal is reached. To see an ideal state, and to sit and do nothing until that ideal state is developed and we are in it, or because it cannot be attained all at once, is entirely contrary to all natural law of which we so far at least, have any tangible knowledge.

With these agencies of political power in our hands we will then be in a position to move along the lines of political and economic advancement untrammelled. We can then take each step and secure each change for political and economic betterment just as quickly as we see such step or such change to be desirable.

We could then institute as several of our progressive states in keeping with some of the more progressive European countries are instituting, or have instituted — the Recall. By means of it when a public official shows himself too subservient to the will or to the interests of public-service corporations, trusts, combines, etc., or shows too fully a disregard of the expressed will of the people, or violates too fully his anti-election pledges, he can, upon petition of a stipulated number of voters, providing it is sustained by a majority of voters when referred in a regular manner to them, be recalled and retired and a true representative of the people's interests be selected in his place. This is a principle long recognized and long established in the business world. No business man would against his will continue in his employ an agent incompetent, or a thieving, dishonest agent. We are certainly capable of exhibiting as much ordinary common-sense in matters of government where such tremendous interests are at stake, as we are in matters of ordinary business.

It would end the public careers of men, quite a little list in our New York State Legislature, for example, who have been there, some for years, in the direct service and in the direct pay of corporations that are filching the people of the State for their own gain, and whose methods, whose influence, and whose subserviency to these interests are more detrimental and more destructive to the people's interest and the interests of the State, than the acts of thousands whom we call criminals in our state penitentiaries to-day. If this volume were given to personalities, this list in the New York Legislature could be given. Those in the Legislatures in other states, as well as in the Councils of various large cities will come to the minds of those at all conversant with these matters.

Then the election of United States Senators by the direct vote of the people, such as practically all are now convinced, is not only desirable but necessary, can be brought about in a comparatively short time, and this great stronghold of monopoly in our national government can be taken. With it can be retired some of the various members that will readily come to the mind of every reader at all conversant with public affairs, that are very carefully watching and upholding even with a grim defiance of the public the interests of the "interests." The following is from an editorial in one of our leading New York City papers:

"The free and intellectual inhabitants of the State of New York are *supposed* to have two representatives in the United States Senate. As a matter of fact a New York express company has one representative in the United States Senate; a very rich family of railroad owners has the other representative in the Untied States Senate, and the people are not represented there by so much as a white kitten. Nice, popular representation, isn't it? Under the circumstances you can hardly wonder that no effort is made to protect the people's interests when corporations are concerned."

And what could be said of a United States Senator from a very small state who could be described quite accurately as an arch enemy of the American people's interests. What could be said also of a member of the Senate from another small state, as also of certain others from states not so small?

The possession of these agencies would enable us to bring about more easily and more quickly a change that the movement now world-wide along the lines of a truer democracy, along the lines of an increasing power in the hands of the sovereign people, is demanding, namely, that all Federal judges and all important officers now receiving their positions by appointment, be made elective at the hands of the people. It is quite as necessary that laws and statutes be construed by representatives of the popular will of the people, as that the laws and statutes be enacted in the beginning by this same agency. Here is a change in a feature of our government that we must now be giving attention to.

The possession of these weapons would enable us to bring about an effective income tax, or an effective inheritance tax, or an effective act limiting, for the greater public good, the accumulations, with constant additions thereto, the vast private fortunes that will become in time as menacing and as poisoning to the greater public welfare, as they have proved to be in all times past. That we must be about this matter in some statesmanlike and *eminently fair manner* is now clearly evident to large portions, and perhaps it is not too much to say, to the majority of thinking men who are more interested in the public welfare — true patriots therefore — than they are in their own selfish personal gain. A wise measure along these lines, moreover, cannot illy effect even the possessors of these vast accumulations for *excessive wealth* is of no advantage, or rather of no real benefit, to any man nor to his descendants.

If we cannot in all cases get at a just basis in the distribution of the products of labour, or in the gains from those properties whose great increase in values is caused by the life and the toil of all the people, then we will have to get at the matter also from the other end. Not the interests of a few individuals, able and shrewd I admit, but the welfare of all the people, must be the motto of a really great and continually progressive nation. That we will be able to find a fair and a just basis upon which we shall build such action, I am confident.

It is perhaps not unwise to say that we must get the agencies of government so into our own hands by these direct methods that we can put an effective end to the gambling and predatory methods of Wall Street, not to any methods that are honourable and legitimate and commendable, but to those that are hellish in their nature and whereby tribute is levied upon every man, woman and child in the nation in order that a few buccaneers may add still more to their already ungodly and illegitimate gains. Their methods enable them to reach out into every state and every city and every hamlet in the nation to gather in their tribute and their toll.

Many of our clearest thinking men are realizing that the time has come that a Federal Bureau of Corporations be established, so that all companies, corporations, trusts, etc., doing in any way an interstate business get their charters and articles of incorporation from the Federal government, and be strictly subject to its scrutiny and regulations. On the basis of certain fair but adequate requirements, those companies and corporations designing to do a business unfair, unlawful and illegitimate, could be weeded out. The present stock watering methods now used so freely and so openly employed by practically all large companies and corporations, and all methods designed to give inflated or fictitious values to their stocks, could then be suppressed and could be dealt with in a systematic and satisfactory manner.

The possession of these weapons will enable us as an intelligent and a determined people, to bring about such regulations or limitations in the methods and aggressions of our great modern trusts and combines as become monopolistic in their methods or oppressive and therefore destructive to the individual citizen's welfare. We could then counterbalance in an effective way the skilful work of the representatives of these agencies that have become intrenched in our various Halls of Legislation. We could counterbalance the efforts of these representatives of the "interests," as they obstruct and fight from within every measure that is designed to protect the people and the public from the aggressions of such of these as are dishonourable and law defying or law breaking in their practices, as well as blighting and corrupting in their influences. We could also in time, and quickly in some cases, cause a complete political extinction to become the lot of the representatives of these interests.

I would not be understood as opposed to any of those interests that are honourable and above board in their methods; or opposed to the advancement of those interests that are not opposed to the greater public interests. Large corporations and large combinations of capital can accomplish results that are unquestionably of great public benefit. Those that are honourable in their methods should in no way be hampered. I do not believe on the other hand that they should be *unduly favoured* for they are abundantly able to take care of themselves. When, however, they secure their favours and their advantages at the terrific price that in the end must be paid by the individual citizen and the public welfare, then I say we cannot, without intelligent and effective protest, sit by and complacently permit these blighting influences longer to ply their trade. Because a man is very wealthy it does not follow that he is a criminal, though many are. That a corporation is large and successful is no sign that it is dishonourable or criminal in its methods. Very many, however, are. Those that are honourable in their methods should be given every respect and every aid up to the point that this respect and this aid is not detrimental to the interests of others and to the public welfare. From those that are not we should not only withhold respect and aids of every kind, but we should find an orderly and effective method not only of checking their aggressions, but if they persist in such methods then, of putting them out of business completely. Are we as a people intelligent and determined enough to do this? Other people are. I believe we are also. When the people *are sufficiently united and determined* these matters are not so complex and difficult of attainment, as they in the ordinary course of events and under a half-hearted method of procedure, appear. But before a people of the right temper these forces of corporation and privilege will listen and will seek cover, and when they are once on the run they are among the greatest of cowards. Ordinarily they will not stand in a square and open fight, but when routed they are liable to pop up again in the most unexpected ways. They must be continually watched.

I think the author of the following paragraph, from a recent number of *The Outlook*, reads aright the signs and the temper of the times:

"The people do not resent wealth, but they do resent predatory wealth. They would not despoil their neighbour of any property honestly acquired; but they would despoil him of the power to monopolize any of the avenues of trade or to control any of the functions of government. To compel plutocracy to act decently is not enough; they wish to destroy plutocracy and re-establish democracy — perhaps I should say to establish for the first time in the world's history, a democracy of industry. And they are quietly but none the less eagerly asking, What next? . . . Not the regulation but the overthrow of monopoly is the popular demand."

It should be the purpose of a wise and liberty loving people to afford every encouragement and protection to each and every honest and legitimate business, be it large or be it small. In this there should be no discrimination. But when through bribery and the debauchery of public servants, and when through the securing of unwarranted favours they are detrimental to practically every other interest, or when by technical evasions or delays in the process of existing laws under the guidance of skilled legal talent, or when through contemptuous disregard or open and apparently fearless violations of existing laws, or when by virtue of the confiscation of vast amounts of the people's property, companies, corporations, vested interests, trusts and monopolies become so great, so contemptuous of the people's rights, of the state, and of the entire public welfare, then it is the plain duty of a worthy, fair-minded and liberty loving people who have or who can have the full agencies of government in their own hands, to come forward and as one man to cry out, thou thief, thou briber and debaucher, thou criminal black in your law defying and law breaking methods, thou despoiler of other men's goods, thou robber of even widows and dependent children, thou traitor to the public welfare, so far and no farther.

Let every vested interest be protected, but let every smaller interest be protected also in like manner. Let no favouritism be shown whereby one class of interests is able to cripple, crush and kill any other interest.

There is no danger of the American people, unless trifled with too long and unless goaded to the last ditch of desperation, manifesting any undue hostility to any vested interests, and certainly none to any that are honourable and straightforward in their methods; and is there a man living who would think or who would be bold enough to proclaim that hostility should not be shown to all that are not? It is only an ignorant, or a weakly or foolishly self-complacent, or an already conquered people, though perchance ignorant of the fact, that will not arouse itself to a sufficient hostility to put an end to an economic slavery of such type, and that unless ended will have as its final end a complete political slavery.

We have this interesting and farcical condition that has come about among us, interesting were it not so notoriously bold and brazen and so degrading and destructive in its results — A body of rich men individually and collectively conspire for their own greater and quicker enrichment, deliberately to violate some fully established law. Many times then through certain other influences they set into operation they are not even molested, or if so they many times go scot free. If, however, they are tried and convicted they are let off with a paltry fine — $5,000 or $10,000, or in rare cases $25,000. An employee of one of these corporations has filched from his employers a few hundred or a few thousand dollars, or another has filched from the city or state. He is promptly arrested, speedily tried and sentenced to the penitentiary for a term ranging say from two to twenty years. Now why not fine him a certain small percentage of what he has filched. Is it five thousand? Make him pay over five hundred of it and call the matter ended? In other words, what effect or rather what deterrent effect, has a fine of five thousand or twenty-five thousand or a million dollars where millions are gained on the part of the managers and proprietors of trusts and large corporations, through their criminal violations of established law? If it is right that the small filcher whom we call criminal be sent to State's Prison, then there is the same right and all the greater reason that these criminals who filch under the most cold-blooded and deliberate methods their millions, who hamper or destroy thousands of businesses, who undermine the very foundations of law, of order, of free institutions, then I say there is the same right and all the greater reason that these be sent to State's Prison, or that they be fined so heavily that it results in a virtual confiscation of their entire business, or both. We should not be at all chary about talking of "confiscation" when it comes to dealing with criminals. We must, as a people, speedily get the machinery of government — the law making and interpreting power — so into our own hands through the simple and direct methods already enumerated, that we can put a speedy end to this travesty on justice and order.

I do not believe in condemning any man. My own errors and shortcomings forbid that. So to a greater or less extent do those of every man. It is only an all-wise and a faultless being that is capable of judging or condemning; only on the part of such would it be at all consistent. But such a being I believe would find no place in his mind or in his heart for condemnation. And understanding so well the frailties of human nature, in all his judgments he would be most lenient. But when a certain order of society is established that men may live harmoniously and mutually advantageously together, certain forms must be established and obedience to them must be compelled.

We must drive the money-changers from the Temple even as the Christ drove them in His day. In connection with all the frailties of human nature He was supremely charitable. The only ones He ever judged harshly or ever really condemned so far as we have any record at least, were those who bound burdens on other men's backs, who never raised even a finger to make them lighter, who sought ever to gain advantage at another's disadvantage, who oppressed or who robbed the people. When we put forth the restraining hand to hold in check or to drive completely out of business men who rend and tear the flesh from other men, simply that they may gorge themselves, not that they need food, then we will manifest somewhat the wisdom and insight that was manifested by Him, who understood so fully our common human nature that He was all compassion and forgiveness for all save those who oppressed, who made burdens heavier, who sought for advantage to another's disadvantage.

I know it is a fascinating game, this financial game. I also know well that great law of life, that we grow into the likeness of those things we habitually contemplate. As is one's dominating thought, so his life becomes. As within, so without — simply the direct law of cause and effect. I therefore know that the game with some natures becomes so fascinating and so irresistible that they are carried to depths and extremes that they never even contemplated at the start. To reach out and gain an additional million now and then that he does not earn, but by hook and crook, by gaining or taking some manifestly unfair advantage, by a contemptuous defiance, or by a brazen, open violation of law, or by a process of indirect murder, as many a million among us has been gained — and the greater shame upon us as a people — becomes fascinating and well-nigh irresistible. But where men are absolutely incapable of exercising self-restraint, but are given to excesses and crimes that are not only detrimental to society, but are destructive to the very forces that hold society together, then it is clearly our duty to deal with such men by way of restraint the same as we restrain the lesser criminal. The point is simply this — we must stop recognizing men and groups of men who are engaged in these practices as among our "successful and representative" citizens. We must look upon these "rich men without moral sense consumed by greed, devoid of scruples and utterly contemptuous of the rights of the people," as the oppressors, as the law-breakers, as the criminals that they actually are. We must deal with them by way of restraint in exactly the same manner as we deal with all other types of criminals. It is only by treatment such as this that we can hope to cope with this type, this most dangerous type of criminal that has become so rampant and so bold and so brazen among us. Just as sensible to attempt to kill an elephant or retard his progress with a pop-gun and its attendant paper wads, as to try to head off or to keep even with the corrupt and criminal practices that these men and federated groups of men are constantly operating under, by meeting to them the penalty of a fine, either nominal or heavy.

In addition to the possession of these weapons, one of the most significant features of the way the people will win out in the great battles that are now on for a clean, a truly representative, and a continually advancing government, is *the type of young men that are now coming into the field of political action* both as voters and as men who will stand for and who will be elected to public office. Here lies one of the most encouraging and significant features or facts of the times. Already in some sections they are throwing out their battle lines, and some of the old time and hitherto secure bosses and machine managers are fighting with a desperate chance to retain their hold. Some are already down and out, others are rapidly on the way. What has occurred at a few points already is enough, as I have heard it aptly put, to drive the old time apostle of "regularity" to drink or to suicide. Some of the old time bosses and machine managers as well as machine wards are already believing in their vague superstitious bewilderment that the methods of Hell have broken loose and have crossed the border, and others that Hell even is crazy. They are asking, what next? and wondering where the next blow will fall.

To the young man who will consent to stand for or who will aspire to public office, I would say, be sufficiently wise and far-sighted as not to aim for or not to stop at the politician's stage. You will have to dirty your fingers continually, and you will have to lower your ideals and your whole trend of life if you do, you will have to associate with and have as your constant and many times unwelcome companions dirty and selfish and scheming men. You will take your orders from a boss, you will become subservient to him. He will keep you as long as he and his like have use for you. Association and like trends of thought will in time mould you into his likeness. You may sink to his level and in time become a boss — a parasite now rapidly becoming despicable in the public estimation; but the chances are that you will get so far and no farther. You will thereby set your own limitations, and in latter years you will confess that your life is a disappointment, as it will indeed be to your family and to all of your *true* friends.

If the stuff is in you then I beg of you to strike for the higher ground. If the stuff is in you, you may reach the statesman stage, but you will reach it only by never making a deal whereby honour is sacrificed, and by being far-sighted enough and brave and resolute enough to stand and to stand uncompromisingly for such measures of public policy and such methods of party management as are always for the *people's* greatest good.

If then the stuff is in you, if you are wise and resourceful, you needn't bother so much about retaining the people's support, about retaining hold on your position. The people will attend to that. We need more such men. We need more such young men that the people find it a pleasure and a duty to support. We need more such young men to come from our farms, which contain to-day one of the most interesting and promising sets of young men in the entire world. We need more such young men from our workshops and from all the ranks of labour. We need more such young men to come from our colleges and universities. We are able to recognize such men when they are really to be found.

It is interesting and somewhat amusing to see how even old-time bosses of his own party as well as kindred types of men in all grades of public office and in party management, those who would have downed and who would have knifed him a hundred times in the past if they could have found the way, are now, as state and congressional campaigns are coming on again, rushing to the support of President Roosevelt and "the policies for which he is standing"— trying in the majority of cases to crawl in under his tent folds. "According to the desires of President Roosevelt," "for the sake of the policies for which President Roosevelt stands," etc., etc. The following from a circular recently issued by the leader of an Assembly District, in the Borough of Brooklyn, is quite typical:

"We believe it to be the duty of every man who has the Republican party's interest at heart, and who desires to aid the cause for which President Roosevelt and the national and State administrations stand, to put forth every effort to elect executive members, county committeemen, and State delegates who will support the — organization as at present constituted under the leadership of —"

There is nothing that so takes hold of men, that so challenges their admiration, that so compels their respect and their support as downright honesty of purpose, as a courage that compels a man to stand firmly or to drive on until he accomplishes what an upright soul that will make no compromise with dishonour compels. Such men compel the support of the people that lesser and compromising and timid men continually *seek.* Does this not give us hope for the future of our country and institutions? Does it not give us renewed faith in our old human nature that we have so many times questioned? Does it not give us a renewed faith for the future of the race?

And to speak fully and frankly what one observes and feels — the great admiration and love the millions among us feel for Mr. Bryan, and entirely irrespective of any party names or lines is because they recognize in him also a brave and an honest man, and a man with a heart primarily of love. A man so endowed will stand always for the people's interest and welfare. A man who so stands is a man of the statesman stature.

One day, several years ago, a certain congressman visited President Roosevelt in the interests of a well-known man, quite prominent in State politics, whose activities in connection with certain postal contracts made it probable that he would be indicted for bribery or conspiracy, or for both. In order that there be no misunderstanding in regard to his position, President Roosevelt followed up their interview with the following letter.

"(Personal.)"

"White House, Washington, October —, 1903.

"My dear Congressman:

"The statement, alleged to have been made by the inspector that I 'ordered' the indictment of —— ——, or anyone else, is a lie,— just as much a lie as if it had been stated that I ordered that anyone should *not* be indicted. My directions have been explicit, and are explicit now. Anyone who is guilty is to be prosecuted with the utmost rigour of the law, and no one who is not guilty is to be touched. I care not a rap for the political or social influence of any human being when the question is one of his guilt or innocence in such a matter as the corruption of the Government service.

"I note what you say, that the circulation of this report about me may alienate the support of many of ———'s friends from my administration. Frankly, I feel that anyone who would believe such a story must be either lacking in intell gence, or else possessed of malignant credulity. If anyone is to be alienated from me by the fact that I direct the prosecution of Republican or Democrat, without regard to his political or social standing, when it appears that he is guilty of gross wrongdoing, — why, all I can say is, let him be alienated.

"If District Attorney —— has anything which should be known to the Attorney-General or to me as regards this suit, I should be delighted to see him. But, frankly, I have not the slightest desire to see him if his visit is to be in the interest 'of the welfare of the party,' or of my 'success.' In a case like this, where the crime charged is one that strikes at the foundations of the Commonwealth, I should hold myself unfit for this office if I considered for one moment either my own welfare, or the interest of the party, or anything else except the interests of justice. Respectfully,

"THEODORE ROOSEVELT."

Why do I cite this? It will give to young men an indication of qualities that compel the confidence and the support of the people; with such qualities subserviency to party boss and party machine, subserviency to low politician methods are made unnecessary. It will offer a suggestion as to one reason why President Roosevelt occupies the position he o-day occupies; also why it can be so truthfully said that he is the only *people's* President we have had since Lincoln's time. It is with scarcely an exception the limitations that a man sets to himself that determine the level to which he will rise.

Again to the young man entering or contemplating entering political life — If you have contemplated employing the methods first enumerated and stopping at the politician stage, then think again and be wise and keep out altogether. Stay in the workshop, on the farm, at your business, your profession, and have thereby a more satisfactory life, and a life of more value to your fellow-men than it would be if you entered politics on this basis. If, however, you have the material in you and a determination sufficient to measure up to the stature of the statesman, then, for God's sake go into political life, and stay in if you can, as long as a well-rounded life will permit. You could do no nobler thing.

IX

THE GREAT NATION

THERE never has been, and from the very nature of human nature there never can be a truly great nation where one class of people rule, and another class or the other classes are ruled. The great nation is that alone in which the people rule, where through their agent — the state or government, they attend to their own affairs, and where they do not allow others to attend to their affairs for them. Government must be thoroughly representative or those in power will gradually get the agents of administration and of production so under their control, and will so use them for their own gain and their continually increasing powers, that in time the very liberties of the people will be stolen away.

Of late, we have been having some very direct revelations of the actual conditions of government in Russia, where a group of eminently "respectable and high-born gentlemen," among them no less than an august company of Grand Dukes, have for many years been directing the affairs, in a sense ruling this nation of considerably over one hundred million people. Some own as high as a dozen or more palaces, all splendidly or even sumptuously equipped, with annual incomes reaching into the millions. This all comes from the people of

Russia, chiefly the working people. What *their* condition is, late events have also revealed to the world, and more clearly than ever before. The hopeless state of inefficiency that this governing class has kept the nation in, and has prevented it from rising out of, the whole world now knows. To think that their greed and rapacity and general debauchery would become so great that through habit they could not keep their hands off of a large and splendidly equipped hospital train, that was starting on its journey during the late struggle with Japan, to give whatever aid it could administer to the wounded and suffering soldiers who in their ignorance were fighting primarily to put more money into the pockets of their rulers! This splendidly equipped train was completely looted and filled with cord wood before it had hardly gotten fully under way, at the instigation or at the connivance of those in authority. But the people of Russia, I hear it said, have not yet attained their freedom and so are not able to prevent other men ruling over them notwithstanding the state of affairs that such a system means. Very true, but there is another truth perhaps even more significant for us. There have been nations where the people have fought for and have won their freedom, but where through lack of due vigilance, and by reason of the growing and in time mastering greed of privileged and excessive wealth, their liberties have been stolen away, and their country, of which they were formerly proud, has through the inevitable resultant internal decay fallen into the hands of the despoiler. The greed for gain becomes so powerful that unless the great common people find some way of checking or controlling it, those that become mastered by it will pillage the very liberties of their country as quickly as they will loot a hospital train. Recent developments in our own nation, even within the last twelvemonth, have clearly demonstrated that there are among *us*, men of otherwise high standing, eminently respectable, in learning, in church standing, in society, but who have gotten so under the drunken sway of the greed for gain that they would not only loot a hospital train, but also a funeral train were the prospective inducements sufficiently large, and were the chances of not being discovered at it of a sufficiently rosy hue. This may be plain speaking. But a man who will cause or connive at death for gain, and many a death has been caused by the scheming, the cunning and the depredations of some of those we term financiers, even within the past few months, is indeed worse in his depredations than the one who will despoil the dead.

"The law of disintegration and destruction never sleeps and only eternal vigilance can check it. Every age brings its own dangers, and those that come stealthily are frequently more fatal than those that come with a mighty noise. . . . Instead of an armed foe that we can meet on the field, there is to-day an enemy that is invisible, but everywhere at work destroying our institutions; that enemy is corruption. It seeks to direct official action, it dictates legislation and endeavours to control the construction of laws . . . The flag has been praised at champagne dinners, while the very pole from which it floated was being eaten off by corruption, and republican institutions were being stabbed to the vitals. A new gospel has come among us, according to which It is mean to rob a hen roost or a hen, but plundering thousands makes us gentlemen.' "

As there can be no great nation without government by the people, so there can be no great nation without a continual vigilance on the part of the people. Vigilance is the price that must ever be paid for continued liberty. Equal advantages and opportunities for all, which is fundamental in any great nation, without active vigilance on the part of the people will be quietly and craftily changed into privilege for the few to be enriched through the toil of the many. And as wealth increases wealth, and power increases power, we can readily see how privilege and its concomitant, oppression, has in time spelled destruction to so many former states.

The fact that we have so much to read from history and so clearly and so repeatedly, makes me so full of hope that there is to come among us a people's movement that is to redeem and save this nation. And certainly there is now no power of any other nature that can do it. Moreover, this movement must not be unduly long delayed, for concentrated wealth and privilege are growing with such gigantic strides that every year, or now, even every month of delay, on account of their continually growing entrenchments, makes the people's task more and more difficult.

The great nation, putting it in another form, is that

in which the people realize the fact that they are not separate from or apart from government, but that they are government. It is indeed strange where this is not a part of the active consciousness of the people, what a little group of men and families is able to do in gaining control of the agencies and necessities upon which the welfare or even the very life of the people depends. And nothing has been more clearly and more repeatedly demonstrated in the history of nations than the fact that he who owns or controls that upon which others depend, owns or controls them also. It is possible for there to be a nation of slaves without the word slave or any word of a kindred nature ever being used. The more shrewd and cunning the owners, the more careful will they be to see that no word or sign or mark describing the actual condition of those owned or controlled be used or even hinted.

Where the people are keen and alert as to who and what they are in relation to government, or rather what government is in relation to them, there will be found a people who see to it that every opportunity is given to those who aim to do right. Such a people will see that among the great mass of their toilers, upon whose sturdy welfare and good keeping the very welfare and ability of the nation to progress, or to continue even to exist at all, depends, there are not untold thousands who are working from early to late year in and year out, getting merely or barely enough for each day's work to provide them with food and clothing and shelter that they may be on hand for to-morrow's work, and to-morrow's and to-morrow's—lives devoid of all learning and art and leisure and hope, those elements that are so essential to any life that is not the life of the slave. This does not conduce to that intelligent and progressive and happy citizenship that makes for a real nation of freemen.

The great nation is again, that in which the agents of production, and especially those that come under the head of natural monopolies, those things upon which all the people depend, are owned and administered as nearly as is possible by their agent, the state, and so administered for the good and the welfare of all, and are not permitted to be monopolized by the few for their own enormous enrichment, and therefore, at the expense of the great mass of the people. It is the private ownership or control of these as we have seen, that has permitted the growth of our enormously rich men and families that are becoming so intrenched that they are now becoming a menace to the very life of a nation of freemen. It is some of these, not all by any means, that have allowed themselves to become so drunken in their greed for an ever-increasing gain that they have resorted, and are to-day resorting, to such practices of criminality and dishonour that they have won for themselves, and deservedly, the term, 'the low-down rich.' And I am inclined to think that as the people get a still greater insight into their methods the application of this term or terms of a similar nature, to them, will be a continually increasing one. But men who gain their riches by these methods are never happy. From the very nature of the laws that govern human life they never can be. Therefore, to save these from their drunken frenzied folly, will be an act on the part of the people that will not deprive them of anything that will take away any really valuable belongings, but will be doing a kindly service for them as well as for the people, by seeing that these great common belongings are held and used as such.

The great nation again, is not that where through this unnatural use of these common belongings we have a small class of rich and powerful men living in their castles with great hordes of hirelings or dependents about them. This is something in regard to which history's lesson is most clearly written.

The nation with which we are dealing is, again, the one quick to see its weaknesses, also the danger of running into and working in ruts, or remaining in ways that were once advisable and reasonable, but where the time has long since passed for it to continue in these ways, and where a continued growth and advancement, to say nothing of its even holding its own, demands that it keep up with the process of evolution and growth that is ever working to lift the minds and the hearts of men, and hence their relations, to continually higher planes.

It is also the nation that is alive and keen to the lessons that can be learned from other nations and peoples. Many times the younger nations where great concentrations of wealth with its debauchery of the agencies of government on the one hand, and its oppression on the other, have not yet gotten a foothold, and which therefore are filled with men and women of lofty purpose and ambitions for a nation better than has yet been, have commendable features that the older ones can adopt and adapt to their own institutions with great advantage.

The welfare of the great nation depends above all things, perhaps, upon the general *intelligence* of its people, and the more general and wide-spread this intelligence the greater, the happier and the more enduring the nation. That it cannot be an intelligence and education on the part of the few, while ignorance or a lack of intelligence holds among the larger numbers, has been shown most clearly in connection with nations that were once among the great, but that are not now known except in history, or that have fallen from their place among the ablest to a position among the backward and the unimportant.

Free and open educational opportunities for all, for the poorest as well as the richest, is undoubtedly the best road to a general diffusion of intelligence among the people. It is possible to have wide-spread educational facilities and still for there to be whole armies of children numbering into the thousands of thousands or into the millions, who, on account of carelessness or greed or incapacity on the part of parents or other causes, are deprived until it is too late, of what should be the privilege, and more, the right, the sacred right, of *every* child.

The state must see to it more carefully than it does, that attendance at school, or some adequate means of education, be made more carefully and more generally compulsory than it now is.

That army of nearly two million child labourers from

five to fifteen years of age, that are this very day toiling in our mills and sweat-shops and factories and mines, must be relieved that they too may have the equipment in mind and in body sufficient to enable them to enter upon the plane of life's activities with opportunities somewhat equal to the other millions of the same ages.

We have an excellent free educational system in the United States; but it is to a great extent and far more perhaps than we realize, offset by this denial of opportunity to this great army of rapidly coming citizens who most of all need these opportunties to enable them to have anything like a fair chance in their struggles for a self-supporting competency, or even for existence at all.

Greed for gain, and clearly illegitimate gain, will prove triumphant and will stifle the higher promptings of the nation's heart, unless we compel every man running a parasitic business or enterprise to be decent.

"To what purpose then is our 'age of invention'? Why these machines at all, if they do not help to lift care from the soul and burden from the back? To what purpose is our 'age of enlightenment,' if, just to cover our nakedness, we establish among us a barbarism that overshadows the barbarism of the savage cycle? Is this the wisdom of the wise? Is this the Christianity we boast of and parade in benighted Madagascar and unsaved Malabar? Is this what our orators mean when they jubilate over 'civilization' and 'the progress of the species'?

"And why do these children know no rest, no play, no learning, nothing but the grim grind of existence? Is it because we are all naked and shivering? Is it because there is sudden destitution in the land? Is it because pestilence walks as noonday? Is it because war's red hand is pillaging our storehouses and burning our cities? No, forsooth! Never before were the storehouses so crammed to bursting with bolts and bales of every warp and woof. No, forsooth! The children, while yet in the gristle, are ground down that a few more useless millions may be heaped up. We boast that we are leading the commercialism of the world, and we grind in our mills the bones of the little ones to make good our boast.

What avail our exports, our tariffs, our dividends, if they rise out of these treasons against God? All gains are losses, all riches are poverties, so long as the soul is left to rot down. . . . "*

There are golden opportunities for earnest men and women to enter upon a determined work in everyone of our states until conditions along these lines in everyone of them are what they should be. Magnificent work has already been and is being done on the part of many; the help of more, those who have a singleness of purpose that does not stop even in the face of defeats until the thing is done, is solely needed.

But *outside* of this great army of children at work at that important period when they should be getting their equipment for life's work and duties, many times at the expense of great bodily injury as well as intellect-

* "The Hoe-Man in the Making," Edwin Markham, in the September (1906) *Cosmopolitan.*

ual and moral, there are almost unbelievingly large numbers that are in school but very little, and still others that are there none at all. *Every child in school until a certain age or until a sufficient equipment to meet the ordinary duties of life is reached,* should be the nation's motto.

It is also eminently fitting that something be said of the *quality* of the education it is proposed to make compulsory attendance upon universal. To come at once to the point in mind and briefly — training of the intellect alone is not sufficient; we shall remain a long way off from the ideal until we make moral, humane, heart-training a far more important feature of our educational systems than we have made it thus far. We are advancing in this respect, but we have great advances yet to make. Kindness and consideration, sympathy and fraternity, love of justice — the full and ready willingness to give it as well as to demand it, the clear-cut comprehension of the majesty and beauty that escapes into the life of the individual as he understands and appropriates to himself the all-embracing contents of the golden rule. The training of the intellect alone at the expense of the "humanities" has made or has enlarged the power of many a criminal, many a usurper of other men's homes and property, many an oppressor, and has thereby added poison and desolation to his own life as well as to the lives of those with whom he has come in contact and who have felt his blighting and withering influence. It is also chiefly from those without this training, that that great body of our fellow-creatures which we term the animal world, receive their most thoughtless and cruel treatment, and perhaps from among none more than among the rich and fashionable.

I think there is another feature in our educational systems that we would do wisely to give more attention to. In a nation of free institutions, more attention could wisely be given to systematic and concrete instruction in connection with the institutions of government, and in connection with this a training in civic pride that sees to it that our public offices are filled with men of at least ordinary honesty and integrity, men who regard public office as a public trust worthy the service of their highest manhood, rather than with those whose eye is single to the largest amount of loot and graft that comes within the range of their vision and the reach of their hand. Such a system would in time spell the end of Tammany Hall — a Democratic organization in New York City, whose chief object is to make politics a cover to divert the largest possible sums of money from the people of the City of New York to line the pockets, and in great abundance, of those in control of the body of loot. It would in time spell the end of the Republican rings and Halls whose object and purpose is identically the same in every city where they have been able to gain control, as well as the Democratic rings in cities other than New York. The methods of the rings of the one are equally black with the methods of the rings of the other; where the motives are the same the resultant action is the same.

Our educational methods are developing. In educational work are some of our noblest, our foremost men and women. There is an element of the practical, the useful, that is now sort of remodelling our earlier methods. It has always seemed to me that not only in our public schools but in our colleges and universities, it is possible to get as great a degree of *training* from branches that are in themselves useful, that will be of actual use later on, as out of those that are used for their training value only. The element of the useful, not at the expense of the training, but combined with it, should be, I think, and is coming to be, the marked feature of our developing educational methods.

The bread and butter problem will be the problem of practically all in our common or public schools to-day. There probably will not be one in a thousand whose problem it will not be. To make our educational systems so that they will be of the greatest *practical aid* to all as they enter upon life's activities should, it seems to me, be one of our greatest aims. That our college courses can be improved to at least from twenty to forty per cent, along this same line I am fully persuaded, in addition to the saving of considerable valuable time for those who, contemplating professional careers, will afterwards have to spend a considerable period in years in professional schools.

When we consider that not more than one tenth of one per cent of those in our common schools ever get as far as the college or university, we can see how important it is that every child be guaranteed what the law of the most ordinary justice demands, that he or she have the benefit at least of what will enable him or her to enter upon the stage of young manhood and young womanhood free from such tremendous handicaps with which so many are entering upon it to-day.

The great nation is a *religious* nation. In order that it be truly religious it is necessary that there be no recognized or established religion, that there be no relation, or rather connection between Church and State.

It is so easy to confound particulars with essentials. The essential, fundamental principle, indeed the sum and substance of all true religion is — The consciousness of God in the soul of man. To come into the conscious living realization of the fact that the Spirit of Infinite Life and Power that is back of all, working in and through all, the life of all, is the life of our life, that there is no life and no power outside of it, and that in it "we live and move and have our being"— to live and to act always in this thought and this realization, is the religious life. Without it one may belong to a thousand churches, or subscribe to the creeds of infinite varieties of man-made religious systems, but without this, one cannot be in the religious life. To dwell consciously and continually in this Life, and thus allow it to manifest through us, is love to God. To recognize it as the life of every other being, manifesting in different stages of Divine unfoldment, gives us the best basis for love of the fellow-man. This marks also the difference between the getting and the giving religion, for it is true in religion that we can get only as we give, the same as is the law in regard to happiness.

The people of the great nation is a patriotic people; it is an intensely patriotic people. I read from the dictionary a definition of "patriotic" — "one who loves his country, and supports its interests." Through lack of discrimination we have done great violence to the word patriotism in the past. In its name many foolish things have been done. Most unpatriotic and most ungodly things have been done in its name, though many times innocently done. We have allowed ourselves to be swayed by the politician's patriotism, by the capitalist looter's patriotism, by the demagogic, self-seeking, self-constituted labour leader's patriotism. They all spring from the same common ground — self-seeking at the expense of everything that is conducive to the highest public welfare. As a people, however, we are gaining wonderfully in discriminating power. As a consequence a new order of patriotism is coming into being and among us. What was at one time confined to the few brave, independent, advanced men, is now becoming common among the people. We are finding that the elements of justice and righteousness, fraternity and godliness, have a very direct relation to, or rather, that patriotism has a very direct relation to them. War, war and the flag, were at one time supposed to be the *only* agents with which patriotism was linked. To hurrah for the flag and to be eager to go to the front when the war bugles sounded, or were likely to sound, was for a long period a prevailing idea of patriotism. It may still be a way in which patriotism may be manifested.

The people are learning the real cause of many wars,

indeed the great majority of them — the bull-headedness or pig headedness, the incapacity on the part of those having to do with affairs; and again, the throwing of an entire nation into war by large and powerful though unscrupulous financial interests solely for gain. These two agents are responsible for the great bulk, indeed for nine out of every ten, of all modern wars, even as they have been for all time past. Men are beginning to realize that instead of having anything to do with this type of war, patriotism lies in *refusing absolutely* to aid or abate it and in using one's influence in a similar way among one's neighbours more blunt and with less power of discernment. When we reach a point where the large body of citizens see to it that these men and their agents — for the large financial interests of the unscrupulous type almost invariably work through agents many of whom they place or have the people place in public positions — when I repeat, the larger body of citizens see to it that these men and their agents are kept out of public office and relegate them to the subordinate place where they rightly belong, then we will witness the full birth of an entirely new and a higher order of patriotism that is soon to be dominant among us.

The highest patriotism that I know is that which impels a man to be honest, kind, hence thoughtful in all his business relations and in his daily life; that impels him to the primary and to give attention to those features of our political institutions that are of even greater consequence than his casting his vote on election day;

that impels him to think and to be discriminating in his thought; that enables him to be not afraid to point out and denounce the pure self-seeker and his demagogic ways, be he in public life, in the ranks of high standing financiers, or in the ranks of organized labour, or in the ranks of the common life. The man whose motto is not "My country, be she right or be she wrong, but always my country"; but, "My country, be she always in the right, and if not in the right then God give me the wisdom and the courage to work as a patriot to help bring her into the right, and *then* may she have every God-given aid that she may prevail." Such is the patriot. A continually and rapidly growing number of such men are appearing among us. Thus patriotism is witnessing the new birth.

It is this patriotism in the common life that is of the high quality. Men who are industrious and honest in their work; who are faithful to whatever tasks are imposed upon them; who are as eager to give justice as to demand it; who are working industriously and intelligently in order to take care of themselves and those dependent upon them, and thus remain self-supporting members of the community; who remain brave and sweet in their natures and who abide always in faith in face of the hard or uncertain times that come at sometime or another and in some form or another into the lives of everyone of us; who are jealous of their country's honour, and of the administration of its internal affairs, for in the life of the nation as in the life of the individual, all life is from within out, and as is the inner so always will be the outer. These I repeat, are the men and these are the conditions that are giving birth to that new and that higher order of patriotism that is now coming among us, and that is to take captive the hearts of men.

That wars in the past have been, and even at the present time are too frequent, all thinking men and women are agreed. That they are in the great majority of cases entirely inexcusable, and that there is and should be very little use for military forces if any, outside of *purposes of defence*, the highest and most intelligent portion of our citizenship thoroughly believes. And so far as effectiveness is concerned it has been proven time and again, that a *citizen soldiery* is the finest in the world. Neither vast bodies of men drawn off from creative and productive enterprises and made into a professional soldier class, nor bodies of hirelings, but men who are citizens of intelligence and training, and who stand with the ear ready for the call to arms when there is just cause for their hearing this call, such are the intelligent, such are the brave and the daring, such are the most effective. Men will not fight effectively for the little price in money they are paid. They will not fight effectively for the glory of another, nor will they fight effectively for a mere tract of land. But where homes are and institutions that they love and revere and care for, then men will fight with all that triumphant intelligence and all that indomitable daring that it is possible to call forth. With a citizen soldiery ready at the just moment to come from the mine, the mill, the counting-house, the farm, thousands of thousands or millions strong, why should there be a vast professional soldiery, a great non-producing class kept primarily for the glory and to do the bidding of a ruling class, but supported almost entirely by the great common people, that is true of the foolhardy military systems of various European countries to-day? Then think of the women and children by the thousands working in the fields by the side of horses and oxen, and then these vast armies of non-producers, and for whose benefit? Royalty, privilege, capitalism in government always depend upon the military arm for their support and at times even for their continued existence. When their demands become too great, however, and too much dead or dead-beat timber is thrown before the car of progress, then even the soldiery itself throws down its arms and goes back to the ranks and to the cause of the people whence they came.

The only excuse for the present gigantic military systems that are in existence to-day is that out of the ruling classes there have not yet come men of sufficient brains and wisdom, to meet similar men from other nations, and come to a sane and common-sense understanding regarding their relations. From the people as democracy grows, and whether it take the name or not, are coming men and forces that will yet break this hellish monstrosity to a thousand pieces and will send these millions of men back to the mills, to the farms, back to the homes that they may be as they should be, producers and equal sharers in the support of their country.

No, it's intelligence and something to fight for that

constitutes the effective in distinction from the ineffective army or navy. Reference has been made in this part to Russia and the condition of her people — the result of allowing one class to attend to the affairs of the others in matters of government. This gives us the basis for an observation regarding her army and navy in view of somewhat recent events. Her navy was larger and supposedly superior to that of Japan, her adversary; but the larger portion of it soon littered the bottom of the sea, and it went there because of the superior intelligence and hence ability of a people whose government aims to make intelligence the common possession of the people. Her army was virtually defeated in every engagement, chiefly through the lack of ability on the part of its officers — for the higher ability cannot be grown on such soil — and through the lack of intelligent and hearty service on the part of her common soldiery. And this because men who are denied opportunities for the growth of intelligence and who have no homes, but who pay excessive tolls and taxes and fees to others, can have neither the power nor the spirit of those who have such opportunities and who have homes. But the deliverance of these, the patient Russian people, out of the hell which results when the people allow themselves to be ruled instead of taking the management of their affairs into their own hands, is near at hand.

Through the treatment the people of Russia have received in their efforts to obtain the most ordinary rights of men, and after exhausting every hope of peaceable methods, they have now declared war to the hilt and the great Revolution is on. There will now be no settlement and no end until Bureaucracy, Czarism and "Holy Synods" are relegated to the place it is a wonder they were not relegated to years ago, and a free and delivered people will stand as the representatives of a new nation. The same forces in power in government that would deny freedom, or that would take freedom from the people, strangle all vitality and life even from the church, so that it becomes a curse and a drawback instead of a blessing.

Can it be that because a man is born a ruler he is born without brains, or without brain power sufficient to read and appreciate the writings that history has so often placed in letters of blood before the vision of the world?

Or can it be that he is born or that he grows to manhood without powers of discernment sufficient to enable him to discern the purposes and the methods of a self-constituted Bureaucracy, composed partly of a body of parasitic Grand Dukes and others of a similar order. which they deliberately plan in their selfish arrogance and greed to surround him with that he may not know the limits of patience and the temper of his people even when respect on their part is turning to hatred, and hatred so intense that it finally demands his extinction? Can it be also that the former become so steeped in their own methods of corruption and oppression that they have not discernment enough to know when their end is nearing and their destruction is close at hand? Or is this the price they finally pay for so continued and so brutal a disregard of all laws of justice and equity and humanity?

"And the struggling masses must suffer through the greed of their rulers, who talk patriotism, but never draw a sword themselves in defence of their country." But, it is said, suppose the ruler went to the front and harm or death befell him, what then for the country? Nonsense, there isn't the King or an Emperor ruling to-day whose place could not be filled, if he fell on the field of battle, most ably by a hundred or a thousand men from his own country, and in many cases it must be truthfully said, more ably.

How often also do those that in legislative halls of whatever nation talk and vote for war, go to the front themselves? Probably not one in 1,000. Were those who instigate or who vote for it compelled to go, war would be most infrequent. So often those that talk the loudest of partiotism in its ordinary sense, are the greatest of cowards. Hasten the day, which should have come long ago, when no war can be declared except through a Plebiscite of the People.

So far then as the soldiery of a nation is concerned, let the interests of all the people be equally taken care of, let there be institutions founded upon justice, upon equal opportunities for all and special privileges for no man, let there be homes and sentiment encircling these homes, and the keeping up of a large military system becomes but a fool's dream. There will come from such a people a citizen soldiery more intelligent, more brave and determined, and therefore more effective, than can ever come from any professional fighting class, and at a cost not a hundredth part as great.

Take sentiment from the battle-field and you take its chief source of heroism away. The people of homes and of just institutions are a people of sentiment. Upon every cartridge-box and upon every rifle and upon every field piece of such a soldiery the word "Invincible" could most rightly be stamped. But of such people and such soldiers let it be said to you, unscrupulous financial jugglers, Kings and Emperors and Grand Dukes, beware, for the people are now beginning to know your tricks. They know that "me and mine," and the ever-ready mockery of a trumped up patriotism is written all over you, and that had you your way, you would continue to make dog soldiers out of great bodies of your fellow-men, you would feed their bodies to the vultures and leave their families to weep in sorrow and cry for bread, that you might add to your already excessive and dishonourable gain, and continue to live in luxury even to your own moral and physical deterioration and destruction.

The great nation again is the nation where that most important class in its make-up, that upon which it depends more than upon any other, that that forms so to speak the backbone of its organism — the farming community — grows and prospers, and has its interests looked after and looks after its own interests more and more. It is to my mind the most natural and normal life there is, and the one — as a general statement —

that is or that can be made the most happy, and the most satisfactory, and in honour second to none.

There is already a growing tendency, and I believe that it will be and should be a continually increasing tendency, for young men of ability and ambition to remain on the farm, instead of leaving it for supposedly superior callings, that is unless the inclination or the aptitude lies so pronouncedly along a different line as to make another course abundantly advisable.

Go then to the school, the college, the university, the agricultural, the horticultural school, — and with this superior equipment, — go then back to conduct a superior type of farm. The outlet for your abilities will be equal to those abilities, both there and as occasion may arise. The possibilities of soil cultivation and all things allied to it under more careful, more scientific, intensive methods, are hardly even dreamed of to-day, notwithstanding the great strides that have been made during the past dozen years or so. And our legislative halls, State and National, have never called so loudly as they are calling to-day for men of such make-up as will yet come to them from these superior types of farms. Nothing to my mind could contribute more abundantly to the welfare of the country than the coming of increasingly large numbers of these into our legislative halls. There is perhaps no class that has suffered economically more from special privilege and maladministration, in short — injustice — during the past two or three decades. In no better way could these abuses be more effectively ended. In no way could a better balance be secured and preserved in all matters of legislative policy and in all matters of national conduct. May there be more organization, an ever-increasing intelligence, more interest in public affairs, and an ever greater determination to have a more equal share in the latter, on the part of this, the most important of our citizenship.

The great nation is again the nation in which the man of great natural executive or financial ability finds contentment in a smaller amount of possessions for himself, and the larger contentment and satisfaction and joy in using that unusual ability in the service of, for the benefit of, his city, his state, the nation. The wonder is that more are not doing this already. What an influence a few such men could have, what results they could accomplish, what real riches they could bring into their lives through the riches they would bring into the lives of multitudes — What gratitude would go to them!

As men continue to see the small satisfaction there is in the possession of great ability of this nature, and in the possession of great wealth when divorced from an adequate or even from an abundant connection with the interests and the welfare of their fellow-men, and as they catch the undying truth of the great law of life as enunciated by One who though He had not even where to lay His head was greater than them all — He that is greatest among you shall be your servant — then they in company with all men will be the gainers. Think what could be accomplished in the nation along the lines we have been considering in this little volume by a company of such men devoted to such ends.

A change is coming and very rapidly. The time has already arrived when we will no longer look upon the possession of mere wealth or the ability to get it as deserving of any special distinction, and especially when the means adopted in its acquirement are other than those of absolute honour and rectitude.

How significant are the following observations from the New York *Outlook*:

"Those who have fallen most completely under the spell of fortune-hunting, and have been consumed by the fever of a pursuit which dries up the very sources of spiritual life, can no longer be blind to the fact that when great wealth ceases to be associated with character, honour, genius, or public respect, it is a very shabby substitute for the thing men once held it to be. There are hosts of honourable men of wealth, and there are large fortunes which have been honourably made; but so much brutal indifference to the rights of others, so much tyrannical use of power, so much arbitrary employment of privilege without a touch of genius, so much cynical indifference to human ties of all kinds, so much vulgar greed, have come to light, . . . that the lustre has very largely gone and wealth, as a supreme prize of life, has immensely lost in attractive power. There are hosts of young men who are ambitious to be rich, but who are not willing to accept wealth on such terms; the price is too great, the bargain too hard."

Men of exceptional executive and financial ability, raise yourselves to the standing-point of real greatness and use these abilities to noble purposes and to undying ends instead of piling a heap of things together that you'll soon have to leave and that may do those to whom it will go more harm than good. The times are changing, mankind is advancing and ascending to higher standing places, and it will be but a short time when your position if maintained as at present will be a very ordinary one or even a very low one in the public esteem —and so will be your memories.

The Bishop of Exeter voices a well-nigh universal human cry at present when he says:

Give us men!
Strong and stalwart ones:
Men whom highest hope inspires,
Men whom purest honour fires,
Men who trample Self beneath them,
Men who make their country wreathe them
As her noble sons,
Worthy of their sires,
Men who never shame their mothers,
Men who never fail their brothers,
True, however false are others:
Give us Men — I say again,
Give us Men!

X

THE LIFE OF THE HIGHER BEAUTY AND POWER

TO be at peace. To be happy. To live in contentment. To have a satisfying and harmonious — a successful life. This echoes the longing of perhaps every normal person. The fact that it so echoes a universal longing, indicates, to me at least, that it should be the natural, the normal life. In order to live a harmonious life there must be something to be in harmony with; and here as I view it is the great secret of life and its successful and satisfactory fulfillment.

That there is a Spirit of intelligence and of love in the universe, no normally constituted mind, and one that has lived at all near the higher revelations that may have come to it, can for a moment doubt. There is a Power, beneficent if worked in harmony with, that pervades and through the channel great and definite systems of law, governs the universe and all that is in it. Every decade we are discovering new laws and forces, and the latter seem to be all the time finer and finer in their nature. This is perhaps on account of the process of evolution so developing, so unfolding us, that we are getting nearer and nearer to the essence, the inner nature — the soul of things.

What was the actual beginning of things no man knows. Nor is it essential or important that we do know. But in the beginning, as now was *Being*, self-existent and all-pervading — the Spirit of Infinite Life and Power that is back of all, working in and through all, the source, the life of all. This seems to be a self-evident fact — Infinite Being projecting itself into ex-istence, therefore the spirit, the substance, the life of all there is. Various terms or names are used by different minds; but to me this Infinite Being is God. To know this as our source, the very essence of our being and from which or from whom we can be cut off, can separate ourselves, only to our detriment, is to recognize ourselves as spiritual beings; it is to be born into the spiritual life, and the spiritual life is the life eternal. Thus we come to know *God* in the degree that we realize that in Him we live and move and have our being. In the degree that we live in the realization of this truth, does this spirit of Infinite Life and Power reveal itself to our consciousness more and more, and it is in this way that we grow and unfold in the spiritual life.

It is through great systems of law, definite and immutable, that God or Infinite Being works. To know these laws and to live, to work in harmony with them brings peace and harmony; wilfully to violate them brings inharmony and struggle and suffering. They all work together for good. To live in harmony with them can bring us only good. To fail to recognize or wilfully to violate them brings necessarily the opposite of good, namely evil. Evil has its origin properly speaking not in *God*, but from a violation of the laws, shall we say, the ordinances of God.

To realize that in essence, though not in degree, we are one with the life of God, and then to open ourselves, our minds and our hearts, so that a continually increasing degree of the God life can manifest itself to and through us, is to understand more and more and to come into a continually greater harmony with the laws under which we live and which permeate and rule in the universe with an unchangeable precision. It is through our non-recognition of the life that is in us and the laws by which all things are governed, in other words, living out of harmony with the laws under which it is decreed we must live, that inharmony and evil with its consequent pain and suffering and despair enters into our lives. There are those who have lived so fully in the realization of their essential oneness with the Divine Life, that their lives here have been almost a continual song of peace and thanksgiving.

As individuals — expressions of Being projected into existence — we are given the power of choice. We can choose to open ourselves so fully to the realization of the Source of our life and open ourselves so fully to its imflux that we will find the attributes of this life manifesting, incarnating themselves more and more in our lives, so that in time we take on more and more the wisdom, the insight and the powers of this Life. In this way we are gradually changed from the natural to the spiritual, from earth-men to God-men, thus fulfilling the undoubted purpose of our being — divine self-realization, and the returning to that from which we came. Coming as babes, returning as fully grown spiritual beings, gaining our experience in contact with this material world through the agency of the material body and for some purpose of which we do not yet know, but that shall be revealed to us in due process of time. What it is, cannot concern us materially now. This will come when we are ready for it. To know the laws under which we are living and to bring our lives into an ever completer harmony with them is what concerns us now. Step by step in this as in all things.

But to know God's laws is first to know the life of God in us. To live then in harmony with these laws and thus to reap the results that follow naturally and unerringly from this course, is the part of the wise. To separate ourselves from the life of God, to lose therefore the guiding wisdom that is its attribute, to fail to live in harmony with these laws, and to be battered and buffetted about as is invariably the result of the violation of law, until through this hard process we are finally driven into harmony with the laws of God, is the part of the unwise, the fool. The laws will have obedience and there has never been a man or a woman powerful enough or rich enough or unique enough to violate them without suffering sooner or later the inevitable results. Many have sought to do so but have learned their lesson in sorrow, in anguish, in humiliation. We go voluntarily and of our own accord, or we are pushed and taught through suffering. God will have obedience. To know God is to know His laws; for His laws are written in the heart of man.

By dwelling continually in this life of God we come into that condition where we are led more and more by the Divine guidance, where the Divine wisdom and power and life so manifest and illumine our being and through this our understanding that we know more and more to do the right thing at the right time; and for such, to know is to do.*

While the end of life is not attained through intellectual processes alone, the mind, the intellect nevertheless is a means to this end. It is through the mind that the connection is made between the human and the Divine. It is through thought operating through the channel of the mind that we are able to realize and keep our connection with Infinite Being, our source. It is by virtue of the mind, working through the brain, that we are connected with the material, physical universe. The body is material, physical. Every particle of it, through the food we take, is from the earth and the air and to the earth and the air every particle of it finally returns.

To realize that the body is not the self, but the instrument by which the self is temporarily related to, and made able to manifest and live in a material world for the purpose of experience, growth, development, is a great aid in arriving at the *realities* of life. The folly then of giving supreme attention to it and the things

*For suggestions as to the method of entering into this higher realization, as also for a much fuller portrayal of its results in everyday life, the reader is directed to the volume by the same author entitled, "In Tune with the Infinite, or, Fullness of Peace, Power, and Plenty."

that pertain to it. To give it sufficient attention to enable it to become *the clearest, the soundest, the most perfect instrument* that it can be made and kept for the real self to use, is the part of wisdom, for it is the true middle ground.

Now, why all this, I hear it asked, in a book of this nature? In order to get a basis in religion, in philosophy, in *reality*, for life, for the individual life; and as is the individual life so is the national life, never higher, never lower. As Dr. Patton, formerly president of Princeton University once said to a class of young graduates:

"Religion is the goal of culture, and the educated man must stand in some relation to God. He must have some philosophy of human life, some theory of society." And as Milton has said: "There is nothing that makes men rich and strong but that which they carry inside of them. Wealth is of the heart, not of the hand." And as Mazzini once said: "Where there is no vision the people perish."

The chase for the material has of late years become so great and so absorbing, whether by fair means or foul, that it has become one of the notorious features or characteristics of the time. And while I believe the heart of the people, and the heart of the nation is sound, by virtue of the vastly superior numbers of splendid, honest, unpurchasable and high-minded men and women among us, both old and young, a strong materialistic *tendency* is nevertheless a marked characteristic of the time. As there is perhaps no greater truth in connection with human life than — As a man thinketh in his heart so is he, and also, that we grow into the likeness of those things we most habitually contemplate, and also that all life is from within out, for as is the inner, so always and necessarily will be the outer, it becomes clearly apparent how essential that the right centre or basis of life be established. We hear it often said, and said in the most well meaning way, that the physical, the material, is the basis of life. Now I would put it in another way, a safer and I think a truer way. The spiritual is the *basis* and the end of life, and the physical, the material, is the channel through which it manifests and works and unfolds and masters. The latter is not to be despised or slighted, but to be used, to be wisely used, but to be subordinated to its proper place. Thus it becomes a great blessing and helper rather than a hindrance and a curse. To have an abundance of the world's goods is good if rightly used, but to make the accumulation of material things the chief object of life can end only in disappointment. Such have but a pinched and stunted life which is unsatisfactory and empty of joy to themselves, and except by way of warning is of but little if any value to the world.

Each one must find a centre for life from which all radiates, or, putting it in another way, a basis, a foundation upon which all else is built. Such a centre or such a basis, one that is true and satisfactory, is earnestly longed for by myriads of people. An instinct for the religious life is born in practically every human soul. So many great chunks as the years have passed, have fallen away from our theological systems, and as many chunks are still continually falling away from them that it is hard or well-nigh impossible for an earnest, mentally honest man to find any satisfactory or even acceptable basis for the religious life there. Such in common with all others will find that the uniform teaching of all the most inspired teachers in the world's history, whatever the religion or system of belief has been, is that the essence, the substance of all true religion is, the Consciousness of God in the soul of man. The rational basis for this I have endeavoured to point out in the early pages of this chapter. "In Him we live and move and have over being." In what a homely, splendid way John Tauler has put it in the following:

> "I have a power in my soul which enables me to perceive God: I am as certain as that I live that nothing is so near to me as God. He is nearer to me than I am to myself. It is part of His very essence that He should be nigh and present to me. . . . And a man is more blessed or less blessed in the same measure as he is aware of the presence of God."

"God made us for Himself, and our hearts are restless until they repose in Him," was St. Augustine's way of putting it. "The only death to be feared is unconsciousness of the presence of God," said Paracelsus. "That the Divine Life and Energy *actually lives in us* is inseparable from Religion," was the keynote to the philosophy of that most spiritual of philosophers, Fichte. "An insight into the absolute unity of the Human Existence with the Divine is certainly the profoundest knowledge that man can attain," said he again. It was the most inspired who has yet lived among us who said: "Neither shall they say, Lo here! or, Lo there! for, behold the Kingdom of God is within you." And again: "Seek ye first the Kingdom of God, and His righteousness, and all these things shall be added unto you." It was He who gave the substance of the moral law and therefore the essence of religion as — Love to God and love to the fellow-man.

To me love to God is this dwelling continually in the conscious living realization of the essential oneness of our life with the Divine Life — Seeking to have no other will than that the Divine will may manifest to and may work through us. How significant then — "Thou wilt keep him in perfect peace, whose mind is stayed on Thee," and also "In all thy ways acknowledge Him, and He shall direct thy paths." How truly in the light of this truth does Fichte say that the expression of the constant mind of the truly religious man is this prayer: "Lord! let but Thy will be done, then is mine also done; for I have no other will than this — that Thy will be done." And how thoroughly in keeping with — "Thou wilt keep him in perfect peace, whose mind is stayed on Thee," is his thought in the following:

"Whatever comes to pass around him, nothing appears to him strange or unaccountable — he knows assuredly, whether he understand it or not, that it is in God's World, and that there nothing can be that does not directly tend to good. In him there is no fear for the future, for the absolute fountain of all blessedness eternally bears him on towards it; no sorrow for the past, for in so far as he was not in God he was nothing, and this is now at an end, and since he has dwelt in God he has been born into light; while in so far as he was in God, that which he has done is assuredly right and good. . . . His whole outward existence flows forth, softly and gently, from his Inward Being, and issues out into Reality without difficulty or hindrance."

Love to the fellow-man is the realization of the fact that we are all parts of the one great whole, that the source and essence of life in each is essentially the same, that love is the established law of life, and that the law will have obedience or it will strike its punishment upon all who do violence to it.

"He that loveth not his brother, abideth in death," said the Master Teacher, and this is simply the enunciation of the law that's written deep in the universe and immutable in its workings.

"All beings are the fruits of one tree, the leaves of one branch, the drops of one sea. Honour is for him who loveth men, not for him who loveth his own," says the Persian.

Truly we are all parts of the one great whole, and one can't suffer or have injustice done him without all sharing in that suffering and none more than the author of that injustice.

It was by virtue of His perceiving so clearly the laws in relation to human life that are so immutable in their workings that enabled and prompted Jesus to give anew to the world an epitome of the laws relating to all human relations when He said, "And as ye would that men should do to you, do ye also to them likewise." It is what is ordinarily termed the Golden Rule. I have never seen any wiser or more suggestive commentary upon it than the following, by the late Hon. Samuel Milton Jones*:

"As I view it, the Golden Rule is the supreme law of life. It may be paraphrased this way: As you do unto others, others will do unto you. What I give, I get. If I love you really and truly and actively love you, you are as sure to love me in return as the earth is sure to be warmed by the rays of the midsummer sun. If I hate you, illtreat you and abuse you, I am equally certain to arouse the same kind of antagonism towards me, unless the Divine nature is so developed that it is dominant in you, and you have learned to love your enemies. What can be plainer. The Golden Rule is the law of action and reaction in the field of morals, just as definite, just as certain here as the law is definite and certain in the domain of physics. I think the confusion with respect to the Golden Rule arises from the different conceptions that we have of the word love. I use the word love as synonymous with reason, and so when I speak of doing the loving thing, I mean the reasonable thing. When I speak of dealing with my fellow-men in an unreasonable way, I mean an unloving way.

*Mayor Jones of Toledo was to my mind one of the most significant men politically that our country has yet known. A man who believed in actually adopting the law of life as enunciated in the Golden Rule as a basis for personal action and for the administration of public affairs. A man who used public office only for the highest public good. A man whom the people therefore so trusted that, running as an independent candidate against the candidates of the two dominant political parties, he was able to pole a vote of nearly 17,000 out of a total voting number of 24,000. It is rather significant, isn't it? — and this against the combined and determined efforts of the machines of both political parties, both local and state, and in face of the united opposition of all the newspapers and corporations in the city, and not a few of the "eminently respectable people." So far as his influence upon the political future is concerned, as it will be, even as it is being already, carried into activity by younger men who are coming into the field of political action, it is unquestionably true that no greater or more valuable man has ever come from or been associated with the State of Ohio.

The terms are interchangeable absolutely. The reason why we know so little about the Golden Rule is because we have not practised it."

Yes, what we term the Golden Rule is an absolute law of life, and it will have obedience through the joy, and therefore the gain it brings into our lives if we observe it, or it will have obedience by the pain and the blankness it drives into our lives if we violate it. As we give to the world so the world gives back to us. Thoughts are forces, like inspires like and like creates like. If I give love I inspire and receive love in return. If I give hatred I inspire and I receive hatred. The wise man loves; only the ignorant, the selfish, the fool, hates.

It is the man who loves and serves who has solved the riddle of life, for into his life comes the fulness, the satisfaction, the peace and the joy that the Law decrees. He it is who is the wise man.

The man who has no sense of service to his fellow-man, whose idea is primarily gain for himself, whether honourable or dishonourable, is the supreme fool in life by virtue of his ignorance leading him into the violation of a law that condemns him to a pinched, a stunted, sunless, joyless life.

"If the gatherer gathers too much," says Emerson, "nature takes out of the man what she puts into his chest; swells the state but kills the owner. Nature hates monopolies and exceptions."

We do well when we remember this — one can never do an injury to another without in some form or another suffering for that injury himself. Why? It is so written in the Law of the Universe, that's all. And we do likewise well to remember — one can never do a real loving, unselfish, kindly act without deriving a benefit from such act himself; and if at any time there are apparent exceptions to this it is, I believe, because our limited vision does not enable us to see the total relationship of human actions.

"No man in the world ever attempted to wrong another without being injured in return,— some way, somehow, sometime. The only weapon of offence that nature seems to recognize is the boomerang. Nature keeps her books admirably; she puts down every item, she closes all accounts finally, but she does not always balance them at the end of the month."*

As the life of a man is of more value to him than the house in which he lives, so the possession and growth of the faculties that enable him to enjoy the things that pertain to and that spring from the inner life are of more value to him by way of bringing him happiness and contentment than any possible accumulation of material things. Wealth is good — as a means to comfort; good as a servant, never as a master; good as a feature, never as the chief end of life.

One of the most pitiable sights that I know is the way some very rich men die; several such deaths have transpired during even the past year. Let the following serve as the type of many. A man has made gain —

* From that excellent little booklet "The Majesty of Calmness," by William George Jordan.

money-getting — the chief object of his life. In time, shall we say through nature's abhorrence of abnormalities, the greed for gain becomes his master and dries up his very powers of enjoyment of the finer things in life. He accumulates a hundred million, with all the care and worry that keeping this invested to the best advantage means. He is of but little use to the world, and through the dwarfing of the finer qualities of his life and the drying up of his powers of enjoyment he has become so also to himself. He dies. Three months after he has gone his name is scarcely ever heard, except perhaps in some long drawn out or bitterly fought will contest. His end is like that of a dog. In short, many a dog, faithful and intelligent and useful, has been more genuinely mourned and longer and more gratefully remembered. And then if it is true, as I believe it must be, that we commence in the other form of life exactly where we leave off here, taking with us only what we have gained by way of soul growth and spiritual unfoldment, but not one cent, not one cent, and having, moreover, no further control over any material possessions, how poor, how pitiably poor is such a life. Contrast it with this as an ideal and a purpose for a life:

"I am primarily engaged to myself to be a public servant of all the Gods, to demonstrate to all men there is good-will and intelligence at the heart of things and ever higher and yet higher leadings. These are my engagements. If there be power in good intentions, in fidelity, and in toil, the north wind shall be purer, the stars in heaven shall glow with a kindler beam that I have lived."

And what a life was the life of this man Emerson who deliberately chose this as his part. And what an influence while he lived, *and truly for all time to come.* Not three months, nor three centuries can forget his name or cease to bless his memory.

Another whom success in the sense of excessive gain develops pride and an itchiness for ostentatious show builds a mansion — a home? costing four million dollars, thinking also that it will be a sort of monument to, a reminder of himself. Within fifty years, or within even a much shorter space of time, it may be the possession of a Barnum and the home of a good up-to-date circus. Such is the security of a man's hold upon material possessions. And how few seem to be able to stand success and remain good, healthy, sensible, normal men. It seems strange that so seldom can a man become successful as to either wealth or power without taking on, mentally at least, the strut of the turkey-cock. A really great man, however, is always immune from this affection. It is rather as Pope said:

Of all the causes which conspire to blind
Man's erring judgment, and mislead the mind,
What the weak head with strongest bias rules,
Is Pride — that never-failing vice of fools.

The law seems to be absolute in that "whosoever shall exalt himself shall be abased; and he that humbleth himself shall be exalted." Nature seems to abhor an abnormally developed pride, snobbery, too marked a consciousness of superiority. And to the — I am holier than thou feeling — she applies always the brand, Hypocrite, and she burns it deep.

Another makes the accumulation of material things the chief object of his life, rising from humble circumstances, possessing unusual abilities, but giving but an infinitesimal amount of these abilities to his city or his state, both badly in need of such service; but rather conspiring with their enemies to make special privileges for a few greater, to secure acts alienating valuable properties from the people of his city and state, to avoid a just share of taxation, thereby defrauding and throwing greater and unjust burdens upon all of his fellowmen, except upon those equally dishonest and contemptible in this practice of tax-evasion. His life here closes considerably before a normal and well-rounded life should close, and on quitting he directs that practically the entire results of his life work go to a couple of young grandsons, not yet in their teens, in order that the family name and business be preserved. "Every man," said Marcus Aurelius, "is worth just so much as the things are worth about which he busies himself." The business may be preserved or it may tumble into ruin. Nature deals so in mockery when a man fancies he can have a controlling hand in the final actual disposition of his material possessions. The family name may be preserved and it may be raised even to a higher esteem, or it may be preserved in the records of an inebriate asylum. A man can have an *actual* say only in regard to his own life, but never in regard to the life of any other. Not by ambition and gain alone for self but,

"By labor, incessant and devout, to raise earth to heaven, to realize, in fact, the good that as yet exists only in idea — that is the end and purpose of human life; and in fulfilling it we achieve and maintain our unity each with every other, and all with the Divine."

Many a rich man's son has found the handicap of great riches too great to allow his making even a decent success of life; the incentive which nature seems to have decreed as a healthy and strength-developing stimulant has been neutralized by the burden which an over-rich father has dumped upon him. "Ungirt loins, unlit lamps, unused talents, sink a man like lead. Doing nothing is enough for ruin." Many a daughter of the unduly rich has found her associations as also her training or lack of training of such a nature that undue pride or a false ambition has taken possession of her, robbing her of one of the chief charms of womanhood, and a designing or worse than empty marriage has fallen to her portion. Surely wealth is of the mind and the heart and not of the hand. And the man who makes as his life work only gain for self and who fails to recognize his inexorable relations with his fellow-men, fails completely in getting from life what he thinks he'll get; for he finds that what he gains turns to a greater or less extent to ashes in his hands, and what he bequeaths to his descendants is far below what it might be, — he or she who is *at all worthy* of receiving such bequest would rather it be a few millions less and be accompanied with a name of honour and a memory to be revered than that it come with the tremendous handicap it many times comes with.

As we come to a fuller appreciation of these facts and of the laws of human life and relations that will not be denied, then more and more will "we measure the degree of civilization not by accumulation of the means of living, but by the character and value of the life lived."

Now I have said, nor would I say ought against wealth. I believe in wealth — sufficient for all the legitimate comforts of life; and I believe in it so thoroughly that I plead for a state wherein it can become the portion of a much larger number than has ever yet been known. And while I do not share in the belief that our time is necessarily more materialistic than other times have been, I do realize and most keenly that the economic conditions during the past few years have produced a class of men so materialistic in their entire outlook, so insatiate in their greed for ever larger gain, so drunk with opportunity and power that they would pull the very pillars of the state to the ground if a united and determined people did not come forward and say, *so far, and no farther*. It is against the aggressions of these and the abuses we have permitted them to give birth to and fatten upon, the aggressions of these against the welfare of their fellows, against the economic and political institutions of the nation, that we must battle for some time to come with an alertness, with a determination and a bravery that can know no defeat.

In the fire of the heart, and with a mind calm and determined and with malice towards none, must these great battles for the redemption of this nation be fought.

And as *excessive wealth* is of no real value to any man nor to his descendants, but becomes more often a veritable curse, and as it makes its possessors a menace to the very welfare of the nation and to the welfare of every man, woman and child in the nation, we will be doing a twofold service through such warfare and subsequent vigilance in saving its possessors and its would-be possessors from their own folly, as well as conserving our own common interests. It's the middle ground that carries with it the satisfactory solution of life. Excesses have to be paid for with heavy and sometimes with frightful interest.

Life, the life of *everyone* has its perplexities, its problems, its struggles and its work to be done. Humanity is brave and there are but few who do not stand up like men and women, some almost like very Gods to the end. It certainly should be the aim of each to throw no hindrance in the path of any fellow-being, to make no load heavier; but rather to lend the hand whenever we can.

Oh the skies are blue and a ribboned road
Shall the pilgrim's heart beguile:
Yet hurry not so fast with your load,
For there is many a mile.

And it's here a friend and there a friend
To bear your hand a while:
But none will go to the journey's end,
And few will stay the mile.

And in connection with the problems and perplexities and *apparent* losses that come and that must be met as the days hurry away, I believe without a question of a doubt, that the time will come when we will see the part that each thing has had to play in our lives and we will give thanks that it came just as it came. I believe, moreover, that a sort of an inborn universal feeling of this nature is a reason why humanity is brave.

A hope that never wearies, a faith that defies defeat, an attitude of mind that compels gladness, will help us to stand like men until we realize this glad culmination. And if one would find the easier way it lies in the ever conscious realization — "Thou wilt keep him in perfect peace whose mind is stayed on thee."

I suppose it is natural for each to find or to form for himself some sort of creed. Here is mine at least as it comes to me to-day; perchance it may contain some little suggestion for another:

To live to our highest in all things that pertain to us; to lend a hand as best we can to all others for this same end;

To aid in righting the wrongs that cross our path by pointing the wrong-doer to a better way, and thus aid him in becoming a power for good; to remain in nature always sweet and simple and humble, and therefore strong;

To open ourselves fully and to keep ourselves pure and clean as fit channels for the Divine Power to work through us; to turn toward and keep our faces always to the light;

To do our own thinking, listening quietly to the opinions of others, and to be sufficiently men and women to act always upon our own convictions; to do our duty as we see it, regardless of the opinions of others, seeming gain or loss, temporary blame or praise;

To play the part of neither knave nor fool by attempting to judge another, but to give that same time to living more worthily ourselves; to get up immediately when we stumble, face again to the light, and travel on without wasting even a moment in regret;

To love all things and to stand in awe or fear of nothing save our own wrong-doing; to recognize the good lying at the heart of all people, of all things, waiting for expression, all in its own good way and time;

To love the fields and the wild flowers, the stars, the far-open sea, the soft, warm earth, and to live much with them alone, but to love struggling and weary men and women and every pulsing living creature better;

To strive always to do unto others as we would have them do unto us.

In brief — to be honest, to be fearless, to be just, to be kind. This will make our part in life's great and as yet not fully understood play truly glorious, and we need then stand in fear of nothing — life nor death; for death is life.

Or, rather, it is the quick transition to life in another form; the putting off of the old coat and the putting on of a new; a passing not from light to darkness but from light to light, according as we have lived here; a taking up of life in another form just where we leave it off here; a part in life not to be shunned or dreaded or feared, but to be welcomed with a glad and ready smile when it comes in *its own* good way and time.

THE END

THE McCLURE PRESS, NEW YORK

ness, to act always upon our own convictions, to do our duty as we see it, regardless of the opinions of others, seeming gain or loss, temporary blame or praise.

To play the part of neither knave nor fool by attempting to judge another, but to give that same time to living more worthily ourselves. To get up no matter how many times we stumble, face again to the light, and travel on without wasting even a moment in regret.

To love all things and to stand in awe or fear of nothing save our own wrong-doing; to recognize the good lying at the heart of all people, of all things, waiting for expression, all in its own good way and time.

To love the fields and the wild flowers, the stars, the far-open sea, the soft, warm earth, and to live much with them alone, but to love struggling and weary men and women and every pulsing living creature better.

To strive always to do unto others as we would have them do unto us.

In brief — to be honest, to be fearless, to be just, to be kind. This will make our part in life's great, and as yet not fully understood play truly glorious, and we need then stand in fear of nothing — life nor death; for death is life.

Or, rather, it is the quick transition to life in another form; the putting off of the old coat and the putting on of a new; a passing not from light to darkness but from light to light, according as we have lived here; a taking up of life in another form just where we leave it off here; a part in life not to be shunned or dreaded or feared, but to be welcomed with a glad and ready smile when it comes in its own good way and time.

THE END